D0243683

BULBS

NORFOLK COLLEGE LIBRARY
3 8079 00055 227 3

THE · PAN · GARDEN · PLANTS · SERIES

BULBS

ROGER PHILLIPS & MARTYN RIX

edited by Brian Mathew

A Pan Original

Acknowledgements

It would not have been possible to complete this book without the help of many people. We are particularly grateful to Brian Mathew for checking the text and the identifications, and answering many questions; to the Royal Horticultural Society's garden at Wisley and especially to Chris Brickell and John Warwick, to Jack Elliott and to Harry Hay, all of whom put up with frequent visits throughout the season, and were always helpful and generous in lending their plants. We would like to thank Lord Skelmersdale of Broadleigh Gardens for giving us a large number of bulbs, Mrs J. Abel-Smith for the modern Daffodils, and Regents Park for the Tulip cultivars. We would also like to thank the following who have given us plants, lent transparencies or helped in other ways: Peter Barnes, Beverley Behrens, Igor Belolipov, Brinsley Burbidge, Tim Brotzman, Jill Bryan, Paul Christian, Jill Cowley, Jenny Deakin, Kath Dryden, Valerie Finnis, Nora Gabrielian, Chris Grey-Wilson, Diana Hewett, John Holmes, Tinge Horsfall, Mary Knox-Finlay, Christopher Lloyd, Roger Macfarlane, Wessel Marais, John Marr, Leuren Moret, Kate Penoyre, Oleg Polunin, Charles Quest-Ritson, Susannah Reade, Alison Rix, Ted Rix, Lyndsay Shearer, Ole Sonderhousen, Walter Stagg, Hugh Synge, John Templer, Anne Thatcher, Romke van der Kaa, and Ursula Wide.

(MK635.934 2P

First published in 1981 by Pan Books Ltd
This revised and enlarged edition published in 1989 by Pan Books Ltd
Cavaye Place, London SW10 9PG
9 8 7 6 5 4 3 2
© Roger Phillips and Martyn Rix 1981, 1989
ISBN 0 330 30253 1
Photoset by Parker Typesetting Service, Leicester
Printed and bound in Great Britain by Springbourne Press Ltd, Basildon, Essex

This book is sold subject to the condition that it shall not, by way of trade or otherwise, be lent, re-sold, hired out or otherwise circulated without the publisher's prior consent in any form of binding or cover other than that in which it is published and without a similar condition including this condition being imposed on the subsequent purchaser.

Contents

Introduction

In this book we hope to show something of the beauty and diversity of bulbous plants. No other group can provide such a display of colour with such ease and reliability. Few indoor plants are as welcome in mid-winter as the sweet-scented hyacinths or graceful paper whites. Tulips make a spectacular show, in every colour except blue, within five months of planting with no intervening attention; while daffodils flower as easily, and go on improving year after year without any replanting or division. Few herbaceous plants are as stately as the 3-metre-high *Cardiocrinum* or the orange formal bells of the Crown Imperial. Some bulbs are like small jewels; sapphire-blue in *Scilla sibirica*, ice-blue in *Puschkinia*, or golden in many crocuses; others like most fritillaries are all sombre purples, greens and browns.

How to use this book

The bulbs are arranged here roughly in flowering order, starting with those which flower in early spring and ending with the autumn. The dates on which the laid out photographs were taken are given and refer to the flowering time in one particular year in south-eastern England. This is roughly equivalent to Washington DC, about a month later than Texas and a few weeks earlier than New York in a normal year. Bulbs which are brought into growth or flowering by the first cold nights of the autumn start earlier in the north, later in the south, as do the autumn colours.

This book may be used to see what a particular bulb looks like, or to identify an unknown specimen, by starting in the right season among similar plants. Most of the commonly grown ones should be found here. Around 1000 different bulbs are shown, most of them hardy enough to stand the cold of winter outdoors in north-western Europe and in America, from New York city and coastal New England southwards, i.e. in zones 6–9. A few need protection from hard frost in the absence of snow cover, and others, coming from California or the European Mediterranean, need greenhouse protection in northern Europe and in the east and midwest of the United States. The habitat and distribution notes for each species are designed to be an indication of its cultivation requirements and of the climates that it is likely to tolerate.

The book is designed not only for gardeners, but also for those who like to travel and find bulbs growing wild. The main areas where bulbs originate are described below.

Measurements are given in metres and centimetres. One metre equals about 3 feet, and 2.5 centimetres equals about 1 inch.

What is a bulb?

In this book we have taken a wide definition of the term bulb, to include all plants which form swollen underground storage roots or stems to survive the dry or cold season. Strictly speaking a bulb, of which the onion is the best-known example, consists of the swollen fleshy bases of leaves. Other storage organs may be formed by different parts of the plant; a corm, such as is found in a *Crocus*, is a swollen stem base, and is usually surrounded by the dry bases of old leaves. There are also swollen underground stems, of which the potato is the best known, usually called stem tubers or rhizomes. A third common type is the fleshy root, which may be either single or branched. If very short it is known as a root-tuber. Some plants, e.g. irises such as *I. rosenbachiana* have both bulbs and tuberous roots, others such as *I. elegantissima* have rhizomes and fleshy roots.

Where wild bulbs grow

The greatest number of bulbous plants is found in areas where the winters are wet and summers are hot and dry, with a short spring. The possession of a food reserve in the bulb enables a plant to grow up very quickly in spring, before annuals and slower-growing herbs have had time to develop. In tropical climates which have alternating wet and dry seasons, bulbs are also common, but very few of them can be grown outside in the cooler parts of Europe and North America; those few that are hardy enough come from high altitudes.

Nearly all hardy bulbs come from areas with a modified Mediterranean-type climate; that is a cool, wet winter and a hot, dry summer. Five areas of the world have this type of climate: the Mediterranean extending eastwards into Central Asia; California; central Chile; the southern tip of South Africa; and western and southern Australia. In the southern hemisphere the Mediterranean climates are found at about 35° S, and in the northern hemisphere at around 40°N. Partly because of this difference in latitude, and partly because they have no continental land masses to their south, the southern hemisphere areas of Mediterranean climate have almost frost-free winters, so that few of their native bulbs can tolerate more than a few degrees of frost. In California the Mediterranean climate is confined to the coast and the lower parts of the central valley. Even this area is sometimes subjected to a big freeze, such as occurred in 1972 and 1989 when arctic air from Canada extended down the west coast and frost and snow reached Los Angeles; consequently many of the Californian plants are cold-tolerant. Others come from higher in the mountains, or from further east across the Sierra Nevada, and some of these can survive in colder climates, on the east coast of North America and in northern Europe, provided they are kept dry in summer.

The majority of hardier bulbs come from the mountains in the Mediterranean area in Europe, North Africa and Asia. The winter rainfall climate extends into Central Asia, almost to the Himalayas, because the mountain ranges, the Alps, the Caucasus, the Tauros, the Hindu Kush and the Tien Shan, run roughly east–west and provide no barrier to the winter storms from the Mediterranean, Black Sea and Caspian Sea. At the same time the proximity of Siberia means that cold air can extend south-westwards, often as far as Turkey and northern Greece. Small areas on the southern shores of the Black and Caspian Seas have summer rainfall too, horticulturally significant as plants from these areas will survive the summer rainfall of northern Europe and the north-eastern states of the USA. North-west Spain and south-west France also have summer rainfall, and this transitional type of maritime–Mediterranean climate produced many of the bulbs such as *Narcissus* which do well in the open garden. On their equatorial side, the Mediterranean climates merge into deserts; these border zones, which are particularly rich in bulbs, provide plants which are most difficult to grow in the eastern United States and northern Europe, but which do well in California and the warmer and drier parts of the mid-west and Texas.

Fewer bulbs come from areas with summer rainfall and dry winters, but one area which is especially rich in bulbs is the Drakensberg mountains in the north-eastern Cape province and Natal in South Africa. These bulbs are relatives of the winter-growing but tender bulbs from the Cape; those which grow in marshes and by streams are especially tolerant of summer rainfall but are little grown. Many should be tolerant of winter frosts down to −10°C. (Hardiness temperatures in this book are expressed in degrees Celsius (°C). To convert Celsius to Fahrenheit, multiply the degrees Celsius by 1.8 and add 32 for the Fahrenheit equivalent. For example, −20°C×1.8=−36°+32=−4°F.)

The hardiness of bulbs from different areas of the world

The hardiest bulbs are those that originate in eastern North America or in northern Europe, Siberia, northern China and northern Japan. They remain underground in winter, where they can tolerate being frozen for several months, and they are protected from extremes of temperature by a covering of snow. They also require or can tolerate rain in summer. Examples of this group are most of the Snowdrops (*Galanthus*), *Crocus vernus* cultivars, *Scilla bifolia* and *S. sibirica*, many *Corydalis*, Trilliums and most daffodils and lilies.

A second group originates in mountains in southern Europe, Turkey, Iran and Central Asia, and the inland parts of California and neighbouring states between the Sierras and the Rockies. These have extremely cold winters with low temperatures and much snow, but also have dry summers, so the bulbs need protection from wet in summer. Many of them can be planted in areas of the garden which naturally dry out, but others require some sort of covering in summer to keep them dry. They are often also the better for some shade from the sun at midday, such as is provided by a deciduous tree, or by the growth of annuals, which flower after the bulbs have finished. Examples of this group are

Collecting bulbs in Kurdistan in 1965

most crocuses and bulbous irises, many fritillaries, tulips, some *Calochortus*, *Eremurus*, and Colchicums. The hardy Oncocyclus irises which require very well-drained alkaline soil, originate in this type of climate, and grow outside very well in the drier parts of the mid-west of the United States. It is worth mentioning that it is important that these bulbs are grown in areas of the garden that are not irrigated in summer.

A third group of bulbs originate in coastal areas in California, Chile, the Cape province of South Africa and the Mediterranean regions of Europe, western Asia and North Africa. Here the winters are wet but mild and temperatures below −5°C are rare. In Mediterranean Europe and Turkey this climate extends to about 1000–1800m altitude. Above that frosts are harder. Bulbs originating in these areas require the protection of a greenhouse in northern Europe and the north-eastern states of America, but would probably survive in a bulb frame in zones 7–9. In California they grow well without protection in winter, but do require a position where they are not irrigated in summer. Examples of this group are *Cyclamen persicum* and *C.repandum*, most Romuleas, *Ranunculus asiaticus*, some tulips and fritillaries and most of the Calochortus and Brodieas.

The fourth major group are those which originate in areas with cool, often rather dry winters and warm wet summers. The coasts of Oregon and Washington, the Himalayas, the Drakensberg mountains in South Africa and southern Chile and Argentina are the main areas with this type of climate where bulbs originate. These bulbs will grow well in the warmer parts of the eastern States, and the hardier ones will survive as far north as zone 6. Examples of this group are the Arisaemas, *Eucomis*, Crocosmias and Nerines, the Tigridias and hardier Hippeastrums, tuberous Tropaeolums, and the tenderer lilies. As these plants mostly die down in winter they may either be lifted and brought indoors in cold areas or protected by a very deep dry mulch to keep their bulbs unfrozen. Evergreen ones such as Dieramas and Moraeas are more difficult as the leaves are evergreen and killed by temperatures below around −10°C.

Conservation and collecting

Apart from surviving the rigours of the climate, bulbs in the wild have to survive two main threats: grazing by animals and collecting by humans. Of these grazing is very ancient, collecting in evolutionary terms very recent.

In the short term grazing is less harmful because the bulb itself is not damaged, and many bulbs have evolved adaptations to protect themselves against it. In some, e.g. *Crocus* and *Colchicum*, the seed head develops below ground, only emerging as the seeds ripen; in others, e.g. *Fritillaria*, the plants produce bulbils which can propagate the plant when the seed pod is eaten: the bulbils are spread through the soil by marmots or gophers. Others, e.g. *Eremurus*, are very slimy and avoided by grazing animals, while others, e.g. some Alliums, have a horrible smell and taste. In other cases the bulb can only survive when growing inside some spiny bush or on an inaccessible rock ledge or in a narrow rock crevice. Fritillaries are common in this kind of habitat.

The threat from human collecting is twofold, for food and for horticulture. In the eastern Mediterranean, a popular gruel called Salep is made from orchid tubers: owing to the similarity of these tubers to testicles (Greek Ορχις = testicle) Salep is thought to have some aphrodisiac properties. Many species are used and this type of collecting probably keeps overall numbers down without threatening rare species in particular. For example, the American Indians ate Camassia bulbs in large quantities, but continued to harvest bulbs from the same fields for generations.

Horticultural collecting is the more dangerous because it is selective and threatens rare species more than common ones. While

Iris cycloglossa (p.65)

Bulb bed showing railway sleepers and wire netting base, with layers of gravel, peat and gritty planting compost; bricks indicate depth of layers.

there are a few examples of bulbs known or believed to be extinct in the wild because of over-collecting – *Tecophilaea cyanocrocus* is one – many are in potential danger of extinction by collectors. A topical example of the type of decimation which can occur is that of *Sternbergia candida*, discovered and described in 1978 as being rare and very restricted in distribution. Within two years, hundreds of bulbs were offered in the trade, recently collected in the wild. If collecting on this scale is continued the plant could very soon become extinct in the wild. Cyclamen, especially the species of more limited distribution, e.g. *C. pseudibericum*, are also in great danger. The importation of collected corms of cyclamen is supposed to be prohibited, but judging by the size and gnarled appearance of some of the corms seen for sale in shops the laws are being ignored. Bulbs of many kinds are still collected in Turkey and exported by the ton, and the sale of these bulbs provides a valuable supplementary income for many peasants. The areas which are being plundered are getting more and more remote, and many bulbs such as snowdrops are now absent from large areas of south-west Turkey. Trilliums are also collected in North America in large quantities, and either sold for wild gardens at home or exported.

Those hardy bulbs considered to be endangered are marked with an asterisk in the index. These should on no account be collected if they are found. Most are in cultivation already, and obtainable through specialist societies or reputable nurseries who propagate their own bulbs and do not import them directly from the wild.

All orchids have been excluded from this book. Some Pleione species are almost hardy, as is *Bletia striata*, and these are easily propagated but hardy wild orchids have not been successfully grown from seed on a commercial scale, and propagation by division is very slow. Few species can be said to be established by cultivation, and gardeners should not collect them unless they are certain to be destroyed anyway, by road widening, ploughing, etc. Most of those offered for sale will, unfortunately, have been collected in the wild, and anyone interested in conservation will avoid buying them.

The pressures of urban development and agriculture threaten many species both in the Mediterranean and in California; the possibility of extinction by this means is very real. *Fritillaria liliacea* is now restricted to about three sites on the outskirts of San Francisco because of the effects of housing developments and agriculture. Fortunately it is not difficult to cultivate and it should be carefully preserved and increased, by seed if possible, by anyone who grows it. Seed is the best means of introduction of a new species and will result in the establishment of the plant sooner, but it is often not present at the time the plant is found. As a general rule bulbs of species which are obtainable in cultivation should not be collected, unless they are unusual individuals of common species. There is never any excuse for collecting more than three bulbs of a species from one area, especially if it does not occur in thousands. Three bulbs will be sufficient for a population to be established in cultivation, by hand pollination and seed sowing. One bulb, unless it is a species or clone which increases very fast by bulbils or division, is a dead end and unlikely to result in the permanent establishment of the plant in cultivation. Twenty or more bulbs are no more likely to do well than three.

Cultivation

Planting bulbs in the garden

Most bulbs should be planted when they are dormant: in early autumn (August onwards) for spring-flowering bulbs, or in early spring for summer-flowering ones. Exceptions to this are snowdrops and snowflakes which are best moved while in flower. Snowdrops bought dry are often difficult to establish, but those transplanted while in flower will do well the following year.

It is important to plant bulbs at more or less the correct depth, and the right way up. As a general rule they should be planted at about their own depth in heavy soil, and in twice or more their own depth in light sandy soil or very dry places, but even the smallest bulbs should have about 5cm of soil above them.

Most bulbs require a well-drained rich soil with much sand and humus. A chalky one, or at least one which is not very acid is preferable. Many of the Dutch bulb fields consist of dune sand which has a large amount of shell in it providing lime, enriched with humus, so that it is both moisture-retentive and well drained, as well as alkaline and fertile.

If bulbs are used only for bedding, and are then discarded, the fertility of the soil is not important. If they are planted permanently, or meant to be used again, then it is essential that the soil in which they are grown is very fertile. The best fertilizers are low in nitrogen, high in potash and phosphate, e.g. bone meal, chrysanthemum or rose fertilizer. These should be applied either before planting or sprinkled on the surface immediately after planting, so that they are well incorporated into the soil before growth begins.

Bulbs in grass

Many bulbs will grow happily in grass, and look most natural in this setting. Snowdrops and snowflakes are both happy, as are some crocus species, especially *C. vernus*, *C. tommasinianus* and Dutch Yellow. These will grow happily in lawns even on heavy soil, but their leaves should not be mowed off until they have begun to go yellow, which is usually in May. Other later-flowering bulbs are less satisfactory in formal grass because their leaves last longer, but they will do well in rough grass which is not cut until July when the leaves of the latest flowers have died down. They associate well in a 'meadow garden' setting, which has been well described by Christopher Lloyd in *The Well-Tempered Garden* and can be seen at Great Dixter. The 'meadow garden' is rather similar in ecology to a mountain hay meadow. The succession of flowers begins in early spring when the grass is short, with snowdrops, spring snowflakes, crocus and *Scilla bifolia*. As the grass becomes longer, larger bulbs flower, such as daffodils, summer snowflakes and fritillaries (*F. meleagris* and *pyrenaica*), *Tulipa sylvestris*, *Ornithogalum*, with cowslips and buttercups. Later come *Tulipa sprengeri* and other cultivated tulips, and possibly *Lilium pyrenaicum*, *Lilium martagon* and *Iris latifolia*, which continue the succession until the end of June. In wetter places Camassias can be especially good. By late July most of the bulbs will have disappeared, and the grass should be cut short and hay made before it is cleared away. One or two mowings, if the summer is wet, will suffice until September when the first of the colchicums and autumn crocus such as *C. speciosus* and *C. nudiflorus* appear, and a final mowing can be done in November after these have flowered, but before any of the bulbs' leaves have emerged.

If the soil is naturally acid and sandy a different range of bulbs can be grown. The crocuses will do well and dwarf narcissus can be grown, e.g. *N. bulbocodium* and *N. cyclamineus*, in the damper places, and *N. triandrus* in the drier areas. So-called 'alpine meadows' of this type can be seen at Wisley and at the Savill and Valley gardens, Windsor. In these cases the grass can be cut rather earlier, in early July or late June, and the wild flower range will resemble a healthy upland hay meadow.

Plastic lattice pots of different sizes, with aluminium labels attached

Bulbs among shrubs and under trees

Many spring-flowering bulbs also grow well among deciduous shrubs and under deciduous trees. They make most of their growth before the tree leaves shade them too much. The roots of the trees and shrubs also help keep the soil on the dry side during the summer, which is beneficial to most bulbs. Snowdrops, aconites (*Eranthis*), cyclamen, scillas, bluebells (*Hyacinthoides*), *Trillium* and *Erythronium* grow well in these conditions, and the very tolerant *Lilium martagon* will also thrive in rather dry shade. The dryness and shade in summer also prevent the grass becoming too thick, and a thin ground cover of a small-leafed ivy can be encouraged. This provides a good foil for many bulbs, especially snowdrops.

Other shade-tolerant bulbs prefer a moister soil such as is found among dwarf rhododendrons, which have more restricted root systems and provide shade without drying out the surrounding soil. This shade is particularly important in spring when the young shoots of lilies are often damaged by late frosts. If the bulbs are planted on the west side of an evergreen shrub or even partly under it, they are less likely to be damaged by the early morning sun. A peat bank is also a very good environment for plants of this type and many other bulbs will do very well in it.

The bulb frame

It will be seen in the text that the 'bulb frame' is often mentioned as a place to grow bulbs. Its purpose is primarily to keep the bulbs quite dry in summer and rather dry in winter in climates where winters are normally warm and wet. The protection the frame gives from cold is incidental and in the absence of snow cover, protection with straw, dry leaves or matting may be advisable for all but the hardiest bulbs. Aluminium frames are expensive to buy, but require no maintenance, and should last for many years. They are also much lighter than steel ones, should they need to be moved, and as they are bolted together, they can be dismantled easily. As much air as possible should circulate inside the frame, and the side should be left open, except in very cold, frosty weather.

The bed in which to plant the bulbs should be raised above ground level to ensure good drainage. The sides may be made of brick, breeze blocks or old railway sleepers, which are the easiest. If there are moles, gophers or mice in the garden, it is advisable to cover the base of the frame with small-mesh wire netting. The sides of the frame can vary in height from about 30cm upwards. Small bulbs can be seen better if the surface of the frame is about waist height.

The bottom 30cm or so should be made up of coarse stones, ash, clinker or gravel, to provide absolutely free drainage. Above this put a layer of peat, leaf-mould, compost or old mushroom manure up to 10cm and above this the compost in which the roots will feed. It should consist of loam, peat or leaf mould, sand and grit in roughly equal proportions for bulbs which want a rich soil; and with more sand and grit for smaller bulbs and for those which require exceptionally good drainage. The addition of crushed limestone, which is sold as poultry feed, is very beneficial to most bulbs. For a small frame, sterilized potting compost which contains loam may be used; otherwise a general fertilizer can be added to the soil as it is mixed: 23–30cm of this soil is ample for all bulbs. The bulbs themselves may be planted on top of this, and the delicate or difficult ones encased in coarse silver sand. This definitely seems beneficial for producing good root growth on fritillaries, crocuses and *Iris reticulata*. The soil around the bulbs can be similar to that for them to root in, or more sandy, and the frame can be topped with 3–5cm of gravel, so that drainage is especially good round the neck of the plant. The bulbs should be carefully labelled, and similar ones not put next to each other, so that they can be separated if they are moved while dormant. Similar species can also be separated by vertical tiles or pieces of slate, or planted in plastic lattice pots sold for planting aquatics. They hardly restrict the root system of the plant, but they prevent the bulbs going astray and make it very easy to move the bulbs while they are dormant. They also have the advantage that the labels can be attached firmly to them, and an aluminium label is especially suitable for this purpose.

Watering and feeding

Most hardy bulbs begin their season's growth in early autumn or with the first rains, when they make roots, and become dormant again in early summer. These are the ones that the bulb frame is designed to accommodate, and the watering regime should take this into account. A very thorough watering should be given in early autumn, to soak the whole frame, and a second about a month later if the weather is hot and dry. No more watering is needed until spring when top growth begins to show and several waterings should be given throughout the spring, preferably on a sunny, windy day, so that the leaves, if they have been wetted, and the surface can dry as quickly as possible. Liquid fertilizer can be incorporated into the spring waterings, using a low-nitrogen compound, such as is used for tomatoes. This will promote healthy growth and flowering, and not produce too much lush leafage, which can encourage botrytis in damp weather. Summer-flowering bulbs from central America such as *Tigridia*, and those from the mountains of southern Africa, such as *Dierama* begin their growth in early spring, and are dormant in winter when they should be kept rather dry.

Bulbs in the alpine house

These will require the same regime as in the bulb frame, but watering will need to be more carefully done, so that there is no drying out while the bulbs are in growth. If they dry out, even for a short time, they become dormant, and nothing will induce them to start again before the following autumn. For this reason bulbs are safer if the pots are plunged in sand which can be kept well watered. The alpine house has the great advantage over the bulb frame that some frost protection can be arranged in exceptionally cold winters, and that winter-flowering bulbs can be admired in comfort. After bulb foliage has died down, the pots can be stored out of the way under the bench or in a cool shed until autumn.

Propagation

Most bulbs are easily propagated, by either division or seeds. Commercial stocks have usually been selected for their vegetative vigour and ease of propagation, so they usually cause little trouble, but the rarer bulbs are often slow to increase and may require more care.

Seed

Seed is the best method of increasing stock. Where several members of one genus are grown together, it is advisable to hand pollinate the flowers to make sure that the seed is true and, if necessary, cover the flowers to prevent cross-pollination by insects. Most species of bulbs with showy flowers are normally self-sterile, so it will be necessary to use two flowers from different clones as parents. Seed of most genera germinates best when fresh, so if planted in September of the year in which it ripens, and kept outside, much of it will germinate the following spring. Some species require a cold period to stimulate germination; some, including many lilies, have more complex requirements, so that germination appears to be delayed for a year. The young bulbs will usually be found clustered around the sides at the base of the pot, so if germination has been good they should be repotted after the first year.

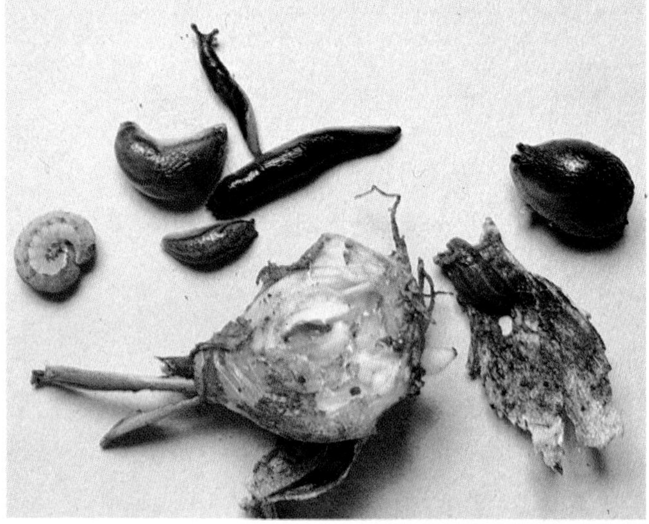

Various slugs, and a cutworm

Division

Division of the bulb is necessary where especially good forms are to be increased or where seed is unobtainable. There are many different ways depending on the type of bulb.

A daffodil, hyacinth or *Allium* can be induced to form bulblets by making a cross cut in the base of the bulb through the basal plate, just into the scales and inserting a small stone to keep the sides apart. These bulblets should be treated as seedlings. The cutting is best done in summer while the bulbs are dormant.

Few-scaled bulbs such as fritillaries can be easily increased by breaking the scales apart and planting each separately. The piece which contains next year's bud will probably flower as well as if nothing had happened, and the other half will make a flowering-size bulb in one year. For larger fritillaries such as *F. imperialis* and *F. persica* the bulb may be cut into many pieces with a sharp knife and the resulting pieces treated like lily-scales. In many-scaled bulbs such as lilies, single scales can be broken off and planted in loose

Larva of large Narcissus fly

Larvae of the Vine Weevil

peaty soil with the tip of the scale just above the soil. A new bulb will soon form at the base, and this can be treated like a seedling.

Corms are more difficult. Crocuses can be induced to make more than one shoot by carefully cutting out the single main shoot, thus stimulating the producing of adventitious buds on the edge of the corm.

Tubers and rhizomes can sometimes be increased by cutting them into pieces, depending on whether they have one or several growing points. Tuberous roots will often make new plants if they are divided at their point of attachment, but will usually fail to grow if cut lower down. One method of vegetative propagation that may be used successfully with trilliums is to remove the soil to expose the growing point of the rhizome, but without disturbing the roots. Then cut off the top at the ring showing the line of new growth; several small bulbs will then form which should be removed in the summer and planted in rich soil. If only a single bulb is available and it is required for flowering, a narrow wedge may be removed around the line of the new growth ring without damaging the growing crown and multiplication along this cut will occur.

Pests and diseases

When grown in small numbers by amateurs, bulbs are remarkably untroubled by pests or diseases, provided that the original bulbs were healthy. It is when a large number of bulbs are grown close together, especially if they are of one genus or family, that troubles are likely to become serious, or spread very quickly.

Pests

Many different animals often attack bulbs, but in my experience four or five are the most serious culprits. Birds can be very destructive, eating the flowers of crocuses and other early bulbs. Mice or squirrels sometimes eat a large number in a very short time once they have developed a taste for bulbs. On rich or heavy soils slugs are the major problem, especially the very small black ones which live underground and eat the young roots and the softer parts of bulbs. Watering with liquid slug killer will kill some, but the best deterrent is to surround the bulbs with a good layer of coarse sand when planting. Lilies are particularly badly attacked, daffodils and snowdrops least affected. Surface-living slugs are less harmful and can be killed with blue slug pellets.

The larvae of vine weevils (*Otiorrhynchus sulcatus*) are very destructive, eating the roots of cyclamen, lilies and other plants grown in pots. Another species, *Agasphaerops nigra* attacks lilies in the Pacific coast states of America. At the first sign of attack, the plants should be carefully repotted and all the old soil burnt. The adults are about 1cm long, and emerge at night, feeding on leaves and flowers. They can be found with a flashlight. Other destructive night-feeders are 'cut-worms', the green or brown caterpillars of various moths, such as the Yellow Underwing (*Noctua pronuba*) and the Turnip moths (*Agrotis* spp). They love the dry conditions and loose soil of a bulb frame and hide several inches down in the day. Again they are best caught at night. Other larvae are stem borers which attack larger stems such as those of lilies.

Iris reticulata bulbs infected with Ink spot (*Mystrosporium adjustum*)

Iris pseudocaucasica and *Colchicum* infected with *Botrytis*

There are a few more specialised pests which are less common but can cause great damage. The Narcissus fly (about three species are involved) lays its eggs among the dying foliage and the larvae feed inside the bulb, finally killing it by eating out its heart. Any sick looking or soft daffodil bulbs should be burnt. The Lily beetle is a beautiful bright red and eats the leaves and buds of lilies; its larvae are horrible, covered in their own excrement, and can soon strip a lily plant of leaves. They also attack fritillaries. Aphids, greenfly or blackfly, can be very common in some seasons and, as well as causing distortion of the leaves and flowers, are the main carriers of virus diseases. Any colonies seen should be sprayed immediately, and a regular spraying programme with a persistent systemic insecticide will prevent the aphids getting a hold on the delicate young growths of lilies, irises, etc.

Diseases

Diseases caused by fungi, bacteria or viruses are less easy to identify but are well described and illustrated for the UK in the Ministry of Agriculture bulletin, *Diseases of Bulbs*, ADAS HPDI (1979), or *Collins Guide to the Pests, Diseases and Disorders of Garden Plants* by S. Buczacki and K. Harris, and for the USA in the bulletins available from your local agent of the US Dept. of Agriculture Extension Service or in *Diseases and Pests of Ornamental Plants*, Fifth Edition, by Pascal P. Pirone.

The worst diseases of the hardy bulbs are the moulds of various species of *Botrytis*. They attack the leaves and stems, particularly in warm wet weather, starting with brown patches on the leaves or at soil level, and finally killing the whole plant. Removal of any infected plants and spraying the remainder with captan, benlate or some other fungicide will usually control an outbreak, but some plants, especially *Iris persica*, always seem to succumb in the end. Small black knob-like 'sclerotia' can often be found on infected bulbs in summer, and they should always be removed and burnt. Soaking the bulbs before planting in a systemic fungicide such as benlate is also helpful in controlling various rots.

A common disease of *Iris reticulata* and related species is the so-called 'Ink Spot' disease, which forms black stains on the bulb tunic, before infecting the whole bulb and killing it. Infected bulbs are best burnt, and healthy ones nearby treated with a fungicide.

Virus diseases do not immediately kill the plants, but they weaken them and cause unsightly spotting and streaking on the leaves and flowers. Most cultivated clones are relatively resistant, and in the case of tulips, the virus causes the beautiful 'broken' effects shown on p.149; these are sold as 'Rembrandt' Tulips and should not be planted near other healthy, more delicate bulbs. The same goes for irises and many other bulbs where the virus shows up as pale yellowish patches on the leaves. Many lilies are especially easily infected, while fritillaries seem almost immune. Viruses can be controlled by ruthless burning of any infected plants, by control of aphids and by keeping newly acquired plants in quarantine, away from healthy ones until they have been 'passed'. There is now the possibility of producing virus-free stocks of infected cultivars by tissue culture, but it is still an expensive business. Viruses are generally not transmitted through seeds, so clean stocks can be raised from seed.

The photographs

When shooting wild flowers in the field it is essential to work from a tripod, so that you can take advantage of the opportunity to use a slow shutter speed and thus a smaller aperture, giving greater depth of field. In practice the best speed is normally 1/15 sec although if there is a strong wind you may have to go up to 1/30 or in extremes 1/60.

²⁄₃ life size Photographed 11 February

(a) Galanthus plicatus Bieb. (*Amaryllidaceae*). Native of western Russia, eastern Romania and the Crimea, growing in woods and scrub, flowering in February and March. Height 12–25cm. Distinguished from other spring-flowering snowdrops by having its leaf-edges folded back in the leaf sheath: the leaves are glaucous and there is a single green spot on each inner petal (cf. *G. byzantinus* p.14). There is also a double form, and an especially fine clone c.v. 'Warham' collected during the Crimean war. Easily grown in good moist soil, in shade or half-shade.

(b) Galanthus plicatus × nivalis (*Amaryllidaceae*). This is a robust garden hybrid, the leaves are partly flat and partly folded back, suggesting that the parentage is *G. plicatus* (a) × *nivalis* (h) (cf. p.17). Baker named plants of this parentage *G.* × *grandiflorus*, and they are reported by E. A. Bowles to be short-lived in cultivation.

(c), (e) Galanthus elwesii Hook. fil. (*Amaryllidaceae*). Native of Yugoslavia, Romania and the Ukraine south to Greece and west Turkey, growing in woods, scrub and among rocks, flowering from February to April. Height 10–30cm. Distinguished from other species by its glaucous leaves, one folded inside the other, and inner petals with two spots which sometimes join so that the whole inner petal is green. Height and width of leaves are very variable (see p.14). *Galanthus* 'Merlin', a beautiful cultivar with a very dark green inner segment, may be a hybrid between this and another species. Easily grown, but better in more well-drained soil than the other species.

(d) Leucojum vernum L. (*Amaryllidaceae*) Spring Snowflake. Native of central Europe from Romania and western Russia to the Pyrenees and Belgium, and naturalised in south England, Denmark and Holland. It grows in woods and on steep shady hillsides often in great quantity, flowering from March to May, as soon as the snow melts. Height usually 15–20cm, but up to 35cm. Plants from the western part of the species range have a green spot on each petal, whereas plants from the eastern part have a yellowish spot, and are somewhat larger: they have been called var. *carpathicum* Sweet (see p.5). Var. *vagneri* Stapf from Hungary is also robust usually with two flowers to a stem as shown here. Easy to grow in any moist soil, in shade or semi-shade.

(f) Galanthus elwesii subsp. **minor** D. A. Webb, syn. *G. graecus* auct. (*Amaryllidaceae*). Native of NE Greece, S Bulgaria and some of the Aegean islands, growing in woods at 100–1300m, flowering in February and March. Distinguished by its narrow twisted leaves and pale yellowish-green ovary. The inner petals have a large green basal spot. Stem 8–12cm. Intermediates between this and subsp. *elwesii* are common in Bulgaria. They have been called *G. maximus* Velen. See also p.14 (e). Easily grown, but better in a sunnier more open spot than the other species, and in well-drained soil.

(g), (h) Galanthus nivalis L. (*Amaryllidaceae*). Common Snowdrop. Native of almost the whole of Europe except for the west, from Russia to Spain and Sicily; naturalised but probably not native in England, Scotland, Holland, Belgium and Scandinavia. It grows in woods and scrub and by streams, flowering from January to March. Height usually 10–20cm. Leaves glaucous, flat in the sheath; flower always with a single green spot. Double forms are common in gardens and some of the many named garden forms and hybrids are shown on pp.14 and 17.

⅔ life size Photographed 11 February

$^{2}/_{3}$ life size Photographed 25 February

(a) **Galanthus nivalis** 'Scharlockii' (*Amaryllidaceae*). A late flowering clone of *G. nivalis*, characterised by its long bifid spathe and small flowers with a pale green mark on each outer petal. It was discovered by Julius Scharlock in the valley of the Nahe river, a tributary of the Rhine, in the mid nineteenth century.

(b), (c) **Galanthus ikariae** Baker (*Amaryllidaceae*). Native of the Aegean islands of Andros, Tinos and Ikaria, and of northern Turkey and the Caucasus, growing in woods and among shady rocks at low altitudes, flowering in February and March.
Two distinct forms are shown here: (b) with a tall stem and inner petals with a small green spot, was collected in northern Turkey. It is similar to a collection from Andros (see p.16); (c) is a cultivated form with shorter leaves at flowering, and larger flowers with the inner petal almost all green. It is illustrated in *Bot. Mag.* 9474, but its origin is not recorded. Both are distinct from other species in their broad shining green leaves, recurving at their ends, and lobed inner petals. Easy to grow in good soil, in shade or half-shade. Source (b) Turkey, Trabzon, Zigana pass, 1100m, Furse & Synge 178; (c) cultivated stock.

(d) **Galanthus byzantinus** Baker (*Amaryllidaceae*). Native of NW Turkey, growing at 100–500m, in fields and scrub, flowering from January to March. Very similar to *G. plicatus* (p.12), differing in its inner petals which have a green blotch at their base. Leaves folded back in the sheath, dark green, somewhat glaucous. Height 10–20cm. Easy to grow in good soil, in sun or shade. Source (d) cultivated stock.
Field shot photographed in NW Turkey, Abant, in March 1975 by B. Mathew 8511.

(e) **Galanthus elwesii** Hooker fil. (*Amaryllidaceae*). A small narrow-leaved form of this variable species (see pp.12 (c) and 2 (e)) collected in NW Turkey. The species is named after H. J. Elwes (1846–1922), an English sportsman and plant collector, author of 'A monograph of the genus *Lilium*' and with A. Henry *The Trees of Great Britain and Ireland* (see also p.94).
Source Turkey, Ankara, Elma Dağ, 1700m, Rix 1524.

Galanthus platyphyllus Traub & Moldenke, syn. *G. latifolius* Rupr. (*Amaryllidaceae*). Native of the central and western Caucasus where it grows in alpine and subalpine meadows, flowering in May and June. Very close to *G. ikariae* Baker, but plant usually larger, flowers on shorter pedicels and inner petals unlobed with a bold green spot.
Photographed in the central Caucasus, by the Georgian Military Highway on the south side of the Krestovje pass at 2500m, in May 1978.

Galanthus platyphyllus on the Georgian Military Highway.

Galanthus byzantinus

¾ life size Photographed 13 February

I. rosenbachiana ½ life size 2 February

Galanthus ikariae Photographed 21 March

½ life size Photographed 13 February

(a) **Galanthus ikariae** Baker (*Amaryllidaceae*) (see p.15 (b), (c).) The form shown here was collected on Andros, and is very similar to that from N Turkey shown on p.14(b); another form. Photographed in cultivation.

(b) **Galanthus fosteri** Baker (*Amaryllidaceae*). Native of Turkey and Lebanon where it grows among mountain rocks and in scrub, at around 1600m, flowering in February and March. It has rather broad dark green leaves like *G. ikariae* but there are two green spots on the inner petals. Reputed to be difficult in cultivation. It has survived well in a dry sunny bulb frame at Wisley. Source Turkey, Adana, above Haruniye, 1400m, P. Davis 26830.

(c) **Galanthus rizehensis** Stern (*Amaryllidaceae*). Native of north-eastern Turkey at c.150m in the foothills of the Pontus mountains above Rize and Trabzon, growing in woods, flowering in January. Very similar to *G. nivalis* in general appearance, but has bright shining green leaves. Easy to grow in the same conditions as suit most other snowdrops.

(d), (e) **Galanthus caucasicus** (Baker) Grossh. (*Amaryllidaceae*). Native of the Caucasus and the Caspian coast where it grows in woods in the foothills, flowering from December to March. Very variable in leaf width, size and in flowering time in cultivation, but can be recognised by its glaucous leaves, one folded inside the other in the sheath. A robust and easy species in good soil in shade.

(f) **Galanthus nivalis 'Magnet'**. A large form of *G. nivalis* raised by J. Allen (see (i)) in the late nineteenth century. The flower hangs on a long graceful pedicel.

(g) **Galanthus nivalis 'Atkinsii'**. A hybrid, *G. nivalis* × *G. plicatus*, named by J. Allen (see (i)) after James Atkins of Painswick in Gloucestershire. The flower has an unusually short pedicel, almost hidden in the spathe.

(h) **Galanthus nivalis 'Lutescens'**. A pale delicate form of *G. nivalis*, requiring more care than the ordinary form. Originated in Northumberland in the nineteenth century.

(i) **Galanthus allenii** Baker (*Amaryllidaceae*). The origin of this species is something of a mystery. It is intermediate between *G. caucasicus* and *G. ikariae* and was spotted by the great Snowdrop grower James Allen of Shepton Mallett, Somerset, in a consignment of bulbs from the Caucasus. Possibly a hybrid.

(j) **Galanthus nivalis 'S. Arnott'**. This fine form was named after Samuel Arnott, Provost of Dumfries (1800–1900) who introduced it into cultivation. The outer petals are very short and broad.

Iris. rosenbachiana Regel, syn. *I. nicolai* Vved. (*Iridaceae*, section *Juno*)). Native of Central Asia, especially the Pamir Alai, and NE Afghanistan, where it grows on stony hillsides and dry earthy slopes flowering from March to April. Plant about 10cm high at flowering, the leaves expanding later to about 15cm long. The form shown was that called *I. nicolai* Vved., and *I. rosenbachiana* was described as purple-flowered, but the two are now considered merely as colour forms of one species, cf. *I. persica* (p.62). **Rare in cultivation and not easy,** but should grow in a very well drained soil, kept rather dry and protected from rain in summer and in winter. Source Tashkent Botanic Garden.

¾ life size Photographed 11 February

(a) **Crocus alatavicus** Regel & Semenov (*Iridaceae*). Native of Central Asia, especially the Ala-Tau, the Tien Shan and the Pamir-Alai, growing in stony places and scrub in the mountains and flowering from February to May according to altitude. It often grows with the yellow *Colchicum luteum* (p.33), whereas the yellow *Crocus korolkowii* grows with the white *Colchicum kesselringii* (p.33). Easy in a bulb frame kept dry in summer. Source Central Asia, Chimgan valley, NE of Tashkent, 1700m, Rix 2765.

(b) **Crocus korolkowii** Regel & Maw (*Iridaceae*). Native of northern Afghanistan, Chitral and Central Asia, especially the Tien Shan and the Pamir Alai, growing in stony and grassy places in the mountains and foothills from 600 to 2600m, flowering from February to May. Easy in a bulb frame but possible in a place outside. Source Central Asia, foothills N of Dushanbe, 1200m, Rix 2728.

(c) **Crocus graveolens** Boiss. & Reut. (*Iridaceae*). Native of southern Turkey and Syria growing in stony fields, scrub and pine forest at c.1000m, flowering in February and March. Distinguished from other yellow-flowered species by its finely divided stigma (about twelve threads), and many narrow, grey-green leaves and parallel fibred corm tunic. The flowers smell of elder. The closely related *C. vitellinus* Wahl. has fewer deep green broader leaves. Cultivation as (a). Source S Turkey, Hatay, near Yayladağ, Rix 1365.

(d) **Crocus nevadensis** Amo (*Iridaceae*). Native of SE Spain and N Africa, growing in mountain meadows, scree, scrub and open pine forest from 1000 to 3000m, flowering from February to April. Petals sometimes, e.g. from the Sierra de Cazorla, unmarked. The whitish fimbriate stigmas are characteristic. Very susceptible to botrytis which infects the dead flowers and if not checked, can kill the leaves and bulb. Source S Spain, Sierra Nevada above Granada, Rix s.n.

(e) **Crocus flavus** Weston × **C. angustifolius** Weston. See pp.25 (f) and 29 (f). The slightly reticulate tunic shows this to be a hybrid. *C. flavus* is native of SE Europe and W Turkey and has a parallel fibred tunic.

(f) **Crocus candidus** Clarke (*Iridaceae*). Native of western Turkey growing in woods and scrub, flowering in February and March. It is especially common in scrub along the Dardanelles and in the pine woods above Troy. Leaves one or two, very wide (see p.25). Styles yellow-orange, much divided. Cultivation as (a). Source NW Turkey, NE of Çanakkale, 130m, N. M. G.Marr 198.

(g) **Crocus sieberi** subsp. **atticus** (Boiss & Orph.) B. Mathew (*Iridaceae*). Native of Greece, growing in stony places in mountains, woods and scrub usually above 1000m, flowering from March to June. Other colour forms are shown and described on p.24 (d), (e). Cultivation as (b). Source Greece, Elion Oros, S of Levadhia, 1100m, Rix 2176.

Crocus tommasinianus Herbert (*Iridaceae*). Native of S Hungary, Yugoslavia and N Bulgaria, where it grows in woods and shady hillsides, especially on limestone, at around 1000m, flowering in January and February. The leaves are always well developed by flowering time. The combination of narrow leaves, purple flower and white tube distinguishes this species from *C. vernus* (p.26). Easily grown in well-drained soil or short grass.

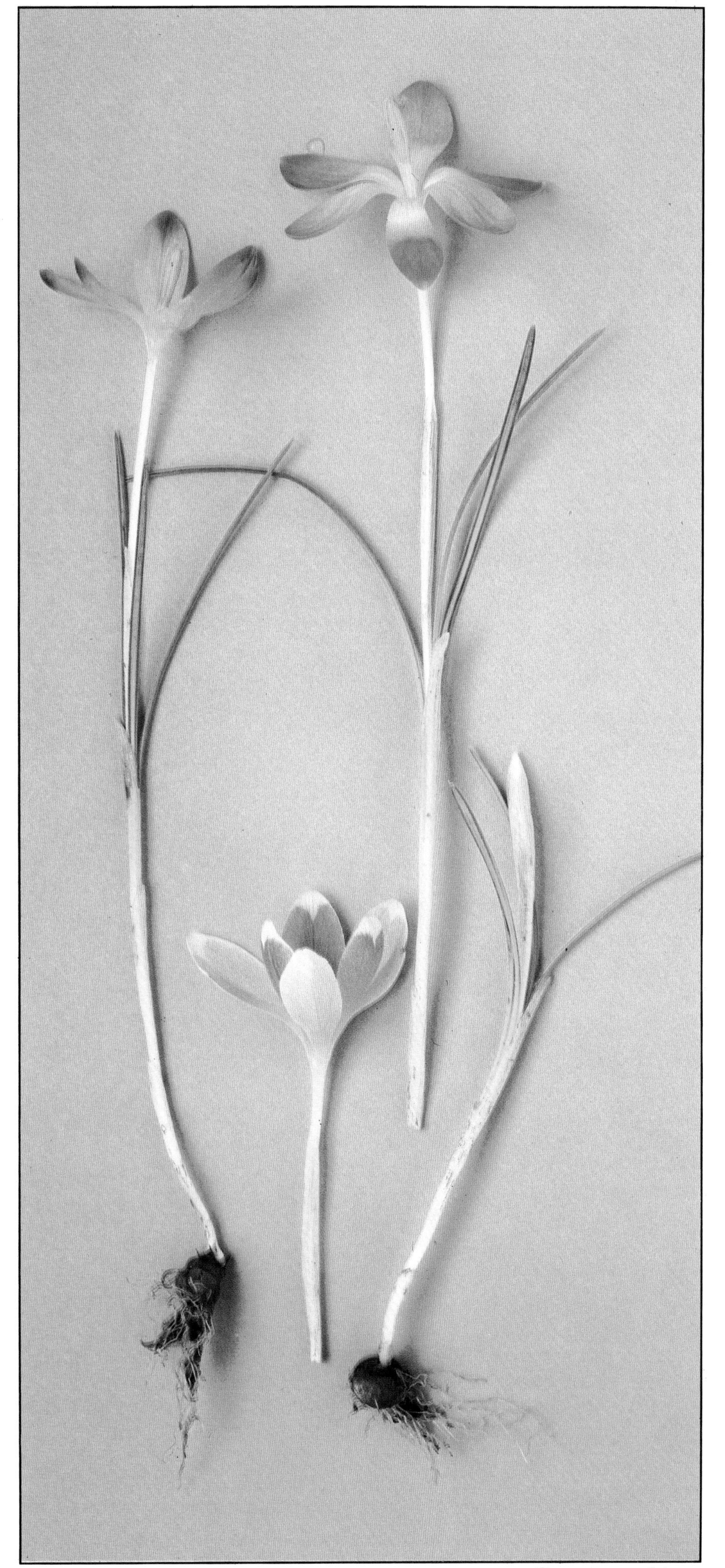

Crocus tommasinianus

life size Photographed 11 February

(**a**) **Crocus biflorus** subsp. **nubigena** (Herbert) B. Mathew (*Iridaceae*). Native of S Greece and western Turkey, growing in evergreen oak scrub and pine forests at 100–1000m, flowering from November till March. Grows outside in stony soil in full sun, but better in a bulb frame because it flowers so early. Source Turkey, Bergama, 260m, Marr 3282. See also p.234 (e).

(**b**) & (**c**) **Crocus chrysanthus** (Herbert) Herbert (*Iridaceae*). Native of Yugoslavia and Romania to Greece and southern Turkey, usually on bare stony or grassy slopes, at 1000–2000m, flowering from March to June, according to altitude. Cultivation as (a). Source Turkey, NW of Maraş, Berit Da., 2000m, Rix 700, and near Pazaçik, 1000m, Rix 1395.

(**d**) **Crocus biflorus** Miller (*Iridaceae*). This very variable species is native from Italy and Sicily eastwards to Georgia, Turkey, and N Iran, growing in woods, on dry open stony hills and alpine turf at up to 3000m, flowering from January to May. The lilac or blue flowers are characteristic of the species (see pp.23, 25 and 27). Source SE Turkey, Bitlis, dry stony hillside, 2000m, Rix 707, (subsp. *tauri*).

(**e**) **Crocus biflorus** subsp. **weldenii** (Hoppe & Furnrohr) B. Mathew, syn. *C. biflorus* var. *albus* Herbert (*Iridaceae*). Native of S Yugoslavia, growing in rocky woods especially on limestone at about 1000m. Cultivate as (a). Source Yugoslavia, Kičevo, Marr 45.

(**f**) **Crocus fleischeri** Gay (*Iridaceae*). Native of western and southern Turkey where it grows on dry rocky hillsides and in evergreen oak scrub at around 1000m, flowering from January till March. Source SW Turkey, Antalya, near Elmali, Rix 1315.

(**g**) **Crocus olivieri** Gay, syn. *C. suterianus* Herbert (*Iridaceae*). Native of Albania, Yugoslavia and Bulgaria to Greece and Turkey, growing on open hillsides in deciduous scrub, or in pine woods, from sea level to 1500m, flowering from January till March. Plants from Greece usually have broader leaves with some purple on the back of the flower. Subsp. *balansae* from W Turkey around Izmir has flowers usually purplish outside, and styles divided into twelve, not six branches. Source Turkey, between Istanbul and Ankara, Rix 651.

(**h**) **Crocus antalyensis** Mathew (*Iridaceae*). Native of south-west and west Turkey, near Antalya and near Bileçik, growing in evergreen oak scrub at c.1000m, flowering in early spring. Best kept in a bulb frame in full sun. Source S Turkey, mountains S of Antalya, 1000m, Rix 1318. (This is the type collection.)

(**i**) **Crocus minimus** DC. (*Iridaceae*). Native of south Corsica at low altitudes, and in Sardinia growing in scrub, flowering from January to April. Cultivation as (a).

(**j**) **Crocus cyprius** Boiss. & Kotschy (*Iridaceae*). Native of Cyprus, especially in the Troodos mountains, growing in stony places, flowering from January to April. Distinguished from *C. hartmannianus* (k) by its papery annulate corm tunic. Cultivation as (a).

(**k**) **C. hartmannianus** Holmboe (*Iridaceae*). Native of Cyprus, in the Troodos mountains where it is said to be rare, growing at about 880m, flowering in mid February. Very closely related to *C. cyprius* (j), but with a coarser tunic with parallel fibres. Cultivation as (a). Source Cyprus, coll. E. Hodgkin s.n.

life size Photographed 13 February

life size Photographed 13 February

Crocus gargaricus on Ulu Dag above Bursa

Crocus scardicus Kosanin (*Iridaceae*). Native of south-western Yugoslavia, where it grows at altitudes of 1700–2500m, by late snow patches, flowering from May to July. Photographed in Yugoslavia, Sar Planina, by Oleg Polunin 7153B.

Crocus sieberi subsp. **nivalis** (Bory & Chaub) B. Mathew (see p.19 (g)). Photographed in Greece, S Peloponnese, Taygetos mts, between Kalamata and Sparta, 1300m, 12 April 1972.

Crocus gargaricus Herbert (see p.25 (m)). Photographed in NW Turkey, Ulu Dağ above Bursa, 2000m, in March 1975 by Brian Mathew 8515.

Crocus biflorus subsp. **tauri** (Maw) B. Mathew (see p.21) (d)). A variable species native from Italy and Sicily eastwards to Georgia, Turkey, and N Iran, growing in damp woods, on dry open stony hillsides and alpine turf at up to 3000m, flowering from January to May. Photographed in central Turkey, Kuruca geçidi, E of Bingöl, 2000m, 10 May 1971.

Crocus chrysanthus cultivars
These were raised by crossing *C. chrysanthus* (p.21) with various forms of *C. biflorus* (pp.21, 25, 27, 31) and selecting far larger flowers and unusual markings and colour combinations. The breeding programme was initiated by John Hoog of the famous bulb firm of Van Tubergen at Zwanenburg Nurseries in Haarlem, and E. A. Bowles (1865–1954) author of *A Handbook of Crocus and Colchicum for Gardeners*, who exchanged bulbs and named their finest hybrids in each other's honour. Other named cultivars are selected clones of either species. Bowles named many of his hybrids after birds, and some are still in commerce today. (a) **'Advance'** (hybrid), (b) **'Goldilocks'**, (c) **'Gypsy Girl'**, (d) **'Saturnus'** (hybrid), (e) **'Blue Bird'** (*C. biflorus*), (f) **'Blue Pearl'** (syn. 'Blue Giant'), (g) **'Snow Bunting'** (hybrid), (h) **'Zwanenburg Bronze'**, (i) **'Cream Beauty'** (hybrid), (j) **'Nanette'**.

Crocus biflorus subsp. **tauri**

Crocus sieberi subsp. **nivalis**

Crocus scardicus

life size Photographed 18 February

(**a**) **Crocus versicolor** Ker-Gawler (*Iridaceae*). Native of the Alpes Maritimes, growing in scrubs and among rocks at up to 1200m, flowering from February to April. Grow in a bulb frame or sunny well-drained place outside. Source P. J. Christian 52.

(**b**) **Crocus biflorus** subsp. **alexandri** (Ničić ex Velen.) B. Mathew (*Iridaceae*). Native of Yugoslavia, especially around Skopje. This striking colour form of *C. biflorus* (p.21 (d)) has been in cultivation for many years. Cultivation as (a).

(**c**) **Crocus etruscus** Parl. (*Iridaceae*). Native of western Italy, growing in deciduous woods and stony fields, flowering from February to April. The form shown here is the cv. 'Zwanenburg'.

(**d**) **Crocus sieberi** Gay subsp. **sieberi**, syn. *C. sieberi* var. *heterochromus* Hal., *C. sieberi* var *versicolor* Boiss. & Held. (*Iridaceae*). Native of Crete, in the White Mountains, where it grows in the hills above the Omalos plain. Better grown in a bulb frame. 'Hubert Edelsten' is a hybrid between var. *sieberi* and var. *atticus*.

(**e**) **Crocus sieberi** Gay forma **tricolor** Burtt. This beautiful form originated in the northern Peloponnese on Mt Chelmos. The plant shown is abnormally small.

(**f**) **Crocus angustifolius** Weston, syn *C. susianus* Ker-Gawl. (*Iridaceae*). Native of the Crimea where it grows on hillsides, and in scrub and Juniper woods, flowering in February and March. Cultivation as (a).

(**g**) **Crocus aerius** Herbert, syn. *C. biliottii* Maw (*Iridaceae*). Native of northern Turkey, especially the Pontus mountains, where it grows in grassy and stony places at c.2000m, flowering in May. The leaves are curved, rather stiff, and glaucous. Cultivation as (a). Source NE Turkey, pass from Bayburt to Of, Rix 1002.

(**h**) **Crocus pestalozzae** Boiss. (*Iridaceae*). Native of north-western Turkey on both the European and Asiatic side of the Bosphorus, near Istanbul, growing in fields and on low hills below 200m, flowering January to March. Has small black spots at the base of the filaments.

(**i**) **Crocus candidus** Clarke (*Iridaceae*) (see p.19 (f)). Source Turkey, near Çanakkale. H. & M. Crook 3026.

(**j**) **Crocus ancyrensis** (Herb.) Maw (*Iridaceae*). Native of western Turkey where it grows on dry hillsides at 1500–2000m, flowering in March and April. Source Turkey, near Ankara, Baytop.

(**k**) **Crocus baytopiorum** Mathew (*Iridaceae*). Native of western Turkey, especially Honaz Dağ, where it grows at about 1400m, flowering in February. The only member of the *C. vernus* group yet found in Turkey. For a bulb frame. Source Turkey, Honaz Dağ, A. & T. Baytop.

(**l**) **Crocus reticulatus** Steven ex Adam (*Iridaceae*). Native of SE Europe from NE Italy and Hungary to Bulgaria, S Turkey and the Caucasus, growing in woods and meadows up to 2000m, flowering from February to April. Source Caucasus, Ordzonikidze, M. Prasil 156–76.

(**m**) **Crocus gargaricus** Herbert (*Iridaceae*). Native of north-western Turkey, especially Ulu Dağ and Kaz Dağ, where it grows in great quantity on grassy slopes (see p.23). Easy to grow in a frame in peaty soil. Source Turkey, Ulu Dağ, above Bursa, 2100m, Rix 1209a.

life size Photographed 18 February

life size Photographed 18 February

(a) **Crocus vernus** (L.) Hill (*Iridaceae*). Native of the mountains of Europe from the Pyrenees eastwards to Poland and Russia, and south to Sicily and Yugoslavia, growing in grassland, scrub and open woods, flowering from February to June. Two subspecies are recognised: subsp. *vernus*, shown here, usually with purple flowers, occurs from Italy eastwards. Subsp. *albiflorus* (Kit.) Asch. & Graeb. is the common white crocus of alpine meadows, found from Czechoslovakia westwards. Subsp. *vernus* is easy in grass, and is the origin of the large Dutch purple crocus. Subsp. *albiflorus* has proved difficult. Source Italy, Naples, nr Giovanni, Mrs P. Saunders.

(b) **Crocus veluchensis** Herbert (*Iridaceae*). Native of Yugoslavia, Bulgaria, Albania and Greece, growing in rocky ground, on mountain grassland and by late snow patches at 2000m, flowering from April to July according to altitude. Easy to grow in well-drained soil in sun. Source NE Greece, Pindus Mts, Katara pass, coll. Mrs F. Baxter.

(c) **Crocus dalmaticus** Vis. (*Iridaceae*). Native of south-west Yugoslavia and north Albania, especially the area around Dubrovnik, growing in limestone hills among oak scrub and in rocky grassland, flowering from January to April. Colour varies from buff to dark violet. Grow in a bulb frame. Source Yugoslavia, above Kotor, B. Mathew 5174.

(d) **Crocus imperati** Ten. (*Iridaceae*). Native of western Italy from Rome southwards, growing in woods, scrub and rough grassy places, flowering from January to March. The form shown here is an albino. The flowers are usually purple to almost white, with the outer petals beautifully striped and feathered outside. Subsp. *imperati*, style deep orange; from Naples southwards. Subsp. *suaveolens* (Bertol.) Mathew, style yellow or orange; Naples northwards. Grow in a bulb frame.

(e) **Crocus malyi** Vis. (*Iridaceae*). Native of NW Yugoslavia, especially the Velebit mountains, growing in grassy places and at the edges of woods from 650 to 1000m, flowering in March and April. Source Yugoslavia, Karlobag to Gospić, P. A. Cox and J. Marr 6.

(f) **Crocus carpetanus** Boiss. & Reut. (*Iridaceae*). Native of central and north-west Spain and N Portugal, growing in stony places in the mountains from 1200 to 2000m, flowering in April and May. The leaves which are U-shaped in section are characteristic as is the very soft fibrous tunic and whitish style. Easy to grow in a bulb frame, but needs frequent replanting as the corms tend to get crowded and smothered by their thick tunic. Source C Spain, Sierra de Guaderrama, near Rascafria, Rix s.n.

(g) **Crocus danfordiae** Maw (*Iridaceae*). Native of central and southern Turkey, especially around Ankara and in the central Tauros mountains, where it grows in rocky places, usually on limestone, at 1200–2000m. Flowers may be yellow or bluish. Grow in a bulb frame. Source Turkey, between Kayseri and Malatya, Rix 1401.

(h) **Crocus biflorus** Miller subsp. **biflorus** (*Iridaceae*). This form of *C. biflorus* is found on the island of Rhodes, off the SW corner of Turkey. Source Mt Profitis Ilias, 600m, among limestone rocks under pines, Rix 1272.

(i) **Crocus vernus** var. **leucostigma**. This differs from normal *C. vernus* in its slender white stigma, rather than the usual orange one. It has been known in cultivation for many years, but its origin is unknown.

life size Photographed 13 February

life size Photographed 13 March

¼ life size Photographed 25 February

Crocus corsicus ½ life size 13 March

Sternbergia candida

(**a**) to (**e**) **Crocus vernus** cultivars (*Iridaceae*). These have been obtained by selection over several centuries from *C. vernus* subsp. *vernus*, p.27 (a). They survive well in grass, increasing by division to form solid patches. They should therefore be planted singly some distance apart, to produce a more natural effect. Shown here are:
(**a**) **'Pickwick'** (The flower is small because it has only just emerged and will expand).
(**b**) **'Remembrance'.**
(**f**) An old cultivated clone of *C. vernus*.
(**g**) **'King of the Whites'**.
(**e**) **'Little Dorritt'**.

(**f**) **Crocus 'Dutch Yellow'** or **'Yellow Giant'**. This old garden clone has been cultivated since the seventeenth century. It was formerly thought to be a form of *C. flavus*, but recent chromosome studies at Kew by C. Brighton and B. Mathew have shown it to be a triploid hybrid between *C. flavus* and *C. angustifolius* (p.25 (**f**)). Easily grown, but happier in better drained soil than the *C. vernus* cultivars.

(**g**) **Sternbergia fischerana** (Herb.) Roem. (*Amaryllidaceae*). Native of Iran and the Kopet Dağ., to the Caucasus, Turkey and Syria, growing on stony slopes at 200–300m, flowering in February and March. A double-flowered form was recently collected in N Iran by Mrs A. Ala, and has been named 'Golestan'. Best grown in a pot or bulb frame where it can receive a good baking in summer to help initiate flowering.

(**e**) **Sternbergia colchiciflora** Waldst. & Kit. (*Amaryllidaceae*). Native of the Mediterranean region from Spain and France to Hungary, Turkey and Iran, where it grows on dry hillsides, flowering in autumn (see p.246). The leaves and seed pod shown here are highly characteristic. Easy to grow in a bulb frame, but rather too small and delicate to place outside. Source C Turkey, Kayseri to Gürün, 1500m, Rix 1599.

Crocus biflorus subsp. **isauricus and Eranthis cilicicus**

Crocus biflorus subsp. **isauricus** (Siehe ex Bowles) B. Mathew. (*Iridaceae*). This variant of the very variable *C. biflorus* (pp.20 (**a**), (**d**), (**e**) and 27 (**h**)) is found mainly in southern and western Turkey. Growing with *Eranthis cilicicus* (see p.39). Photographed in S Turkey, Antalya, above Akseki, by O. Polunin.

Crocus corsicus Vanucci ex Maw (*Iridaceae*). Native of Corsica where it grows in stony and grassy places in the mountains, up to 2000m, flowering from January till June according to altitude. Tunic fibrous and finely reticulate. Easy to grow in a bulb frame or in a dry sunny place outside in the south of England. Always one of the last crocuses to flower. Source Corsica, Monte D'Oro, c.1800m, Rix s.n.

Sternbergia candida Mathew & T. Baytop (*Amaryllidaceae*). Native of south-western Turkey, near Fethiye, where it was discovered as recently as 1976 by Oleg Polunin. It grows in scrub and among rocks at the edge of cedar forest, flowering in January and February. The only white *Sternbergia*. Petals 4.5–5cm; height 12–20cm. Photographed near Fethiye in February 1980 by O. Sønderhousen.

life size Photographed 25 February

Romuleas are similar to Crocuses, but most species have flowers on distinct stems. The leaves of the Mediterranean species generally appear in winter, and are killed by frost below −10°C, unless protected by snow. The bulbs are also tender. Most of the South African species are even more tender, and grow well in the warmer parts of California. A few, from the high Drakensberg grow in summer, and are hardy. Two are shown on p.216.

(a) **Romulea columnae** Seb. & Mauri (*Iridaceae*). Native of the Azores, western England (Devon), and the Channel Is, S to Spain and N Africa, Turkey and Israel, usually in sandy places near the sea, flowering in February and March. The flowers are always small, 1–2cm long, and are usually pale lilac, with a yellow throat. The inner bract is scarious. Easy to grow in very sandy soil in a bulb frame or pot. Source France, St Tropez, sandy cliff top, Rix s.n.

(b) **Romulea crocea** Boiss. & Held. (*Iridaceae*). Native of southern Turkey, where it grows in sandy places near the sea, flowering in March. Easily recognised among Mediterranean species by its yellow flowers, but otherwise very similar to *R. bulbocodium*. Easy to grow in a very sandy soil in a bulb frame. Source Turkey, Manavgat to Alanya, fixed dunes by the sea, Rix 1334.

(c) **Crocus biflorus** subsp. **pulchricolor** (Herbert) B. Mathew (*Iridaceae*). A well-marked form of *C. biflorus* (see p.23 (c) etc.) from Ulu Dağ, north-west Turkey. Flowering late, but easily grown and increasing well with striking dark bluish flowers. In wild it grows with *C. gargaricus* (p.23). Source Turkey, Bursa, Ulu Dağ, c.2000m, Rix 1209.

(d) (e) (h) **Romulea bulbocodium** (L.) Seb. & Mauri (Iridaceae). Native of the Mediterranean region from NW Spain and N Africa to S France, Yugoslavia, Turkey and Israel, growing in sandy and rocky places near the sea and in scrub up to 1000m. Very variable in flower size (20–35mm) and colour, varying from white to pink and lilac. The flowers are often of two sizes, the smaller flowers being pollen-sterile, which makes the anthers appear white – see (d) and (h): this phenomenon is commoner in cultivation in some years than in others. Easy to grow in a bulb frame, but not long-lived in the open. Keep dry in summer and replant regularly in good, very sandy soil. Source (d) S Italy, above Matera, Rix 453; (e) Greece, Corfu, 800m, Rix 459; (h) N Africa, J. Archibald 839.

(f) **Romulea nivalis** (Boiss. & Kotschy) Klatt (*Iridaceae*). Native of Syria (Anti-lebanon) and the Lebanon, growing at 1400–2000m, flowering in May and June near the melting snow. Distinct in its rather stiff upright growth, smallish flowers (20–25mm) with a very short tube. Easy to grow in a bulb frame, but not increasing as do many of the other species. Source Mt Hermon.

(g) **Romulea tempskyana** Freyn (*Iridaceae*). Native of SW Turkey from Izmir southwards, Rhodes and Cyprus, growing on low hills and sandy places up to 1000m, flowering in March. Distinguished from other species by its dark purple flowers 15–26mm long, with a long slender tube, exserted from the bracts. Easy to grow in a bulb frame and very striking when the starry deep-purple flowers open wide in the sun. Source Rhodes, dry sandy maquis, Rix 1243.

life size Photographed 11 February

life size Photographed 11 February

Iris pseudocaucasica in northwestern Iran.

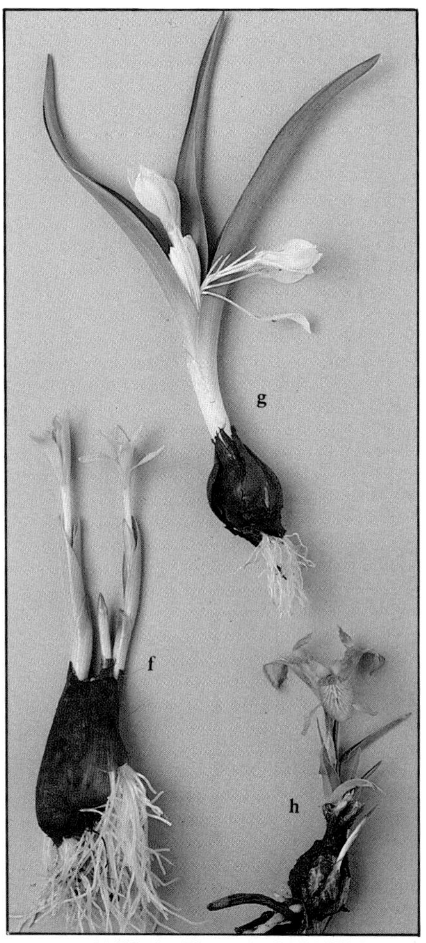

½ life size Photographed 25 February

(a) Colchicum szovitsii Fischer & C. A. Meyer, syn. *C. nivale* Boiss. & Huet, *C. bifolium* Freyn & Sint. (*Liliaceae*). Native of Turkey, Iran, Soviet Armenia and the Kopet Dağ, growing in alpine meadows from 2000 to 3000m, and flowering from March to June. Flowers pink or white. Leaves usually two, glabrous. Easily grown in a bulb frame or raised bed, and probably better if not baked in summer. Source Turkey, Kayseri, Erciyes Dağ, alpine meadows, 2300m, Mathew & Tomlinson 4530.

(b) Colchicum falcifolium Stapf syn. *C. serpentinum* Woron, ex Miscz., *C. tauri* Siehe ex Stef. (*Liliaceae*). Native of the Caucasus, Iran and Turkey, growing on dry stony hills at c. 1000m, flowering from February to April. Leaves sometimes hairy (*C.hirsutum* Stef.). Not difficult to grow in a dry bulb frame but slow to increase. Source Turkey, Malatya, limestone hills west of Darende, 1500m, Rix 1591.

(c) Colchicum kesselringii Regel (*Liliaceae*). Native of Central Asia, especially the Tien Shan and the Pamir Alai, and northern Afghanistan, from 1500 to 3000m, flowering from February to June depending on altitude, and growing on stony hillsides and alpine meadows. The flowers emerge as soon as the snow melts, and fade within a day or two to be followed by rather narrow leaves (up to 1cm wide). E. A. Bowles records that it grew well on a sunny bank until eaten by slugs. Cultivation as (a).

(d) Merendera hissarica Regel (*Liliaceae*). Native of Central Asia, especially the Pamir Alai and the Tien Shan, N. Afghanistan, growing in stony places at 2400–4000m, flowering in spring. Flowers are rather similar to *Colchicum kesselringii*, but petals rounded and filamentous at the base. Anthers long compared with *M. trigyna* (g). Has survived and flowered in a bulb frame, but not increased. Source Afghanistan, SO623.

(e) Colchicum hungaricum Janka (*Liliaceae*). Native of south-eastern Europe, growing on stony hills, flowering from December to April. Leaves two or three, ciliate. Flowers purplish-pink to white. Leaves usually well developed at flowering. Cultivation as (a). Source Yugoslavia, Mathew & Tomlinson.

(f) Colchicum luteum Baker (*Liliaceae*). Native of Afghanistan, north-west India and Central Asia, especially the Tien Shan and the Pamir Alai, from 2000 to 3800m, growing on earthy slopes, flowering from March to July, at the edge of the melting snow. Not easy. The dead flowers are liable to botrytis which soon spreads to the developing leaves. Probably best planted in very gritty soil in a bulb frame and kept covered to protect from rain.

(g) Merendera trigyna (Adams) Woronow (*Liliaceae*). Native of the Caucasus, Turkey and N Iran, growing on dry slopes at about 1500–1800m, flowering from January to April. *Merendera* is close to *Colchicum*, but the petals are separate, so that the flower falls to pieces as it goes over. *M. kurdica* Bornm., from eastern Turkey and Iran, has broader petals and leaves. Easily grown in a bulb frame.

(h) Iris planifolia (Miller) Fiori & Paol., syn. *I. alata* Poiret (*Iridaceae*, section *Juno*). Native of the Mediterranean region from southern Spain and N Africa to Greece, Crete and Sicily, flowering from December to February. The plant shown here is unusually small. Not easy to grow, but will survive in a dry, sunny bulb frame. Hardy to −5°C. Source N Africa.

Iris pseudocaucasica Grossh. (*Iridaceae* section *Juno*). Native of N Iraq, north to Armenia, and N Iran, growing on stony hillsides from 600 to 3450m, flowering from April to June. Distinguished from *I. caucasica* (p.65) by the high wings on the erect part of the falls. The flowers vary from pale blue, through greenish, to yellow. Photographed in Iran by Brian Mathew, BSBE 744.

Colchicum luteum

life size Photographed 18 February

(a), (c), (d), (e), (f) Cyclamen coum Miller, syn. *C. atkinsii* T. Moore, *C. orbiculatum* Miller (*Primulaceae*). Native of the Crimea, Bulgaria, Turkey, NW Syria, the Caucasus and NW Iran, growing in beech or pine woods and scrub from sea level to 2000m, flowering from February to May according to altitude. Very variable; pink forms are commonest in S Turkey and N Syria, dark pink or magenta forms from around Istanbul and the Black Sea coast. From eastern Turkey eastwards, the flowers become progressively larger and the leaves more heart-shaped. Plants from this area are called var. *caucasicum* (C. Koch) Meikle (q.v.). The easternmost forms from forest along the Caspian coast of Iran have been called *C. elegans* Boiss. & Buhse; its flowers are large and pale pink, the leaves narrowly heart-shaped. Various intermediate forms are found in the southern Caucasus, and have been called *C. circassicum* Pobed., *C. adzaricum* Pobed., and *C. abchasicum* (Medw. ex Kusn.) Kulak. Illustrated here are: **(a)** E Georgia, above Telavi, 1000m, Rix 2647; **(c)**, **(e)** S Turkey, Hatay, above Osmaniye, 1000m, Rix 1379; **(d)** cultivar 'Album'; **(f)** N Turkey, near Trabzon, 1800m, Rix 1010. Easily grown in sun or light shade, in a well-drained leafy soil. Will often produce self-sown seedlings.

(b) Cyclamen trochopteranthum O. Schwarz, syn. *C. alpinum* Saunders (*Primulaceae*). Native of south-west Turkey around Muğla and Denizli, growing in scrub and under pine trees in stony ground from 350 to 1100m, and flowering from February to April. Said to smell of heather honey. Probably less hardy than *C. coum*, and safer grown in a frame or a pot in the alpine house.

(g) Cyclamen parviflorum Pobed., syn. *C. coum* subsp. *alpinum* O. Schwarz (*Primulaceae*). Native of northern Turkey, in the Pontus mountains above Trabzon and Rize, where it grows in pine forests, or under bushes of *Rhododendron* from 1200 to 2300m, flowering from April to June as soon as the snow melts. The leaves appear in autumn and are uniformly dark green with a slightly scalloped edge. Easy to grow in rather dry peaty or leafy soil in semi-shade, but easy to lose because it is so small. The round tuber often has a long delicate shoot on which grow the leaves and flowers. Should not be dried out in summer. Source N Turkey, above Of, under *R. caucasicum*, Rix 1003a.

(h) Cyclamen pseud-ibericum Hildebr. (*Primulaceae*). Native of southern Turkey in the Amanus mountains and in the Anti-Tauros, E and NE of Adana, growing in pine forests and beech and hornbeam woods, from 550 to 1500m. Rather similar to *C. coum*, but with much larger, always magenta, flowers. The flowers smell of violets. Should be grown in a pot, or in a rather dry spot in sun or semi-shade. Good in a bulb frame, where it can be kept rather dry in summer.

(i) Cyclamen libanoticum Hildebr. (*Primulaceae*). Known only from the Lebanon where it is very rare, growing in the mountains E of Beirut from 750 to 1400m, among limestone rocks and under trees. It was thought to be extinct but was recently rediscovered in small quantity. The young leaves appear in winter and will survive slight frost but are safer if protected in an alpine house or frame. The leaves are thick, fleshy and heart-shaped, with well rounded lobes; underneath they are deep shining red. Best grown in a pot or pan in the alpine house, in leafy, stony soil with limestone, and kept dry and cool in summer. A careful watch should be kept for vine-weevil larvae, which can do great damage to the roots of all cyclamen, especially in pots.

life size Photographed 13 March

½ life size Photographed 14 April

Leucojum trichophyllum

Cyclamen repandum f. **vividum (b)**

Cyclamen repandum subsp. **peloponnesiacum** in the Peloponnese.

Trillium nivale ½ life size 13 March

(a) Cyclamen persicum Miller (*Primulaceae*). Native of the eastern Mediterranean from Greece (where it is very rare) to Turkey, Cyprus and Lebanon, growing in woods, scrub and among limestone rocks, at altitudes of up to c.1000m, flowering from February to April. The tuber can be large, up to 15cm in diameter, rooting from the lower surface. The leaves appear in winter before the flowers, and are variously marbled with silver. The flowers vary from white to purple in the wild, and smell sweetly like lily-of-the-valley. The flower stalk does not coil and pull the seed head to the ground. Not reliably hardy. If grown in a pot, it should be kept dry in summer and very carefully watered while in growth. The cultivated florists' cyclamen have all been bred from *C. persicum* by selection.

(b)–(e) Cyclamen repandum Sibth. & Sm. (*Primulaceae*). Native of the north-east Mediterranean region from S. France to Yugoslavia, Greece and Rhodes, growing among shady rocks and in walls, in woods or scrub, at altitudes up to 500m. The leaves appear in early spring, the flowers from March to May. Very variable in leaf and flower colour. Subsp. *rhodense* (Meikle) Grey-Wilson from Rhodes has a greyish marbled leaf which appears in winter and white or pale pink flowers, usually with a darker eye, see p.75. In Corsica and Italy, the leaves are dark green, marbled pale green and irregularly toothed, and the flowers are deep pink with no eye (d). In the central Peloponnese, subsp. *peloponnesiacum* Grey-Wilson (c, e), the leaves are heavily marbled and spotted with white, and the flowers are pale pink with a deep pink eye. This form has received the cultivar name 'Pelops'. In the eastern Peloponnese, the flowers are crimson and the leaves are dark green, sometimes unmarked, sometimes faintly marbled f. *vividum* Grey-Wilson (b). Other Mediterranean islands have closely related species; *C. balearicum* Willk. from the Balearic Islands and S. France has marbled leaves emerging in spring, and whitish, small pink-veined flowers; *C. creticum* Hildebr. from Crete has pure white (or rarely pink) flowers and smaller leaves than *C. repandum*, which appear in autumn. All have a flattish corm, rooting from the middle. All forms of *C. repandum* are sensitive to hard frost and are better with protection in cold areas. Source: (b) Greece, SE Peloponnese, near Neapolis, Rix 2131; (c), (e) Greece, C Peloponnese, near Sparta, Rix 2107; (d) Corsica, near Ajaccio, Rix s.n.

Trillium nivale Riddell (*Liliaceae*) Native of eastern North America from Pennsylvania to Minnesota, south to Missouri and Kentucky, growing in woods, clearings and shady ledges, flowering from March to May. Grow in leafy soil in a cool, shady place, kept moist in summer. Good for a pot or pan in the alpine house.

Leucojum trichophyllum Schousboe (*Liliaceae*). Native of south-west Spain, S Portugal and Morocco where it grows in sandy places, often in dunes, flowering from January to April. Flowers usually white; petals 12–20mm long. The rather similar. *L. longifolium* (Gay) Gren. & Godr. has smaller flowers about 10mm long and rounded petals. Best grown in a pan in the alpine house or in a bulb frame kept dry in summer. Photographed by Paul Furse.

½ life size Photographed 11 February

(a) **Gymnospermium alberti** (Regel) Takht., syn. *Leontice alberti* Regel (*Podophyllaceae*). Native of Central Asia, especially the Tien Shan and the Pamir Alai growing among shrubs and rocks at c.2000m, flowering in April and May, as soon as the snow melts. Height c.10cm at flowering, up to 20cm in fruit. Leaves digitate. Often considered to belong to the *Berberis* family. Should be kept rather dry at all times and completely dry in summer. Source C Asia, Tashkent, Chimgan valley, Rix 2768, and photographed in May, 1980.

(b) **Hyacinthella acutiloba** Persson & Wendelbo (*Liliaceae*). Native of Turkey, where it grows in rocky places in the mountains, flowering in spring. The specimen shown here is a very poor one. Leaves with raised nerves, and ciliate. Easy to grow, but does not increase well, and is susceptible to botrytis. Source C Turkey, between Kayseri and Malatya, among limestone rocks, 2000m, Rix 1609.

(c) **Scilla sibirica** Haw. in Andrews (*Liliaceae*). Native of S Russia, the Caucasus and Turkey southwards to Syria, growing in woods, scrub and among rocks, up to 2000m, flowering from March to May. Naturalised in E Europe. Very variable. The form shown here is a rather small pale one, from the south part of the species range. (See also pp.43 and 44). Easy to grow in a bulb frame or dry shady place outside. Source S Turkey, Gaziantep, Nurdağ pass, 1000m, Rix 1375. (Probably = *S. ingridae* Speta.)

(d) **Eranthis hyemalis** (L.) Salisb. (*Ranunculaceae*). Winter Aconite. Native of France, Italy, Yugoslavia and Bulgaria, but widely naturalised elsewhere in Europe. It grows in woods and rocky places, flowering from January to March. *E. cilicicus* (e) differs in its narrower leaves and larger flowers, and var. *bulgaricus* Stephanof from Bulgaria tends towards it. The garden form *E.* 'Guinea Gold' is also intermediate with extra large flowers. Easy to grow, and naturalises best in well-drained alkaline soil, under deciduous trees. Good under Horse Chestnuts (*Aesculus*).

(e) **Ornithogalum fimbriatum** Willd. (*Liliaceae*). Native of Romania and Bulgaria to Greece and Turkey, growing on dry hillsides, flowering from February to May. Leaves hairy beneath and often ciliate at base. Easy to grow and increases well. Very early flowering in cultivation usually beginning in December. Source Greece, Euboea, Mt Dirphys, Rix s.n.

(f) **Eranthis cilicicus** Schott & Kotschy (*Ranunculaceae*). Native of Turkey, N Iraq and Afghanistan, growing on open hillsides and in pine and fir woods, flowering from February to May. Very similar to *E. hyemalis*, and now considered synonymous with it, but leaf segments usually narrower and flowers larger. See also p.29. Grows well in a bulb frame or pot and will tolerate drying in summer. Source Turkey, Mathew & Tomlinson 4138.

Leontice leontopetalum L. subsp. **eversmannii** (Bunge) Coode (*Podophyllaceae*). Native of E Turkey, N Iraq, Iran, Afghanistan and C Asia, growing in fields and on stony hillsides from 400 to 2200m, flowering from March to May. Subspecies *leontopetalum* has broader leaflets, which are usually orbicular, apiculate or emarginate. It grows further west than subsp. *eversmannii*, i.e. from Bulgaria, Greece and Turkey to Iran and Iraq, Israel and N Africa. Photographed in C Asia, Amankutan valley, S of Samarkand, April 1979, Rix 2378.

Eranthis longistiptitatus Regel (*Ranunculaceae*). Native of Central Asia, especially the Kopet Dağ, Pamir Alai and the Tien Shan, growing in woods and among scrub from 1000 to 2000m, flowering from February to May. A very small delicate plant with flowers about 15mm across. The seed pods are held on long slender stalks, not sessile as in *E. hyemalis*. Probably better in a bulb frame. The plants collected in 1979 have grown but not flowered yet. Photographed in C Asia, Tashkent, Chimgan valley, 1800m, in May 1980.

Leontice armenaica Boivin, syn. *L. minor* Boiss. (*Podophyllaceae*). Native of S Caucasus, Syria and Jordan to Iran, growing in stony places from 1500 to 2400m, flowering in spring. Differs from *L. leontopetalum* in its smaller size, up to 20cm, and unbranched inflorescence. Best grown in a bulb frame and kept on the dry side as it is susceptible to too much damp in winter. Keep dry in summer. Photographed in NE Iraq by Oleg Polunin.

Leonticc armenaica

Gymnospermium alberti

Eranthis longistiptitatus

Leontice leontopetalum subsp. **eversmannii** near Samarkhand

¾ life size Photographed 13 March

(**a**), (**b**) × **Chionoscilla allenii** hort. (*Liliaceae*). This hybrid between *Chionodoxa luciliae* and *Scilla bifolia* is frequent in gardens where the two parents grow together and has also been found in the wild. Very variable, and many different forms have received cultivar names. The starry flowers are rather similar to *Scilla bifolia*, but the petals are joined at their base.

(**c**) **Scilla sibirica** Haw. in Andrews, c.v. **'Spring Beauty'** (*Liliaceae*). Native of S Russia southwards to Syria (see p.39 (c)). This robust cultivar has more purple in the flower than most wild forms. It is very similar to the original illustration of the species in Andrews' *Botanist's Repository*, a beautiful early nineteenth-century journal similar to the *Botanical Magazine*. Requires a rich sandy soil to grow well and tends to fade away if planted in thick grass (see p.43).

(**d**), (**e**) & (**f**) **Scilla bifolia** L. (*Liliaceae*). Native of central and southern Europe from Spain to Belgium and eastwards to the Ukraine, south to the Caucasus and Turkey, growing in woods, meadows and among rocks, flowering in spring. Very variable in size, chromosome number and flower colour, from pale violet to deep blue. The rather large starry flowers and two or three sheathing leaves are characteristic of the species. Easily grown in sunny places or half-shade in short grass or amongst shrubs, where it will naturalise itself if happy. Source (d) cultivated stock; (e) Greece, Euboea, Mt Dirphys, 1700m, Rix 626 (close to *S. nivalis* Boiss.); (f) forma *rosea*.

(**g**) **Chionodoxa luciliae** Boiss. (*Liliaceae*) Glory-of-the-Snow. Native of western Turkey, especially near Izmir, where it grows on stony hillsides, flowering in May and June by the melting snow at c.2000m (see also p.45 (c)). Leaves usually two. Flowers few, with a small white eye. The nomenclature of Turkish *Chionodoxa* is very confused, and most of the stocks in commerce are wrongly named. Easy to grow in well-drained soil in a sunny situation.

(**h**) **Scilla miczenkoana** Grossheim, syn. *S. tubergeniana* Hoog ex Stearn, (*Liliaceae*). Native of the southern Transcaucasia and NW Iran where it grows in mountain meadows and among rocks flowering from March to May. Like *S. sibirica* but flowers larger, palest blue or white, opening as soon as they emerge from the ground. Easily grown in a bulb frame, or a well-drained soil in the open where it will seed itself. The form sold as *S. tubergeniana* is slightly larger than the wild form shown here. Source NW Iran, pass from Ahar to Tabriz, 1800m, shady rocks, Rix 983.

(**i**) **Hyacinthella siirtensis** Mathew (*Liliaceae*). Native of south-east Turkey, growing on stony hillsides, flowering in early spring. The small pale sessile flowers are characteristic. The specimen here is rather smaller even than usual. Easy to grow in a bulb frame, flowering very early, often in December, and increasing well. Source Turkey, Siirt, pass between Eruh and Şirnak, Rix 417 (type collection).

(**j**) **Scilla messenaica** Boiss. (*Liliaceae*). Native of Greece, especially the Peloponnese, growing on rocky hillsides, at c.1000m, flowering in April. Like a robust small-flowered *S. bifolia* but has up to seven leaves per bulb and seven to fifteen pale blue flowers per stem. Easy to grow in well-drained soil in sun or half-shade. Source Greece, Peloponnese near Kalamata, H. & M. Crook 517.

¾ life size Photographed 18 February

life size Photographed 13 March

Puschkinia Rix 1926

Scilla sibirica 'Spring Beauty'

Scilla puschkinioides

Puschkinia scilloides near Hoşap in southeast Turkey

(a), (d) **Puschkinia scilloides** Adams, syn. *P. libanotica* Boiss., *P. hyacinthoides* Baker (*Liliaceae*). Native of the Caucasus, S Turkey, N Iraq, Iran to Lebanon, growing in scrub, in stony places and in meadows in the mountains, at up to 3000m, flowering from April to July according to altitude. Like *Chionodoxa* the petals are united at their base, but the flower is smaller and never opens flat. Easy to grow in good, well-drained soil and very attractive if planted in a large mass, as it often grows in nature. The pure white form is common in cultivation and very beautiful. Source Turkey, Hakkari, near Yukşekova, 2000m, Rix 1943, and photographed in May 1971.

(b) **Scilla puschkinioides** Regel (*Liliaceae*). Native of Central Asia, especially the Pamir Alai and the Tien Shan, growing above 1000m, in scrub and stony places, flowering from March to July, according to altitude. The stem may be up to 20cm. Rather feeble, and has not done well in cultivation, though often introduced. Source C Asia, Tashkent, Chimgan valley, 1800m, Rix 2773, and photographed in April 1979.

(c) **Scilla armena** Grossh. (*Liliaceae*). Native of the south Transcaucasus and NW Turkey, where it grows on grassy places and stony slopes from 1500 to 2400m, flowering in May and June, usually by late snow patches. Close to *S. sibirica* (p.41) but leaves short, lanceolate, and flowers usually solitary with short, broad petals. Has grown well in a shady bulb frame and would probably be happy in a well-drained peaty soil outside. Source NE Turkey, Tahir Dağ, 2500m, Rix 1638.

(e) **Chionodoxa cretica** Boiss. (*Liliaceae*). Native of Crete, especially the White mountains, where it grows in *Berberis* scrub, at c.2000m, flowering in April. The stem can have several flowers, blue with a clear, white centre. Rather small and delicate, and safer in a bulb frame.

(f) **Chionodoxa lochiae** Meikle (*Liliaceae*). Native of Cyprus, especially the Troodos mountains, where it grows in stony soil under pines. The flowers are usually one or two, but may be up to six, blue without any white in their centre, with a long tube at the base and usually not opening fully. Easy to grow in a bulb frame or in a well-drained soil outside. Source Cyprus, Troodos Mts, W. K. Aslet s.n.

(g) **Chionodoxa albescens** (Speta) Rix, comb. nov., syn. *Scilla albescens* Speta in Naturk. Jahrb. Stadt Linz 21: 19 (1976), *Chionodoxa nana* auct. (*Liliaceae*). Native of Crete, growing at 1200–1800m, in the White mountains, usually among rocks. Flowers the smallest of the genus and usually white, pinkish or pale blue. Small and delicate and better in a bulb frame or alpine house.

Puschkinia sp. (*Liliaceae*)
This green variant of *P. scilloides* is as yet unnamed. It has been collected in Hakkari, and Bitlis, south of Lake Van, and in Azerbaijan by Brian Mathew. It grows in the same area as the common form, but in separate populations and usually at a rather lower altitude, flowering by late snow patches. Photographed in Turkey, Hakkari, near Yukşekova, May 1974, Rix 1926. In cultivation the Turkish collections have proved very sensitive to botrytis, but the Azerbaijan collection has grown well in a bulb frame.

Scilla sibirica 'Spring Beauty', syn. 'Atroviolacea'. Photographed in the RHS Gardens, Wisley, April 1980, by Roger Phillips.

¾ life size Photographed 28 March

(a), (h) Gagea peduncularis (Presl) Pascher (*Liliaceae*). Native of Yugoslavia and Bulgaria to Crete, Greece and Turkey, growing in stony places and among rocks at up to 1000m, flowering in March and April. Distinguished from other species by its long and very slender basal leaves, which are solid, its long pedicels and its obtuse petals, up to 20mm long. Easy to grow in a bulb frame. Source: (a) Cyprus, Halefka, H. & M. Crook 973; (h) Rhodes, Mt Profitis Ilias, 780m, Rix 1269.

(b) Scilla melaina Speta (*Liliaceae*). Native of S Turkey, in woods, scrub, meadows and rocky places, flowering in March to May. Stem to 25cm tall. Easy to grow and striking in its relatively late flowering, and pure blue flowers. Source: Turkey, limestone rocks west of Gaziantep, 600m, Rix 1380.

(c) Chionodoxa luciliae Boiss, syn. *C. gigantea* Whittall (*Liliaceae*). Native of western Turkey, especially the mountain of Boz Dağ, east of Izmir, where it flowers in May and June by melting snow at c.2000m, growing in very stony soil. The form shown here, usually called *C. gigantea*, is simply a larger form of *C. luciliae*. Flowers rather few per stem with a short tube, and outer petals much wider than inner. Easy to grow in well-drained rich soil in full sun.

(d) Chionodoxa forbesii Baker (*Liliaceae*). Native of southern Turkey, reputed to be from Ala Dağ above 2500m, flowering probably in May. The largest species in cultivation, and usually triploid, with a very large white centre to the flower, which is 12–19mm long. Rather smaller plants, diploid, are recorded from hills east of Izmir, from 900 to 1100m, flowering in March. They have shorter, broader petals. There is also a pink form in cultivation, called 'Pink Giant'. Easy to grow in well-drained soil in full sun, and good under deciduous shrubs.

(e) Chionodoxa sardensis Whittall ex Barr & Sugden (*Liliaceae*). Native of western Turkey, in the hills E of Izmir, in shady woods among mossy rocks, at 100–700m, flowering from February to April. This is one of the more distinct species, with rich blue flowers, 8–17mm long with only a small white eye, up to twelve on each inflorescence. Easy to grow in the same conditions as the other species.

(f) Ornithogalum balansae Boiss. (*Liliaceae*). Native of north-eastern Turkey at c.2500m. This is one of the more distinct and striking species with its short conical raceme of flowers, and rather broad leaves. Easy to grow in good soil in sun or semi-shade.

(g) Gagea pusilla (F. W. Schmidt) Schultes & Schultes fil. (*Liliaceae*). Native of central and southern Europe from Czechosolvakia and Hungary to Greece and Turkey, growing on stony hillsides, flowering from February to April. Characterised by its single narrow leaf, opposite stem leaves and glabrous flowers and stem. Easy to grow in well-drained stony soil in full sun. Source: V. Horton 1795.

(i) Ranunculus kochii Ledeb., syn. *Ficaria fascicularis* C. Koch (*Ranunculaceae*). Native of S Transcaucasus, N Iran and the Kopet Dağ to S Turkey and N Iraq, growing in bare, stony places at up to 3000m, flowering from March to May. Cf. *R. ficaria*, Celandine (p.73). Easy to grow in a bulb frame, and better kept dry in summer. Source: Turkey, Hakkari, Mor Da., 2800, Rix 2440.

life size Photographed 25 February

½ life size Photographed 13 March

Tecophilaea cyanocrocus ½ life size Photographed 28 March

Scilla verna

(a) **Muscari commutatum** Guss. (*Liliaceae*). Native of Italy and Sicily and the east Mediterranean south to Israel, growing in scrub and rough grassland, flowering from February to June. Distinguished from other species by its very dark blackish flowers without white lobes. Easy to grow in well-drained soil in a sunny place. Source Greece, Argolis, near Didymi, 250m, Brickell & Mathew 8010.

(b) **Hyacinthus orientalis** L. (*Liliaceae*). Native of western Asia, in Turkey, Syria and Lebanon, growing among rocks, at up to 2000m, flowering from February to May. Close to the cultivated 'Roman Hyacinth' (p.249). Easy to grow in well-drained sandy soil in full sun. Source Turkey, Kayseri to Malatya, 1980m, among limestone rocks, Rix 1606.

(c) **Muscari chalusicum** Stuart (*Liliaceae*). Native of northern Iran, in the Chalus valley, where it grows on rock ledges from 300 to 1100m, flowering in March and April. The leaves lie flat on the ground. Grows easily in a bulb frame or sunny warm place outside. Source Iran, Chalus valley, P. Furse.

(d) **Hyacinthus litwinovii** E. Czem. (*Liliaceae*). Native of N Iran, and the Kopet Dağ in western Central Asia, growing at 1500–2000m, flowering in March and April. Distinguished from *H. orientalis* by its fewer broader leaves and narrow petals; in *H. transcaspicus* Litw. the tube is longer than the free part of the petals. Easy to grow in a bulb frame kept dry in summer. Source Iran, Kopet Dağ, stony slopes and rocks, P. Furse 7894.

(e) **Hyacinthella leucophaea** (C. Koch) Schur. (*Liliaceae*). Native of eastern Europe from Poland southwards to Greece, Romania and S Russia, growing in dry grassland and on stony slopes, flowering in spring. Distinguished by its upright rather broad leaves, and flowers on spreading stalks (see p.39 (b)). Better grown in a bulb frame or pot in the alpine house where it can be kept rather dry in summer. Shown here is the variant which has been called *H. atchleyi* Feinbrun. Source Greece, Kozani to Grevena, Linzee Gordon, 0009.

Bellevalia atroviolacea Regel (*Liliaceae*). Native of Central Asia, especially the Pamir Alai, and NE Afghanistan, growing on bare dry hills and rocky places from 600 to 1500m (and rarely up to 2200m), flowering in April. Grow in a dry bulb frame, baked in summer. Photographed in C Asia, south of Samarkand, April 1979.

Tecophilaea cyanocrocus Leyb. (*Tecophilaeaceae*). Native of Chile in the Cordillera of Santiago at around 3000m, where it grows on stony slopes kept dry and protected by snow cover in winter, flowering in October and November. It is now possibly extinct in the wild through overcollecting. Shown here are the type form with flowers all blue, and var. *leichtlinii* in which the flowers are paler with a white centre. The closely related *T. violiflora* with purplish flowers grows on the coastal ranges north of Santiago, from Valparaiso to Coquimbo. Keep rather dry in winter, so that the leaves which are tender to hard frost do not develop in winter, or grow in a pot in the alpine house where it can be protected from frost. Requires a rich sandy soil. The best results have been obtained in mild gardens on the east coast of Ireland where it has grown well outside. Will set seed after careful hand pollination.

Bellevalia atroviolacea

Scilla verna L. (*Liliaceae*). Native of the Atlantic coast of Europe from Portugal to the Faroes, but absent from the south and west coasts of Ireland, growing on sea cliffs and grassy places, flowering from March to June. Distinguished by its short, 5–15cm stems and relatively large flowers, 10–16mm in diameter, usually purplish blue; bracts longer than the pedicels. Photographed in S Wales near St Davids by Roger Phillips.

Bellevalia forniculata in an alpine meadow near Sarikamis, Turkey

Bellevalia rixii

Merendera kurdica

Scilla rosenii

Bellevalia forniculata (Fomin) Deloney (*Liliaceae*). Native of NE Turkey near Erzurum and Kars, and possibly also in Soviet Armenia, growing in large numbers in wet peaty meadows at 1800–2400m, flowering in May. Stem 12–30cm; leaves usually 2–8mm wide. Flowers 5–6mm long.

Bellevalia rixii Wendelbo (*Liliaceae*). Native of SE Turkey near Hoşap (Guzelsu), on limestone screes at 2800–3000m, flowering in May. A dwarf species to 10cm, with flowers of an unusual combination of blue and brown, and large, inflated capsules to 12mm across. Easily grown in a bulb frame, but hardly showy! Source: Rix 2305.

Merendera kurdica Bornm. (*Liliaceae*). Native of NE Iraq and SE Turkey, on dry slopes at 1800–3000m, flowering from May to July by late snow patches. Leaves expanding to 17cm long when mature. Flowers pale to deep purple. A beautiful species which proved very prone to *Botrytis*. Source: Sat Dağ above Yukşekova, 2800m. Rix 105.

Galanthus nivalis L. subsp. **cilicicus** (Baker) Gottlieb-Tannenheim (*Amaryllidaceae*). Native of the island of Kastellorhizo, NE of Rhodes, and of the foothills of the Tauros Mts near Tarsus, growing among limestone rocks at up to 600m, flowering from November to March. Leaves usually well-developed at flowering time, very glaucous, recurved. Easily grown in well-drained soil. Source: Kastellorhizo, Rix 4010.

Scilla rosenii C. Koch (*Liliaceae*). Native of Soviet Armenia, Georgia and NE Turkey, growing in moist subalpine meadows, flowering from May to July by late snow patches. Stems to 15cm, but usually less than 5cm; leaves 6–10mm wide, linear. Petals recurved. Easily cultivated in well-drained limy, peaty soil, kept shaded and moist in summer, but much favoured by slugs.

Gagea minima (L.) Ker-Gawler (*Liliaceae*). Native of Europe from France to Russia, and south to Greece and the Caucasus, in meadows and damp woods, flowering in March to June according to altitude and latitude. Basal leaf 1, flat, to 3mm wide. Flowers nodding in bud, with narrow, acuminate petals 10–15mm long. Easily grown in moist leafy soil in deciduous shade. Photographed near Leningrad in May.

Tulipa humilis Herbert (*Liliaceae*). The form shown here is variously called *T. pulchella* var. *albocaerulea-occulata* or *T. violacea* var. *pallida*. It is early flowering, with a stem to 15cm. The source of the commercial stock is not known, but it probably originated in central Iran. See also pp.136, 143, 144.

Tulipa montana Lindl., syn. *T. wilsoniana* Hoog (*Liliaceae*). Native of N Iran in the Tabriz region, in the Elburz and in the Kopet Dağ, and in Soviet Turkmenia, in rocky and stony hills at up to 3000m, flowering in April to June. Flowers may be yellow. Close to *T. maximowiczii* Regel and *T. linifolia* Regel, but differs in its broader basal leaves; all three are characterised by their smooth filaments and bulbs with a tuft of wool protruding from their apex. Source: seed received from Aschabad Botanic Garden, collected in the Kopet Dağ.

Crocus vernus (L.) Hill subsp. **albiflorus** (Kit. ex Schultes) Asch. & Graeb. (*Iridaceae*). Native of the Pyrenees, the Alps, the Appenines and the Balkan Mts south to Albania, and of E Europe east to Czechoslovakia, in subalpine meadows at 600–2500m, flowering in March to July according to altitude, usually by melting snow. Flowers small, usually white. This is the form of *C. vernus* which is so common in alpine meadows. The larger, usually purple-flowered subsp. *vernus* is more common in woods, rough ground or grassy clearings. Photographed in the Valais, Switzerland, above St Luc.

Crocus versicolor Ker-Gawl. **'Picturatus'**. The species is described on p.25. 'Picturatus' is one of the few, or possibly the only named clone still in cultivation.

Crocus cvijicii Kosanin (*Iridaceae*). Native of E Albania, S Yugoslavia, and N Greece in alpine meadows on limestone and in clearings in forest at 1800–2500m, flowering in May to June, by melting snow.

Gagea minima

Crocus versicolor 'Picturatus'

Galanthus nivalis subsp. **cilicicus**

Crocus vernus subsp. **albiflorus**

Tulipa montana

Tulipa humilis

Crocus cvijicii

life size Photographed 21 March

Corydalis rutifolia

Corydalis glaucescens

Corydalis emanueli

Corydalis ledebouriana

(a) **Corydalis popovil** Nevski (*Papaveraceae*). Native of Central Asia, especially the Pamir Alai mountains, growing in scrub and rocky hillsides above 2000m, flowering from March to July according to altitude. Only recently introduced, but apparently not difficult to grow either in a pot in the alpine house, or in a bulb frame; will not require baking in summer. Source: Central Asia, Ferghana district, Rix 2794.

(b) **Bongardia chrysogonum** (L.) Griseb. (*Podophyllaceae*). Native of western Asia from Turkey to the Pamir Alai and the Kara Kum desert, growing in cornfields and on stony hillsides, flowering from March to May. *Bongardia* differs from *Leontice* (p.39) in having all the leaves arising from the tuber, not from the stem. Easy to grow in a bulb frame, but must be kept dry in summer, and not allowed to get too wet in winter. Source: Turkey, near Gaziantep, Rix 1854.

(c) **Corydalis aitchisonii** M. Popov (*Papaveraceae*) Native of Soviet Central Asia in the Kopet Dağ and Badgis, and of NE Iran and Afghanistan, at 650–2300m, flowering from March to May. Tuber more or less spherical. Has grown well in a dry bulb frame at Wisley but has not increased since 1964. Source: Iran, near Meshed, 1800m, granite rocks, P. Furse 5280.

(d) **Corydalis wendelboi** Liden (*Papaveraceae*). Native of C Turkey, growing on stony hillsides at 1000–2000m, flowering in May and June, often by late snow patches. Stems to 15cm, usually less. Leaves and bracts deeply divided. Easy to grow in a bulb frame or alpine house. Source: Turkey, Elma Dağ, near Ankara, Rix 1532.

Corydalis rutifolia subsp. **erdelii** (Sibth. & Sm.) DC. Native of Crete and Turkey eastwards to Pakistan, growing in stony places at 1300–2800m, flowering from April to July. Distinguished from *C. bulbosa* (L.) DC. by its opposite, not alternate, stem leaves, and fewer-flowered raceme. Flower colour variable. Grow in a pot in the alpine house or a bulb frame, kept dry in summer. Photographed in central Turkey, near Malatya, 1900m, May 1970, Rix 1584.

Corydalis ledebouriana Kar. & Kir. (*Papaveraceae*). Native of Central Asia and NE Afghanistan, to Kashgar and Chitral, growing in rocky places and in scrub from 800 to 3700m, flowering from March to June. Characterised by upward-curving or horizontal spur and deflexed lower lip. Cultivation as (a). Photographed in Central Asia, S of Ferghana, c.12000m, in April 1979.

Corydalis glaucescens Regel. Native of Central Asia, especially the Tien Shan, the Pamir Alai and the Ala Tau, growing in woods and scrub at up to 1500m, flowering from March to June. Cultivation as for *C. popovii* (a). Photographed in Central Asia, in the mountains S of Frunze, c.2000m, May 1980.

Corydalis emanueli C. A. Meyer (*Papaveraceae*). Native of the Caucasus, from Taberda to Kasbek, growing among shady rocks at 2400–2500m, flowering in July and August. The thick, fleshy root has 2–5 lobes. Photographed in the Baksan valley, 2500m, in August 1975.

¾ life size Photographed 14 April

Gagea chrysantha

Gagea fistulosa

Gagea bohemica

Lloydia serotina

Corydalis macrocentra in the Varsob gorge, Tadjikistan

(a) **Corydalis caucasica** DC. (*Papaveraceae*). Native of the Caucasus where it is widespread, growing in forests and in scrub, flowering in April and May. Flowers usually pinkish-purple, but the white form shown here, var. *albiflora* DC., is common. Easily grown in shady places in peaty sandy soil.

(b) **Corydalis macrocentra** Regel. (*Papaveraceae*). Native of Central Asia, especially Tadjikistan and NE Afghanistan, growing on low sandy hills from 900 to 1300m, flowering in March and April. Source C Asia, Dushanbe, low bare sandy hills at mouth of Varsob gorge, 1200m, Rix 2723, and photographed in April 1980.

(c) **Gagea gageoides** (Zucc.) Vved. (*Liliaceae*). Native of eastern Turkey and Iran to Central Asia especially Tien Shan, Pamir Alai and Kopet Dağ, growing on bare hills and rocks at up to 3000m, flowering in April and May. Easily distinguished by the numerous leafy bulbils in the leaf axils. Easy to grow in a bulb frame. Source Turkey, Hakkari, near Yukşekova, Rix 1954.

(d) **Gagea fibrosa** (Desf.) Schultes & Schultes fl., syn. *G. rigida* Boiss., *C. commutata* C. Koch (*Liliaceae*). Native of the S Caucasus, Turkey and Greece to Israel and N Africa, growing on dry hillsides, flowering in March and April. Distinguished by its very long tapering petals, flat spreading leaves, and stem which usually branches below ground. Source Greece, Parnon Oros, c. 1000m, Rix 2143.

(e) **Gagea chrysantha** (Jan) Schult., syn. *G. amblyopetala* Boiss. (*Liliaceae*). Native of Sicily and Crete to Yugoslavia and S Russia, and western Turkey growing in rocky places and in scrub, flowering in March and April. Distinguished by its two narrow basal leaves, small (less than 10mm) rounded petals, and glabrous stems with diffuse branching. Flowers often reddish outside. Source Greece, Elion Or. W of Thebes, c. 1200m, Rix 2178, and photographed near Sparta by Roger Phillips.

Gagea fistulosa Ker Gawl., syn. *G. liotardii* (Stern.) Schultes & Schultes fil., (*Liliaceae*). Native of Europe from the Pyrenees to Russia, Greece, Turkey and the Caucasus, growing in damp grassy meadows in the mountains, flowering from May to July. Distinguished by its hollow fleshy leaves, opposite stem leaves and usually hairy pedicels. Sometimes produces bulbils instead of flowers. Photographed in the Serrat valley, Andorra, in June 1977 by Brinsley Burbidge 565.

Gagea bohemica (Zauschn.) Schultes & Schultes syn. *G. saxatilis* (Mert. & Koch) Schultes & Schultes fil. (*Liliaceae*). Native of Europe from Wales and France to Turkey and Syria and the Caucasus, at up to 1000m (in the south), growing in rocky places often in small pockets of soil, flowering from January to April. Distinguished by its narrow filiform basal leaves, rather large flowers with blunt petals, usually hairy pedicels and alternate stem leaves. Photographed in Wales on rock ledges in March.

Lloydia serotina (L.) Rchb. (*Liliaceae*). Native of the Arctic and mountains of Europe and the Caucasus, growing in tundra and on rock ledges up to 3000m, flowering from June to August. Very rare, and protected in Wales. Photographed in the Caucasus, Dongus Orun, in August 1976.

Fritillaria carica subsp. **serpenticola**

Corydalis bulbosa white form

Fritillaria karelinii

Lloydia tibetica

Lloydia tibetica Baker (*Liliaceae*). Native of W China, in NW Yunnan (Lijiang) and SW Sichuan around Kangding (Tachienlu), growing in alpine meadows at 2000–4000m, flowering in June and July. Stems 15–25cm. Stems 2 to 5 flowered. Petals c.3cm long. Photographed by Chris Grey-Wilson near Lijiang, NW Yunnan in early June.

Fritillaria karelinii (Fisch.) Baker (*Liliaceae*). Native of the deserts of Central Asia from the Caspian Sea eastwards to the Ili valley in NW China, growing in salty scrub and steppe, flowering in March to May. Distinguished from *F. gibbosa* (p.59) by its narrower, spotted petals, the upper only with a large indented nectary. It requires rather dry sandy soil in a bulb frame or pot in the alpine house. Source: desert steppes near Tashkent: I. Belolipov.

Fritillaria carica Rix subsp. **serpenticola** Rix. Native of SW Turkey, growing on serpentine scree at c.1700m, flowering in April. This very dwarf sub-species has only recently been discovered by Mr & Mrs O. Sonderhousen. It requires careful cultivation in a frame or alpine house.

Corydalis cashmeriana Royle (*Papaveraceae*). Native of Kashmir eastwards to N Sikkim, Bhutan and SE Tibet in scrub, alpine meadows and screes at 3000–4900m, flowering in May to August. Stems to 10cm in cultivation; rootstock tuberous, increasing by bulbils. *C. cashmeriana* requires cool conditions in full light and well-drained soil, not drying out in summer. The Japanese blue-flowered *C. ambigua* is rather similar, but has a 2-lobed lip and less finely dissected leaves. Photographed in Kildrummy Castle Garden, Aberdeenshire.

Corydalis solida (L.) Swartz **'G. P. Baker'**. This beautiful red-flowered clone of *C. solida* was long-known as *G. transilvanica* in cultivation and was preserved by Messrs Ingwersen's nursery in Sussex. It is now becoming more common in gardens and increases well in a bulb frame, less freely in the open garden. Another pink-flowered clone is called 'Beth Evans', named recently after the wife of Alf Evans of Edinburgh Botanic Gardens.

Corydalis bulbosa (L.) DC (white form) (*Papaveraceae*). Native of much of Europe, and naturalised in England and Belgium, growing in woods, flowering in March to May. Flowers usually pinkish-purple, sometimes white, and cream or yellowish in subsp. *marshalliana* (Pallas) Chater. *C. bulbosa* is distinguished from *C. solida* by its entire bracts, and by its lack of a scale below the leaves. Both are easily cultivated in ordinary garden soil, preferably with the addition of sand and leafmould, and planted in the shade of a deciduous tree. This very fine white form was distributed from the garden of Sir Cedric Morris at Benton End, Suffolk, and comes true from seed, with the odd purple-flowered individual among the white.

Corydalis darvasica Regel (*Papaveraceae*). Native of C Asia, in the W Pamir-Alai and W Tien Shan, growing on rocky slopes and screes, at 1000–2000m, flowering in April to June. Stems to 6cm high and more across. Leaves finely divided, very glaucous. Flowers 18–20mm long, pinkish or yellowish, with pink spots. Often long-lived, producing a very large tuber. For careful cultivation in the alpine house or bulb frame, kept dry in summer, but not drying out during its growing period in winter and spring. Photographed in the Chimgan valley, NE of Tashkent.

Corydalis maracandica M. Pop. & Zak. (*Papaveraceae*). Native of C Asia growing in scrub and on earthy slopes in the hills south of Samarkhand, at c.1800m, flowering in April. Stems to 15cm. Very close to *C. ledebouriana*, but with yellowish flowers fading to pink.

Corydalis bulbosa white form at Benton End Suffolk

Corydalis cashmeriana

Corydalis solida 'G. P. Baker'

Corydalis maracandica

Corydalis darvasica in the Chimgan valley, central Asia

¾ life size Photographed 11 February

Iris × sindpur ⅓ life size 25 February

Iris wendelboi

½ life size Photographed 25 February

(a) Iris histrio Rchb. fil. (*Iridaceae*, section *Reticulatae*). Native of S Turkey, Lebanon, Syria and Israel, growing on stony hillsides, and among rocks at up to 2000m, flowering in February and March. Flowers usually paler than shown here. Easy to grow in a bulb frame, kept rather dry and baked in summer. Benefits by frequent division. Source S Turkey, Nur Dağ pass above Osmaniye, 1000m, Rix 1557.

(b) Iris histrio var. **aintabensis** (*Iridaceae*, section *Reticulatae*). Native of S Turkey and Syria (?) growing in pockets on limestone rocks west of Gaziantep, at c.1000m. Like *I. histrio* but smaller with more delicate, paler flowers. Cultivation as (a).

(c), (i) Iris histrioides (G. F. Wilson) S. Arnott, c.v. 'Major' (*Iridaceae*, section *Reticulatae*). Native of central Turkey recorded from near Amasya and from Erzinçan district; very rarely collected probably because of its early flowering. Close to *I. histrio* but usually leafless at first flowering. Two or three very similar clones are in cultivation, one named 'Lady Beatrix Stanley' with more spotted falls. Cultivation as for (a).

(d), (e), (f) Iris reticulata M. Bieb (*Iridaceae*, section *Reticulatae*). Native of Turkey, Iran, S Transcaucasus and Iraq, growing on scree and bare stony places and among scrub from 600 to 2700m, flowering from March to May. Variable in colour, the pale blue forms from Talysh and N Iran (f) have been called *I hyrcana* Woron., but occur mixed with the normal purple form (d), (e). (See also pp.58 and 60.) Easy to grow in a bulb frame or in very sandy soil in the open, kept dry if possible in summer. Sources NW Iran, Tabriz district, Rix 875 and 973.

(g) Iris winogradowii Fomin (*Iridaceae*, section *Reticulatae*). Native of the southern Caucasus, in the west above Gagra, and in the south, inland from Batumi, growing in the subalpine zone, but very rare and poorly known. Very striking for its pale yellow colour, and the only species of the section better grown outside, in sandy peaty soil. New root growth begins in summer, so it should be replanted as soon as the leaves begin to fade, and never dried out completely.

(h) Iris 'Katharine Hodgkin'. This beautiful hybrid was raised in 1958 by E. B. Anderson and named after the wife of Eliot Hodgkin (1900–1972), a great grower of rare bulbs. The parentage was said to have been *I. histrioides* 'Major' × *I. danfordiae*, but it looks as if *I. winogradowii* is a more likely parent because of its large standards compared with the minute ones of *I. danfordiae* (p.58). Easily grown and increases very quickly in a bulb frame, more slowly in the open.

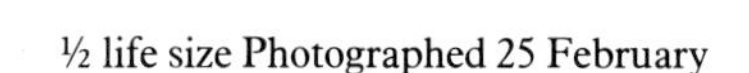

Iris × sindpur (*Iridaceae*, section *Juno*). A hybrid between *Iris aucheri* (p.63) and *I. persica* (p.62) raised by the Dutch bulb firm of Van Tubergen, in an attempt to combine the robustness of *I. aucheri* with the dwarf habit and early flowering of *I. persica*. Probably better grown under cover in the British Isles.

Iris wendelboi Grey-Wilson & Mathew (*Iridaceae*, section *Juno*). Native of south-western Afghanistan, growing on dry sandy hills among *Pistachia* scrub, at c.1700m, flowering in March and April. Photographed in Afghanistan, ten miles NE of Gulestan, by C. Grey Wilson, G.-W./H. 575.

¾ life size Photographed 25 February

(a), (b), (d), (e) Iris reticula M. Bieb. (*Iridaceae*) (see pp.57 and 61). Four of the many cultivare of *I. reticulata* are shown here. They have been obtained by selection of collected forms and by hybridisation. Some of them are infected with virus, which shows itself by a dark and light mottling of the young leaves, so they should be kept separate from wild-collected bulbs which may not be as resistant. They are often also infected with 'Ink disease', a fungus which forms dark stains on the tunic, before infecting the whole bulb.
(a). Old commercial form, which is very sweetly scented. It is very rare in the wild, being recorded only once, in NE Iran by Paul Furse, P. F. 5179
(b) 'Clairette'. Probably a hybrid with *I. reticulata* var. *bakeriana*.
(c) 'Cantab'. Raised by E. A. Bowles.
(e) 'Joyce'. Raised by Van Tubergen. The large blue flower and shorter stouter leaves suggest that it may be a hybrid with *I. histrioides*.

(c) Iris danfordiae Boiss., syn. *I. bornmülleri* Hausskn. (*Iridaceae*, section *Reticulatae*). Native of central Turkey, where it has been recorded from several widely separated areas, in the Taurus, in west Malatya, in Amasya and in Gümüsane, at 2000–3000m, on bare, earthy hills, flowering probably in March and April. Will flower well the first year after planting but difficult to keep going in the open garden.

(f) Fritillaria stenanthera Regel (*Liliaceae*). Native of Central Asia, especially the Pamir Alai and the Tien Shan, where it grows in the foothills up to 2000m on earthy slopes and screes, flowering in March and April. Nectaries all equal. Should not be difficult to cultivate in good soil in a bulb frame kept dry in summer. Source Central Asia, Tashkent, Chimgan valley, c.2000m, Rix 2779.

(g) Fritillaria ariana (A. Los. & Vved.) Rix (*Liliaceae*). Native of Central Asia, especially at the southern edges of the Kara Kum desert, and NE Iran and N Afghanistan, growing on sandy steppes flowering in March. Not easy to grow and probably best kept dry until late March, when, if watered, it will grow and flower in a few weeks.

(h) Crocus michelsoni B. Fedtsch. (*Iridaceae*). Native of the Kopet Dağ in NE Iran, and S Central Asia, where it grows on stony hills from 1200 to 2300m, flowering in March and April. The style is whitish; the flowers always bluish or white inside, marked with blue purple outside; corm tunic with reticulate fibres. Best grown in a bulb frame, kept dry in summer.

(i) Iris kolpakowskiana Regel, syn. *I. winkleri* Regel (*Iridaceae*, section *Reticulatae*). Native of Central Asia from the mountains near Tashkent eastwards to Alma Ata from 1100 to 3000m, flowering from April to June, growing on grassy or stony slopes and in scrub. An atypical member of the *Reticulatae* section in its flat leaves and large standards, and found far to the east of all other members of the section. Not easy to grow, but the same treatment as given to other delicate bulbous irises should suit it.

Fritillaria gibbosa Boiss. (*Liliaceae*). Native of Iran and Afghanistan, south Caucasia and the Kopet Da., growing on dry hills and steppes from 1000 to 2000m, flowering from March to May. Close to *F. ariana* (g) but has broader leaves with less contrast between basal pair and the rest, and papillose stems. Flowers usually spotted. Cultivation as (g). Photographed in the Elburz mountains by Paul Furse.

⅔ life size Photographed 13 March

Fritillaria gibbosa

¾ life size Photographed 25 February

⅓ life size Photographed 28 March

(a), (b), (c) **Iris reticulata** M. Bieb. (see p.57). These three forms are from further south than those shown on p.56, where there is a tendency for the flowers to be bi-coloured. Source (a) Turkey, Hakkari, gorge of Habur River, c.1200m, Rix 2437; (b) Iran, central Zagros Mts, Razan pass, E of Khorramabad, 1950m, P. Furse 1864; (c) Iran, Kuh-i-Sahand, P. Furse 2364.

(d) **I. reticulata** var. **bakeriana** (Foster) Mathew & Wendelbo (*Iridaceae*, section *Reticulatae*). This variety of *I. reticulata* is distinguished by its eight-ribbed leaves, not four-ribbed as in *I. reticulata* itself, but intermediates are found in the southern Zagros. Wild plants usually have pale blue flowers and dark falls without the yellow spot. Shown here is a commercial stock sold under the name *I. bakeriana*.

(e) **Iris pamphylica** Hedge (*Iridaceae*, section *Reticulatae*). Native of southern Turkey, confined to one small area NE of Antalya, where it grows in pine forest, among oak scrub and between limestone rocks at c.1250m, flowering in March. It has not proved easy to cultivate, but has survived and increased slowly in a sunny bulb frame in very sandy soil. Sensitive to botrytis, so it is wise to lift and treat with captan or benlate each summer. Source Turkey, Antalya, Rix 1340.

(f) **Hermodactylus tuberosus** (L.) Miller, syn. *Iris tuberosa* L. (*Iridaceae*). Snake's Head Iris, Widow Iris. Native of S France eastwards to Yugoslavia, Greece, Turkey and Israel, where it grows in scrub and on grassy banks and hillsides, flowering in March and April. It is naturalised in Devon and Cornwall. The long soft, *reticulata*-like leaves emerge in autumn. Easily grown in well-drained sunny places where it will sometimes increase greatly. Protect from slugs. Source Greece, Peloponnese near Githion, Rix 514, and photographed in March 1964.

Gynandriris sisyrinchium (L.) Parl., syn. *Iris sisyrinchium* L. (*Iridaceae*). Native of the Mediterranean region, from Portugal to Italy and Greece, Turkey and Israel and eastwards to Pakistan, growing at altitudes of up to 2000m, flowering from February to April. Very variable in size from 10 to 60cm. Flowers usually opening in the afternoon and faded by morning. *Gynandriris* is a mainly S African genus close to *Morea* (p.184). The corm is rather similar to *I. reticulata*. Photographed in Greece, near Sparta, in April 1980 by Roger Phillips.

Gynandriris sisyrinchium

Hermodactylus tuberosus

life size Photographed 13 February

Iris aucheri ⅓ life size Photographed 28 March

I. willmottiana ⅓ life size Photographed 28 March

Iris orchioides in the Chimgan valley

(a), (d) Iris persica L. (*Iridaceae* section *Juno*). Native of southern Turkey, N Iraq, Syria and Lebanon, growing on bare eroded hills, on screes and among oak scrub at 600–2000m, flowering from February to April. Flowers usually solitary, greenish, brownish-yellow or greyish. The leaves should be kept as dry as possible at all times, dead flowers removed, and the centre of the leaves dusted with captan to prevent infection by botrytis. Source (a) Turkey, Adiyaman near Kahta, Linzee Gordon 5152; (d) Turkey, Silifke to Karaman, Linzee Gordon 5108.

(b) (c) Iris stenophylla Hausskn. & Siehe ex Baker, syn. *Iris tauri* Siehe ex Mallett (*Iridaceae*, section *Juno*). Native of central Turkey, where it grows on stony slopes and screes usually on limestone, at c.2000m, flowering in March and April. Very similar to *I. persica*, but is usually slightly smaller, and always a deep purple colour. Cultivation as for *I. persica*. Source Turkey, Eğredir to Beyşehir, Linzee Gordon 5065.

Iris aucheri (Baker) Sealy, syn. *I. sindjarensis* Boiss. & Hausskn. (*Iridaceae*, section *Juno*). Native of SE Turkey, W Iran, N Syria, and N Iraq, growing on rocky hills from 550 to 2600m, flowering in March and April. Height 15–40cm. Flowers pale blue crowded at the top of the stem above the lush leek-like leaves. Easy to grow in a bulb frame where it makes a dense clump. Keep dry in summer. Source SE Turkey, Bitlis, Pelli Da, 2600m, Rix 796.

I. willmottiana Foster (*Iridaceae*, section *Juno*). Native of Central Asia, especially low hills near Derbent where it flowers in May. This species is still in commerce, and is worth trying in good soil outside, preferably where it will become rather dry in summer.

Iris orchioides Carr. (*Iridaceae*, section *Juno*). Native of Central Asia, especially the Tien Shan, the Kara Tau and the Ala Tau, at up to 2000m on stony slopes, flowering from March to July. Grow in a sunny bulb frame in very gritty soil. Photographed in C Asia, Tashkent, Chimgan valley, c.1600m, in May 1980.

½ life size Photographed 14 April

(a) **Iris bucharica** Foster (*Iridaceae,* section *Juno*). Native of Central Asia, especially the Pamir Alai and Tadjikistan, and NE Afghanistan where it grows on stony and grassy hills from 800 to 2400m, flowering in March and April. Height 15–45cm. The form shown here is the usual commercial form. The wild form is shown on p.66. Easily grown in good well-drained soil in full sun.

(b) **Iris magnifica** Vved. (*Iridaceae,* section *Juno*). Native of Central Asia, especially the mountains south of Samarkand where it grows among limestone rocks at c.1600m, flowering in March and April. The largest species with stems up to 1m, and whitish or pale blue flowers. Easily grown in deep well-drained soil, in full sun. Photographed in Central Asia, Samarkand, Amankutan valley, April 1979.

(c) **Iris caucasica** Hoffm (*Iridaceae,* section *Juno*). Native of S Caucasus, NW Iran, E Turkey and N Iraq, growing on screes and stony mountain steppe at 2400–3000m, flowering in May. Most Turkish records, including the specimens illustrated here, belong to subsp. *turcica* B. Mathew, with smooth, not ciliate or scabrid leaf margins. The erect part of the fall is winged, but the wings are flat, not turned up as in *I pseudocaucasica* (p.33). Has survived and flowered in a bulb frame but not increased. Possible outside in very well-drained soil. Sources: Turkey, Agri, Tahir Dağ, 2500m, Rix 1640, and photographed in NE Turkey, west foothills of Mt Ararat, 2000m, in May 1972.

Iris vicaria Vved. (*Iridaceae,* section *Juno*). Native of Central Asia, especially the Pamir Alai, growing on stony slopes and among rocks, at c.2000m, flowering in March and April. Height 20–40cm in the wild. Plants few flowered; flowers always pale bluish, the upright part of the falls without a wing. Probably not difficult in cultivation. Photographed in Central Asia, Dushanbe, 2000m, Rix 2701.

Iris cycloglossa Wendelbo (*Iridaceae,* section *Juno*) (see Introduction). Native of SW Afghanistan where it grows in low valleys flooded in winter, dry in summer, at 1450–1700m, flowering in April. Plant up to 40cm, with about six narrow leaves on the lowest part of the stem. Flowers scented and unusually shaped for a Juno Iris with wide flat falls, and horizontal standards. This seems likely to be one of the best Iris introductions of recent years, being easily grown in a bulb frame or outdoors. Source: Afghanistan, near Farah, Wendelbo, Hedge & Ekberg 7727.

Iris magnifica in the hills south of Samarkhand

Iris caucasica

Iris vicaria

Iris drepanophylla

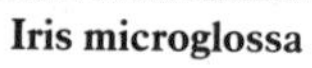

Iris microglossa

Iris bucharica

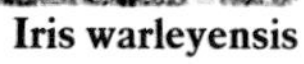

Iris warleyensis

(a) **Gagea glacialis** C. Koch (*Liliaceae*). Native of the Caucasus and northern Turkey, growing in wet places in alpine meadows, flowering in May and June. Like a small *G. fistulosa* (p.53). Source Caucasus, Georgian Military Highway, 2500m, Rix 2630.

(b) **Anemone caucasica** Willd. ex Rupr., syn. *A. blanda* var. *parvula* (DC.) Boiss. (*Ranunculaceae*). Native of the Caucasus, northern Iran and NE Turkey, where it grows in subalpine meadows from 500 to 2000m, flowering from April to June. Differs from *A. blanda* primarily in its small size. Suitable for a sink in a well-drained peaty soil. Source SW Caucasus above Sukhumi, c.2000m, Rix 2659, and photographed in April 1978.

(c) **Bellevalia hyacinthoides** (Bertol.) Persson & Wendelbo, syn. *Strangweja spicata* (Sibth. & Sm.) Boiss. (*Liliaceae*). Native of Greece, growing on rocky hillsides, olive groves and abandoned fields at up to 1000m, flowering in March and April. The flat leaves develop in autumn. Easy to grow in a bulb frame. Source Greece, Parnassus above Delphi, Rix 2130.

(d) **Anemone gortschakovii** Kar. & Kir. (*Ranunculaceae*). Native of Central Asia, especially the Tien Shan and the Ala Tau, growing on rocky slopes at up to 2000m, flowering in April and May. Distinguished from *A. petiolulosa* (p71) by its very long flower stalk, and by the divisions of the basal leaves being sessile. Source C Asia, Ferghana, Chamsabad, 1800m, Rix 2784.

Iris bucharica Foster (*Iridaceae*, section *Juno*) (see p.65 (a)). Photographed in Central Asia, near Dushanbe, on dry grassy hills at c.1000m, in April 1979. Growing in great quantity; flowers all deep yellow with a variable amount of brown on the falls.

Iris warleyensis Foster (*Iridaceae*, section *Juno*). Native of the Pamir Alai mountains of Central Asia from Samarkand to Derbent, growing on sandy slopes at around 1300m, flowering in March and April. Height 20–40cm. Will grow outside in a well-drained sunny place. Photographed in C Asia, S of Samarkand, on steep, loose scree at 1500m, in April 1979.

Iris microglossa Wendelbo (*Iridaceae*, section *Juno*). Native of NE Afghanistan, where it grows on dry grassy hillsides often among Junipers from 1700–3000m, flowering from April to June. Height up to 60cm. Flowers pale blue to white. One of the easier of the Afghan species to cultivate, and some of the collections are reported to have grown well. Photographed on north side of Salang pass, 1900m, by C. Grey-Wilson, G.-W./H. 705.

Iris drepanophylla Aitch. & Baker (*Iridaceae*, section *Juno*). Native of NE Iran, NW Afghanistan and SW Central Asia, growing on dry slopes often of loess, from 600 to 1800m, flowering in April. The margin of the upright part of the falls is turned down, not turned up as in most species. Photographed in Afghanistan, Paropamissus, N of Herat, by C. Grey-Wilson, G.-W./H. 477.

Primula fedtschenkoi Regel (*Primulaceae*). Native of N Afghanistan and Central Asia, especially Uzbekistan, growing on dry grassy slopes from 700 to 1600m, flowering in March and April. Height 4–12cm. Has a tuft of tuberous roots, which become dormant in summer. Photographed in C Asia, S of Samarkand, Amankutan valley, at 1600m, in April 1979.

¾ life size Photographed 28 March

Anemone caucasica

Primula fedtschenkoi

Iris parvula

Iris narbuti

Iris rosenbachiana

Iris nusariensis

Iris parvula Vved. (*Iridaceae* subgenus *Scorpiris* (Juno)). Native of Central Asia in the Pamir Alai, growing on bare earthy or clay slopes in the mountains at 2500–3000m, flowering in May and June. A delicate plant to 12cm high, with very small narrowly diamond-shaped falls. Source: mountains south of Ferghana near Khamsabad, on loose muddy slopes among *Artemisia*.

Iris rosenbachiana Regel (*Iridaceae* subgenus *Scorpiris* (Juno)). Native of Central Asia in the Pamir Alai (with paler-flowered forms in NE Afghanistan) growing on rocky slopes at up to 2000m, flowering in March to April. This is the original purple colour form, distinct enough in cultivation, though not always distinct in the wild from the pale greyish-flowered form called *I. nicolai*, p.17. Photographed in the bulb frames at Wisley.

Iris nusariensis Mouterde (*Iridaceae* subgenus *Scorpiris* (Juno)). Native of Syria, especially in the Jebel Nusairi, growing in rocky places, flowering in April. A fine plant for the alpine house with large flowers 6–7cm across on a short 7–10cm stem. Photographed in the Alpine House at Wisley.

Iris narbuti O. Fedtschenko (*Iridaceae* subgenus *Scorpiris* (Juno)). Native of Soviet Central Asia in the Tien Shan and Pamir Alai, or foothills near Samarkhand and Tashkent, flowering in March to April. A dwarf species up to 15cm, usually c.10cm, with deep purple falls and pale blue, rather large standards. For cultivation in a bulb frame, but has not proved long-lived. Source: from near Samarkhand, collected by Diana Goatcher.

Iris xiphium L. (*Iridaceae*). Native of SW Europe from Spain, Portugal and Morocco to France, Italy and Tunisia, growing in grassy places usually on sandy soils damp in spring, flowering in April to May. The flowers vary in colour from blue and yellow to white in Morocco and Algeria, (*I. battandieri* Forter). Photographed in S Spain near Medina Sidonia in April.

Iris lusitanica Ker-Gawl (*Iridaceae*). This is usually considered part of the variable species *I. xiphium* (q.v.). Yellow-flowered forms are commonest in C Portugal and E Spain, but said to occur elsewhere also. They are reported from dry rocky places in contrast to *I. xiphium* which is commonest in places which are damp in spring. Source: from Coimbra Botanic Garden seed at Margery Hall Pig Farm.

Iris tingitana Boiss. & Reut. (*Iridaceae*). Native of Morocco and Algeria, among limestone rocks and in damp fields, flowering in February to May according to altitude. Stems to 60cm. Leaves silvery, appearing in autumn and requiring protection from frost. Flowers variable in colour from pale to dark blue and purplish. Photographed at Kew; M.J.W.6.

Iris filifolia Boiss. (*Iridaceae*). Native of S Spain including Gibraltar and of Morocco, growing on rocky limestone slopes with *Cistus* species, flowering in April and May. Stems to 45cm. Leaves usually very narrow, to 3mm wide, appearing in autumn, and requiring protection from hard frost. Flowers generally rich reddish-purple. Photographed between Ronda and the coast in late April.

Iris xiphium in southern Spain

Iris lusitanica

Iris filifolia

Iris tingitana

life size Photographed 25 February

Anemone petiolulosa in Tadjikistan near Dushanbe

Anemone petiolulosa × tschernjaewi

Geranium transversale

Anemone tschernjaewi

Anemone blanda Schott & Kotschy (*Ranunculaceae*). Native of the eastern Mediterranean region from Albania and Greece to Lebanon, growing in rocky places and in scrub at up to 2000m, flowering from March to May. The flowers are usually white or dark blue in Greece, and often a uniform pale blue in Turkey. The leaves are hairless beneath. *A. appenina* L., with a more elongated rhizome, and leaves hairy beneath, is found from Corsica to Yugoslavia and Greece. Several cultivars of *A. blanda* have been selected and put into commerce by Van Tubergen; shown here are: p.70 (**a**) **'Radar'**, flowers rich pink with a white centre; p.70 (**b**), (**c**), (**d**), wild forms from near Delphi, Greece, Rix 563; p.70 (**h**) **'White Splendour'**, large flowers up to 5cm across; p.70 (**i**) **'Atrocaerulea'**. All are easily grown in full sun or light shade under deciduous trees. The plants shown are at the beginning of their flowering, and would become larger in a few days.

Anemone petiolulosa Juz. (*Ranunculaceae*). Native of Central Asia, especially the Tien Shan, Pamir Alai and Kopet Dağ, where it grows on stony steppes and mountainsides, flowering in March and April. Close to *A. biflora* (p.73) but flowers always yellow, smaller and less globular. Division of the leaf more pointed. Not well known in cultivation, but will probably require bulb-frame treatment, kept dry in summer. Photographed in C Asia, east of Dushanbe, 2000m, in April 1979.

Anemone tschernjaewi Regel. (*Ranunculaceae*). Native of N Afghanistan and Kashmir, and Central Asia, especially the Tien Shan and the Pamir Alai, growing on rock ledges and among scrub, from 900 to 2000m, flowering from March to May. Flowers whitish to pale violet, leaves three-lobed, the lobes almost entire. Grow in a bulb frame or pot in the alpine house, kept dry in summer. Photographed in Central Asia, east of Dushanbe, 2000m, in April 1979.

Anemone petiolulosa × tschernjaewi. This probable hybrid was a single plant growing with the parents, and is close to the description of *A. eranthoides* Regel, recorded from the same area. Photographed in Central Asia, east of Dushanbe, 2000m, in April 1979.

Geranium transversale (Kar. & Kir.) Vved. (*Geraniaceae*). Native of W Siberia, Central Asia and N China, growing on plains and low hills, flowering in April and May. Leaves with 7–9 linear lobes. Photographed near Tashkent, Chimgan valley, in May 1980.

½ life size Photographed 14 April

Anemone nemorosa L. (*Ranunculaceae*). Native of northern Europe, eastwards to Turkey and NW Asia, growing in woods and shady hillsides, flowering from March to June. Flowers usually white in the wild, often pinkish outside, but in Ireland where some of the cultivars originated, often bluish. Shown here are: (**a**) **'Robinsoniana'**, Named after William Robinson, an influential Victorian gardener and journalist, who found it in the Oxford botanic garden to which it had come from Ireland. Robinson himself came from Stradbally, Co. Laois. Flowers pale blue, greyish outside; (**b**) **'Vestal'**, pure white button double. Origin not recorded; (**c**) **'Bracteata'**, a loose white double in which some of the petals are green. Cultivated since the sixteenth century; (**d**) **'Allenii'**, named after James Allen of Shepton Mallet, Somerset, who raised it some time before 1890. Flowers pale blue, pinkish outside; (**f**), a wild form from Kent, S England; (**g**) **'Grandiflora**, a large-flowered white form, possibly the same as 'Leeds' Variety' mentioned by Graham Thomas in his account of the varieties. Other cultivated varieties include 'Lismore Blue' (pale blue) and 'Lismore Pink' (a uniform pale pink), both originating in Co. Waterford, Ireland. The closely related *A. altaica* Fischer from Russia and Siberia has flowers blue-veined inside. All are easily grown in shade of deciduous trees in moist leafy soil.

(**e**) **Anemone × lipsiensis** Beck, syn. *A.* × *intermedia* Winkler (*Ranunculaceae*). A variable hybrid between *A. nemorosa* and *A. ranunculoides* which is often found where the parents grow together. Cultivation as for *A. nemorosa*.

(**h**), (**i**) **Anemone blanda** Schott & Kotschy (see p.71); (**h**) c.v. **'White Splendour'**; (**i**) c.v. **'Atrocaerulea'**.

(**j**), (**k**) **Anemone ranunculoides** L. (*Ranunculaceae*). Native of northern Europe and western Asia from Belgium and Spain eastwards to the Caucasus and Siberia, growing in deciduous woodland and heaths and flowering from March to June. Two subspecies are described: subsp. *ranunculoides*, a large plant, up to 30cm tall, with a far-creeping rhizome, and subsp. *wockeana* (Asch. & Graeb.) Hegi, a smaller plant with a short rhizome, which makes a dense clump. Cultivation as for *A. nemorosa*.

Anemone biflora DC. (*Ranunculaceae*). Native of Iran, Afghanistan, Pakistan and Kashmir growing on stony hillsides flowering from March to May. Flowers either red or bronzy yellow, larger than *A. petiolulosa* (p.71), up to 5cm across. Leaves with obtuse segments. Grow in a bulb frame, or pot in the alpine house, kept dry in summer. Photographed in Iran, Zagros mountains, Shuturunkuh, 2300m, BSBE 714, by Brian Mathew.

Ranunculus ficaria L. (*Ranunculaceae*). Celandine. Native of the whole of Europe except the Atlantic islands, eastwards to Central Asia (near Alma Ata), and Siberia, flowering from January to May, growing usually on shady or grassy banks or in woods. Very variable, each form being able to spread widely by dispersal of the tubers. Shown here are: (**l**), (**m**), two semi-double forms; (**n**), a button-eye double form; (**o**), a bronze-flowered form; (**p**) subsp. **ficariiformis** Rouy & Fouc., a very large form, native of S Europe, characterised by its yellowish sepals and size; (**q**), a white form. All are attractive plants for damp places in wild garden, but are apt to become too invasive in more cultivated parts of the garden.

½ life size Photographed 17 April

Anemone biflora in the Zagros mountains

Anemone lancifolia in the Blue Ridge Mountains, Virginia

Anemone lancifolia

Anemone coronaria

Anemone lancifolia Pursh (*Ranunculaceae*). Native of eastern North America, from S Pennsylvania to Georgia, growing in deciduous and mixed forest, flowering in April and May. Stem up to 15cm. This is the American equivalent of the European *A. trifolia* L., distinguished from the commoner *A. nemorosa* L. (in Europe) see p.72 or *A. quinquefolia* L. (in America), by its simply tripartite leaves. Leafy soil, with shade in summer from deciduous trees. Photographed in Virginia, in the Blue Ridge Mountains, near Charlottesville.

Anemone ranunculoides L. **'Pleniflora'** (*Ranunculaceae*). This form has twice or three times the number of petals as the normal form, but normal stamens.

Anemone coronaria L. (*Ranunculaceae*). The pinkish-mauve colour form of this eastern-Mediterranean anemone is frequently found in cultivation. The red form, photographed here in southwest Turkey, is probably the one found most often in the wild. It is recorded, in the *Flora of Turkey*, that the commonest colour forms, red, pink, blue or white occur in pure populations in natural habitats, but in mixed colours in disturbed ground.

Anemone hortensis L. syn. *A. stellata* Lam. (*Ranunculaceae*). Native of France, Corsica, Sardinia, Italy and the coasts of Yugoslavia and Albania, growing in scrub and rocky places, flowering from February to April. Stems usually about 15cm. Lowest leaves with broad lobes. Petals 12–19, usually 15, pale mauve. A. × *fulgens* Gay p.82, probably originated as a hybrid between this species and *A. pavonina*. Photographed near Nice in April.

Ranunculus ficaria L. **'Brazen Hussy'** (*Ranunculaceae*). This striking purple-leaved Celandine was found by Christopher Lloyd and Romke van de Kaa, growing wild in a wood near Northiam, Sussex, in about 1976 and is now becoming widespread in gardens in southern England. The almost-black leaves are a fine foil for the shining deep yellow flowers. Grow in a position sunny in spring, partially shaded in summer, in rich heavy soil.

Cyclamen repandum Sm. subsp. **rhodense** (Meikle) Grey-Wilson (*Primulaceae*). Native of Rhodes, growing in pine woods and oak scrub at 150–460m, flowering in March to May. This variety of *C. repandum* is distinct in its white or very pale pink flowers, with a deeper eye, and is closest to the pale pink form from the southern Peloponnese in flower colour, but in leaf to the form from Italy and Corsica: see p.36. Like all forms of *C. repandum* the leaves, which are formed in January, are sensitive to more than about 5°C of frost, so they need protection in cold climates.

Gentiana olivieri Griseb. (*Gentianaceae*). Native of central and eastern Turkey, and N Iraq eastwards to Central Asia in the Tien Shan, on grassy hills and valleys at up to 2300m, flowering in April to July. This species is unusual in that the woody vertical rootstock becomes completely dry and dormant in summer, sprouting roots when wetted in autumn. Can be cultivated in a bulb frame, but shy-flowering in cultivation.

Anemone ranunculoides 'Pleniflora'

Ranunculus ficaria 'Brazen Hussy'

Anemone hortensis

Gentiana olivieri

Cyclamen repandum var. **rhodense** in Rhodes

½ life size Photographed 14 April

(a) **Ornithogalum collinum** Guss., syn. *O. tenuifolium* Guss. (*Liliaceae*). Native of the Mediterranean region, where it grows on hillsides and in scrub flowering in April and May. There are many very closely related dwarf narrow-leaved species, differing in details of bulb and leaf hairiness, in the presence or absence of a white stripe, and in flowering time (see pp.38 and 82). Most are easily grown in sunny well-drained soil and among short grass. Source Turkey, Hakkari, c.1200m, Rix 2443.

(b) **Scilla lilio-hyacinthus** L. (*Liliaceae*). Native of central France and N Spain, growing in woods and damp grassy places, flowering in May. Easily recognised by its strange lily-like bulb with several separate scales, and rather few (up to fifteen) flowered inflorescence. The specimen here is unusually short; stems normally 15–40cm. Easily grown in moist rich soil in shade, or half-shade.

(c) **Anemone pavonina** Lam. (*Ranunculaceae*). Native of the Mediterranean region from France eastwards to Turkey, flowering from February to April, growing in fields and on hillsides, often carpeting the ground under olive trees. Flowers variable in colour, pink, purple or scarlet. Close to *A.* × *fulgens* (p.83) which has more (twelve to nineteen) narrow petals, and *A. coronaria* (p.83) which has more finely divided leaves. Easily grown in full sun and well-drained soil. Source Greece, SW Peloponnese, Rix 502a. Photographed in Greece in April 1980 by Roger Philips.

(d) **Muscari tubergenianum** Hoog. ex Turrill (*Liliaceae*). The native range of this plant is not certain, but Brian Mathew says that it comes from N Iran. It is very close to *M. aucheri* (Boiss.) Baker from Turkey and may be a selection of it. Flowers pure blue. Easy to grow in any good soil in sun.

(e) **Muscari armeniacum** Leichtlin ex Baker (*Liliaceae*). Native of Bulgaria and Yugoslavia, Greece, Turkey and the Caucasus, growing on grassy hillsides. Very variable. Leaves three to five, up to 1cm wide. Flowers often have a purplish tinge. Easily grown in well-drained good soil in sun. There is a weird form c.v. 'Blue Spike' in which each flower has become a miniature inflorescence, giving a monstrous effect. (see p.83.)

(f) **Muscari botryoides** (L.) Miller (*Liliaceae*). Native of Europe from France, Germany and Poland southwards, though rare in Greece. Plants variable up to 30cm. Leaves shorter than the stem, two or three. The form shown here is an albino frequent in commerce. Easily grown in any good soil.

Ornithogalum nutans L. (*Liliaceae*). Native of Bulgaria and Greece to Turkey, growing in fields and waste places, flowering in April and May. Naturalised in many other parts of Europe. The large (15–30mm long) nodding flowers are characteristic, and appear long after the leaves. Will survive in grass on well drained soil or among shrubs, and naturalise itself if happy.

Anemone pavonina in Greece

Ornithogalum nutans

½ life size Photographed 2 April

(a) **Muscari azureum** Fenzl (*Liliaceae*). Native of Caucasus and NW Turkey, growing in damp mountain meadows. Easily grown in good well-drained soil, in a sunny place or in a pot in the alpine house. Common in cultivation as is a very good white form.

(b) **Scilla furseorum** Meikle (*Liliaceae*). Native of NE Afghanistan, near Faisabad, growing on stony hillsides at c.1500m. The rather similar *S. griffithii* has a larger inflorescence and pendulous not erect flowers. Easily grown in a bulb frame or in a pot in the alpine house, kept dry in summer. Source Afghanistan, Faisabad, limestone slopes, 1600m, P. Furse 6254.

(c) **Bellevalia trifoliata** (Ten.) Kunth (*Liliaceae*). Native of S Italy to Greece, Turkey and Egypt (naturalised in S France), growing in fields and waste places, flowering in April and May. There are several very similar species in the Middle East. All are easy to grow in full sun. Source Adiyaman, near Kahta, Linzee Gordon 5150.

(d) **Scilla cilicica** Siehe (*Liliaceae*). Native of Cyprus and SE Turkey southwards to Israel, growing on limestone rocks at up to 1000m, flowering in spring. Distinguished by its long leaves which develop before the flowers appear, and purplish blue upright or horizontal flowers in a lax raceme. Easily grown in a bulb frame or semi-shaded place outside, kept dry in summer. Source Turkey, coll. P. H. Davis.

(e) **Allium paradoxum** (Bieb.) G. Don (*Liliaceae*). Native of the Caucasus, northern Iran and the Kopet Dağ, where it grows in forests from sea level to 2300m, flowering in April and May. Plant 15–30cm high with one flat leaf and one to four large white nodding flowers. Sometimes the flowers are replaced by bulbils. Differs from *A. triquetrum* (p.161) in its rounded petals and single leaf. Easily grown in shady places, and naturalised in NW Europe (esp. S Scotland) where it usually has many bulbils and only one flower. This form can become a weed, but some Iranian plants with no bulbils are very beautiful. Source N Iran above Chalus, coll . P. Furse.

(g) **Muscari neglectum** Guss. ex Ten., syn. *M. atlanticum*, Boiss. & Reut., *M. racemosum* (L.) Lam. & DC. (*Liliaceae*). Native of Europe, from north France southwards to N Africa, Lebanon and eastwards to the Caucasus, Iran and the Altai; naturalised in England. Distinguished by its blackish-blue flowers with white teeth. Very variable in size. Easy to grow in any well-drained soil, and increasing by numerous bulbils.

(f) **Muscari armenaicum** Leichtlin ex Baker (*Liliaceae*). Native of SE Europe, from Yugoslavia and Bulgaria southwards to Turkey and the Caucasus, growing in grassy or rocky places at up to 2000m, flowering in April and May. See also p.83 (a) and (b). Shown here is a commercial cultivated plant. Easily grown in well-drained soil in a sunny place.

(h) **Muscari commutatum** Guss. (*Liliaceae*). Native of N Africa and Italy, eastwards to Lebanon, Turkey and the southern Caucasus, growing in stony places and scrub, flowering from March to May. Distinguished from other species by its dark blackish flowers, with black teeth. Easily grown in any well-drained soil in a sunny place. Source Cyprus, coll. W. K. Aslet.

$^2/_3$ life size Photographed 21 March

½ life size Photographed 2 May

(a) **Bellevalia pycnantha** (C. Koch) A. Los, syn. *Muscari pycnanthum* C. Koch (*Liliaceae*). Native of eastern Turkey, north-west Iran and Soviet Armenia, growing in medows and marshy fields in the mountains at 1000–2000m, flowering in May and June. Easily grown in good soil in full sun, wet in spring and will tolerate summer drought, though it does not require it.

(b) **Bellevalia romana** (L.) Rchb. (*Liliaceae*). Native of SW France and the Mediterranean region from France to Greece, growing in meadows and waste ground, flowering in spring. Easy to grow in well-drained soil in a sunny position.

(c) **Muscari latifolium** Kirk (*Liliaceae*). Native of NW Turkey, growing in open pine forests at c.1000m, flowering in April. Very distinct with its single broad leaf which encircles the stem at the base. Cultivation as (b).

(d) **Iris × warlsind** hort. (*Iridaceae*, section *Juno*). A hybrid between *I. warleyensis* (p.67) and *I. aucheri* (syn. *I. sindjarensis*) (p.63), easily grown in well-drained soil and full sun.

(e) **Ranunculus asiaticus** L. (*Ranunculaceae*). Native of the eastern Mediterranean from Crete, Rhodes and S Turkey to S Iran and Israel, and N Africa, growing on stony hillsides and on rocks, flowering in April and May. Usually red, but also yellow, purple, pink or white. Easily grown in a bulb frame or pot in the alpine house. Tender and killed by frosts below −10°C. Source Rhodes, on limestone rocks, Rix 1240.

(f) **Muscari caucasicum** Griseb. ex Baker (*Liliaceae*). Native of Turkey, south Transcaucasus, N Iran and the Kopet Dağ, at up to 3000m, growing in mountain meadows, on stony slopes and in scrub, flowering from April to July. Distinguished from *M. comosum* by its shorter stemmed sterile flowers, which do not elongate to form a tassel-like head. Cultivation as (b). Source Iran, coll. P. Furse.

(g) **Fritillaria lusitanica** Wikstrom, syn. *F. hispanica* Boiss. & Reut. (*Liliaceae*). Native of E, C and S Spain, C and S Portugal, growing in open pine forest at low altitudes, among rocks and in alpine scree up to c.3000m in the Sierra Nevada, flowering from March to July. Very variable in leaf length and flower colour and shape, but intermediates occur between all the forms which have at some time been considered distinct. Easy to grow in a bulb frame, or pot in the alpine house, kept dry in summer. Source Portugal, near Lisbon, open pine forest, c.100m, R. Macfarlane.

(h) **Scilla ramburei** Boiss. (*Liliaceae*). Native of Portugal, SW Spain and N Africa near Tangiers, growing in sandy places at low altitudes flowering from March to June. Sometimes considered a subspecies of *S. verna* (p.47), but taller with a looser inflorescence, and smaller flowers on longer stalks. Easily grown in well-drained sandy soil in a sunny place.

(i) **Scilla monophyllos** Link. (*Liliaceae*). Native of Portugal, W Spain and N Africa around Tangiers, growing on heaths, in pine woods and sandy ground, flowering from February to June. Easy to grow in sandy peaty soil in a sunny position.

(j) **Scilla persica** Hausskn. (*Liliaceae*). Native of SE Turkey, NE Iraq and W Iran, where it grows in wet meadows at c.1700m, flowering in May. Stem 15–20cm. Easy to grow in a bulb frame or in a sunny place outside. Source Iran, Sanandaj, P. Furse.

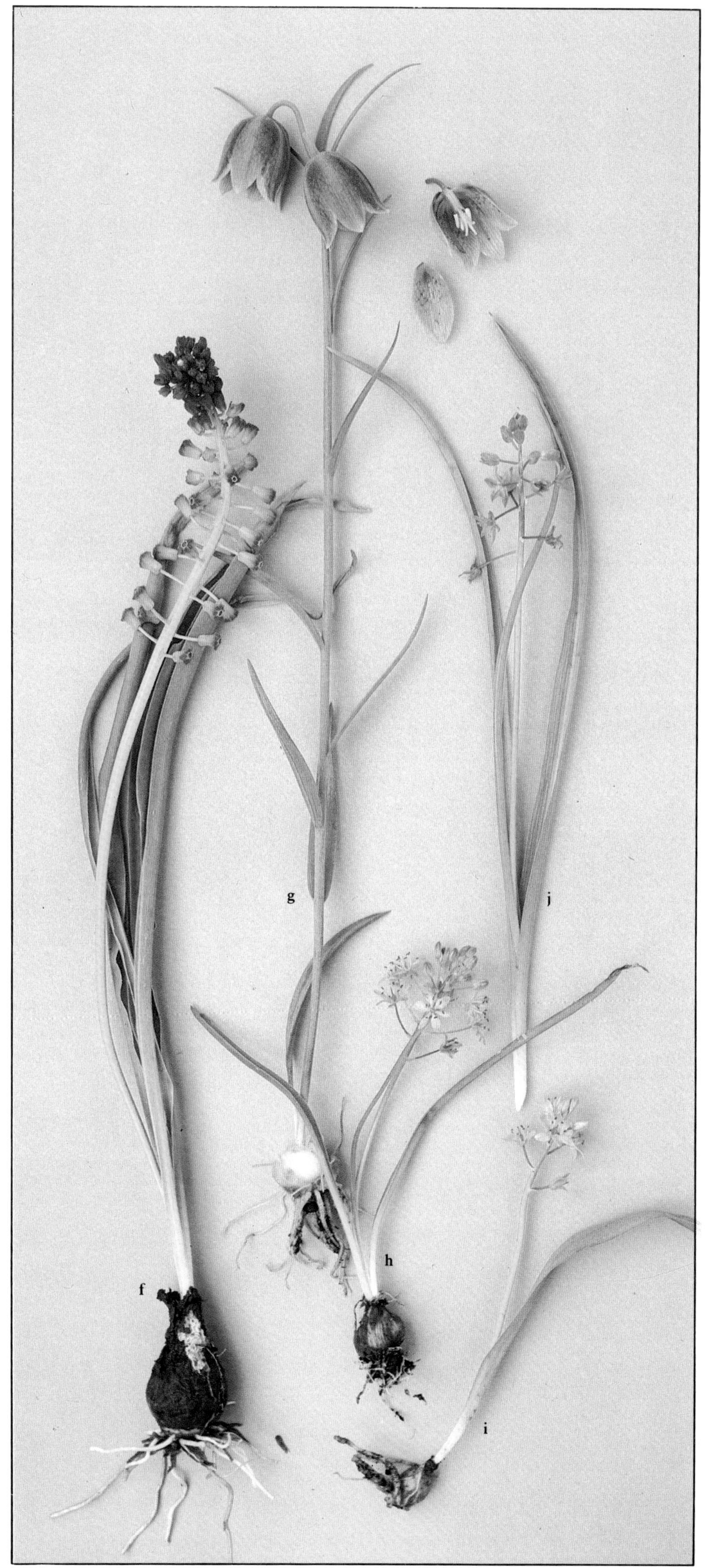

½ life size Photographed 17 April

½ life size Photographed 2 May

(a) **Anemone coronaria.** L. (*Ranunculaceae*). Native of the Mediterranean region from Spain and France to Greece, Turkey and Algeria; found also in Central Asia, where it is often called *A. bucharica* Regel. The flowers can be bluish, pink, red or white. Cultivation as for (d). (see also p.83)

(b) **Anemone x fulgens** Gay (*Ranunculaceae*). This probably arose from hybrids between *A. hortensis L.* and *A. pavonina* Lam, found wild in the south of France. The usual bright-red flowered form was found in vineyards near Dax. The St Bavo strain, shown here, varies from pink to purple. This colour form has been named *A. variata* Jord., and was recorded from near Grasse. All forms flower in early spring and require a well-drained, sunny position, rather dry in summer. Hardy to −10°C.

(c) **Geranium macrostylum** Boiss. syn. *G. tuberosum* subsp. *macrostylum* (Boiss.) Davis (*Geraniaceae*). Native of the E Mediterranean region, as far as S Turkey near Adana, growing in stony places and scrub, flowering from April to June. The N African *G. malviflorum* Boiss. & Reut. is a better garden plant, with larger, bluer flowers.

(d), (e) **Muscari armeniacum** Leichtlin ex Baker (*Liliaceae*). Native of SE Europe from Yugoslavia and Bulgaria to Greece, Turkey and the Caucasus, growing in grassy and rocky places up to 2000m, flowering in April and May. Easy to grow in a well-drained soil and sunny position. Source: (d) Turkey, Elma Da., above Ankara (an albino), Rix s.n.; (e) between Malatya and Kayseri, limestone plateau, c.2000m, Rix s.n.

(f) **Gagea graeca** (L.) Terr., syn. *Lloydia graeca* L. (*Liliaceae*). Native of Greece, Crete and Turkey, growing in pockets of soil on rock, flowering in March and April. Easily grown in a sunny bulb frame or in a pot in the alpine house in full sun, kept dry in summer. Source: Turkey, Izmir, Rix 1218.

(g) **Gagea confusa** Terr., syn. *G. minimoides* Pascher (*Liliaceae*). Native of E Turkey, N Iraq, W Iran, Kopet Dağ, and S Transcaucasia, growing in grassy places, usually by late snow patches from 1000 to 3000m, flowering from April to July. Easily grown in a bulb frame, kept wet in spring, dry in summer. Source: Turkey, Van, near Hoşap.

(h) **Muscari macrocarpum** Sweet (*Liliaceae*). Native of Greece, especially the Aegean islands and Crete, and western Turkey, growing on limestone cliffs, flowering in April and May. Distinguished from *M. muscarimi* med., p.85, by its yellow flowers, purplish in bud. Easy to grow in a well-drained sunny place.

(i) **Bellevalia longipes** Post (*Liliaceae*). Native of Turkey, Syria, Iraq and Iran, growing in fields and on hillsides from 900 to 2000m, flowering in March and April. One of a complex group of species with pedicels which elongate in fruit, close to *B. sarmatica* (Pallas ex Georgi) Woron. from the steppes of S Russia and Romania. Cultivation as for (h). Source: Iran, coll. by Paul Furse.

Muscari comosum (L.) Miller (*Liliaceae*). Native of most of Europe, N America to Lebanon, Turkey and Iraq, at up to 2200m, flowering from March to July, growing especially in dry meadows and as a weed of cultivation. Photographed in Greece, Peloponnese, near Sparta, in April 1980 by Roger Phillips.

⅓ life size Photographed 22 April

Muscari comosum

Bellevalia dubia

(j) **Ornithogalum fimbriatum** Willd. (p.38).

Bellevalia dubia (Guss.) Reichenb. (*Liliaceae*). Native of Italy and Yugoslavia to Greece and Turkey, growing on rocky hillsides on limes at up to 1000m, flowering in March and April. Photographed in the S Peloponnese near Githion, in April 1980 by Roger Phillips.

Scilla peruviana near Ronda in Spain

Scilla bithynica

Leucojum tingitanum

Scilla peruviana L. (*Liliaceae*). See also p.64. In spite of its name (Linnaeus thought that it came from Peru), this species is native of the western Mediterranean region. Many different forms have been named. It often grows in really wet, marshy ground, as shown here, but these areas are probably dry and baked hard in summer. Photographed in S Spain near Ronda in April.

Scilla bithynica Boiss. (*Liliaceae*). Native of Bulgaria and NW Turkey growing in damp meadows, woods, and scrub at sea level (up to 20m) flowering in March to April. Leaves 5–15mm wide. Flowers 11–18mm across, on a stem 9–30cm tall. Easily grown in partially shaded grassy places or in shrubberies, and sometimes naturalising. *S. amoena* L. a species of unknown origin, but possibly a fertile hybrid, is naturalised in France and SE Europe. It has bright blue flowers and pedicels without bracts.

Leucojum tingitanum Baker (*Amaryllidaceae*). Native of Morocco, growing in sandy soil near the coast south of Tangier, flowering in February and March. Stems to 20cm. Leaves about 1cm wide. Flowers c.9mm long. A most beautiful species, rare both in the wild and in cultivation. Photographed in a garden in Suffolk.

Muscari macrocarpum Sweet (see p.83). Photographed on granite cliffs on the island of Cos, in April.

Muscari muscarimi Medikus syn. *Muscari moschatum* Willd. (*Liliaceae*). Native of south-west Turkey, growing on screes and dry hillsides at 800–1920m, flowering in May and June. Stem to 18cm with 12–30 flowers, like *M. macrocarpum* p.75, but with greenish or white flowers 7–9mm long. Long cultivated for its powerful musky scent by the Turks and as early as 1596 by Clusius in Holland. Photographed in Turkey by T. Baytop.

Ornithogalum reverchonii Lange (*Liliaceae*). Native of SW Spain especially near Ronda, and Morocco growing in crevices in limestone rocks, flowering in April. An elegant plant with up to 20 pure white, nodding flowers and floppy linear leaves. I have had this species for several years since receiving seedlings from Ivor Barton. They have been growing in a crevice between two limestone rocks, and flower every year. Photographed near Ronda in April.

Ornithogalum lanceolatum Labill. (*Liliaceae*). Native of SW Turkey, Syria and Lebanon, growing in pine forests, rocky slopes and in alpine steppes at 1000–2500m, flowering in March to April. A dwarf species with leaves 15–20mm broad and 5–20 flowers at ground level. Easily cultivated in a bulb frame, dry in summer and flowering in England in January. Source: S Turkey, Cilician gates.

Muscari macrocarpum in Cos

Ornithogalum reverchonii near Ronda, Spain

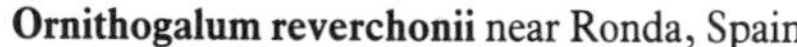

Muscari muscarimi

Ornithogalum lanceolatum

Ornithogalum reverchonii

Bluebell wood in the Chilterns near Ibston, Buckinghamshire

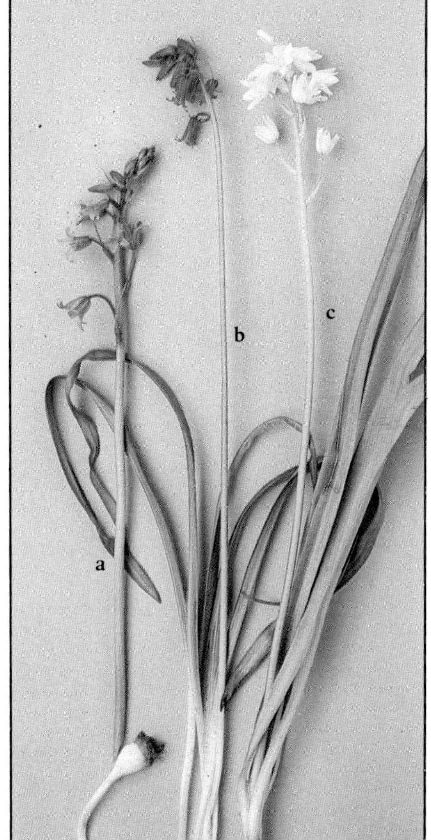

¼ life size Photographed 2 May

¼ life size Photographed 17 April

(b) **Hyacinthoides non-scripta** (L.) Chouard ex Rothm., syn. *Endymion non-scriptus* (L.) Garcke, *Scilla non-scripta* (L.) Hoffmans. & Link (*Liliaceae*). Bluebell. Native of W Europe from western France, Belgium and Portugal, growing in woods and meadows, flowering from April to June. Naturalised further east. Easily grown in leafy soil near the Atlantic coast of Europe, and requiring cool shady conditions further east. Photographed in S England, Chiltern Hills near Ibston, Buckinghamshire, by Roger Phillips.

(c), (a) **Hyacinthoides hispanica** (Miller) Rothm., syn. *Scilla hispanica* Miller (*Liliaceae*). Native of Spain, Portugal and N Africa, especially Morocco and Algeria, naturalised elsewhere, growing in woods and among shady rocks, flowering from March to May. Distinguished from *H. non-scripta* by its erect racemes, erect and more open flowers, as well as its broader leaves. Hybrids are common in cultivation and one is shown here (a) which has an infloresence intermediate between the parents. White (as shown) and pink forms are also common in cultivation.

(d) **Fritillaria meleagris** L. (*Liliaceae*). Snake's Head Fritillary. Native of most of Europe from N Yugoslavia and S Russia to Poland, central France and S England. Naturalised in Scandinavia. It grows in the flood plains of rivers usually in rather dry fen vegetation on alkaline soils, often in great numbers. The colour varies from dark purple to white. Easily grown in grass or in well-drained soil in sun or half-shade, not dried out in summer. Photographed in Gloucestershire in April 1964.

(e) **Leucojum aestivum** L. (*Amaryllidaceae*). Summer Snowflake. Native of Europe and SW Asia to north Iran, growing in wet fields, woods and swamps especially near rivers, flowering from March to May. Distinguished from *L. vernum* by the smaller flowers, and by having three to seven flowers in the umbel. The leaves emerge in winter. The seed pod is swollen and filled with air so that it will float and be dispersed by water. The larger flowered form, is c.v. 'Gravetye', named after the garden of William Robinson in Sussex. Easily grown in damp rich soil and happy in waterlogged conditions.

Fritillaria meleagris

¾ life size Photographed 13 March

(a) **Fritillaria pinardii** Boiss., syn. *F. syriaca* Hayek & Siehe, *F. alpina* Freyn & Sint. (*Liliaceae*). Native of S Armenia, most of Turkey, Syria and Lebanon, growing on stony hillsides especially by late snow patches, at above 1800m, flowering in May and June (see also p.91 (d)), (j)). Very variable, but characterised by its alternate rather broad leaves, purplish or reddish flowers, yellow or green inside, and papillose style. The short-stemmed form shown here was called *F. syriaca*. Easy to grow in a pot in the alpine house or in a bulb frame. Source Turkey, mountains south of Malatya, 200m, Rix 1624.

(b) **Fritillaria zagrica** Stapf (*Liliaceae*). Native of SE Turkey and Iran, especially the central Zagros mountains from 1800 to 3000m, growing in mountain steppe, often by late snow patches, flowering from March to May. Characterised by the small yellow tips to the otherwise dark purple petals, and rather slender, papillose style. Stem 4–12cm. Cultivation as (a).

(c) **Fritillaria assyriaca** Baker, syn. *F. canaliculata* Baker (*Liliaceae*). Native of E Turkey, W Iran, N Iraq and possibly S Armenia, growing in fields, on steppe and stony hillsides, from 100 to 2500m, flowering from March to May. Distinguished from *F. pinardii* by its narrower leaves, usually taller stem and very short stout style. (Height 10–35cm.) Cultivation as (a), but many forms have proved susceptible to botrytis. Keep rather dry. Source NE Turkey, Ağri, Tahir Dağ, 500m, Rix 1658.

(d), (e) **Fritillaria chlorantha** Hausskn. & Bornm. (*Liliaceae*). Native of Iran, especially the NW Zagros mountains, growing on steep and stony slopes from 1800 to 3000m, flowering in April and May. Characterised by its shining green, not glaucous leaves and green flower, sometimes marked with purple. Style short, stout, divided at the tip. Height 4–10cm. Cultivation as (a). Slow to increase. Source (d) Iran, Zagros, S of Thuin, 2310m, Archibald 1609; (e) Iran, SW of Arak, Shuturunkuh, 1800m, BSBE 695.

(f) **Fritillaria assyriaca × caucasica** (*Liliaceae*). Hybrids are rare in *Fritillaria*, but this form is frequent in NE Turkey around Erzurum and Kars. It has the tall stem of its parents, but broader leaves than *F. assyriaca*, and a stouter, more papillose style than *F. caucasica*. It is usually found near the parents, but often growing in separate colonies. Robust and easy to cultivate in a bulb frame, and might succeed outside. Source Turkey, Ağri, Tahir Dağ, stony slopes, 2400m, Rix 1641.

(g) **Fritillaria armena** Boiss. (*Liliaceae*). Native of north-eastern Turkey, especially around Erzurum, where it grows on stony hillsides in bare earth by late snow patches at 1800–2800m, flowering in May and June. Characterised by its small, deep purple flowers, dark inside, and stout papillose style. Cultivation as (a). Source Turkey, Erzurum, Çakmak Dağ, 2200m, Rix 855.

Fritillaria raddeana Regel, syn. *F. askabadensis* M. Micheli (*Liliaceae*). Native of NE Iran, and SW Central Asia, especially the Kopet Dağ, growing on rocks and among scrub, flowering from March to April. Like a small delicate Crown Imperial, with pale yellow flowers and a much smaller nectary. Easy to grow, but flowering so early that it is better in a bulb frame. Source cultivated stock, probably originating from a large seed collection by P. Furse in Golestan Forest, NE Iran.

Fritillaria raddeana ½ life size Photographed 13 March

²⁄₃ life size Photographed 28 March

(a) **Fritillaria conica** Boiss. (*Liliaceae*). Native of S Greece, especially the Peloponnese, where it grows on limestone hills near the sea in low evergreen oak scrub, and at the edges of fields. Distinguished from other small yellow-flowered species by its tall stem, up to 25cm, and deeply divided style. Easy to grow in a bulb frame and in very well-drained, good soil outside, in full sun. Source Greece, near Pylos, Rix 485.

(b) **Fritillaria uva-vulpis** Rix, syn. *F. assyriaca* hort. non Baker (*Liliaceae*). Native of N Iraq, W Iran and SE Turkey, growing in cornfields and hay meadows from 1000 to 2500m, flowering in March and April. Distinguished from *F. assyriaca* Baker (p.89 (c)) by its few flat, shining green leaves; style very stout. This plant was misidentified as *F. assyriaca* and is widely cultivated under that name. Cultivation as (a). Source Iran, Rezaiyeh, SE of Mahabad, 1700m, Furse 2173.

(c) **Fritillaria caucasica** Adams, syn. *F. tulipifolia* M. Bieb. (*Liliaceae*). Native of NE Turkey, NW Iran and the Caucasus, growing in grassy subalpine meadows, and on shady rock ledges from 1700 to 3000m, flowering from April to June. Distinguished by its usually tall (up to 30cm) stem, few leaves and long, 9–17mm, slender usually smooth style and stamen filaments. Always grows in peaty soil in the wild, but difficult to cultivate satisfactorily. The specimen shown here is shorter than normal. Source USSR, Armenia, hills above Lake Sevan, Rix 2623.

(d) **Fritillaria pinardii** Boiss., syn. *F. alpina* Freyn & Sint. (*Liliaceae*) (see p.89 (a)). The form shown here is close to *F. alpina*, with its tall stem, and flowers yellow inside. It grows on stony hills in NW Turkey south to Ankara. Source Turkey, Elma Dağ above Ankara, Rix 1526.

(e) **Fritillaria forbesii** Baker (*Liliaceae*). Native of the extreme south-western corner of Turkey around Marmaris, where it grows in scrub, usually on serpentine, flowering in February and March, from 50 to 350m. Requires careful treatment in a bulb frame or alpine house, as it tends to emerge very early and be damaged by frost. Collected plants grow poorly, and as the species is very restricted in the wild, it should not be dug up. The form shown here has been in cultivation for many years, and grows well, but increases slowly.

(f) **Fritillaria carica** Rix (*Liliaceae*). Native of south-western Turkey, Samos and Chios, where it grows on rocky hillsides, often among scrub, or in open pine woods from 200 to 1500m, flowering from March to May. Distinguished from *F. forbesii* by its broader leaves and shorter stem, and from *F. bithynica* which often grows nearby, by its fat, papillose style. Capsule not winged. Easily grown in a bulb frame or a pot in the alpine house. Source Turkey, Izmir, by the ruins of Ephesus, C.M.W. 2508.

(g) **Fritillaria aurea** Schott, syn. *F. cilicicotaurica* Hausskn., *F. bornmuelleri* Hausskn. (*Liliaceae*). Native of central Turkey, growing among limestone rocks and on cliffs, often by late snow patches from 1800 to 3000m, flowering from May to July. The large yellow flowers distinguish it from all other species except *F. collina* (p.95 (e)), which has narrower leaves and petals greenish on the back, with finely ciliate margins, and the larger paler *F. tubiformis* subsp. *moggridgei* from the Alps. Cultivation as (f). One of the best small species, increasing well. Source Turkey, Sivas, Yildiz Dağ, Rix 2030.

2/3 life size Photographed 28 March

(h), (i) **Fritillaria aurea × pinardii** (*Liliaceae*). Two hybrid individuals and the likely parents are shown here. Hybrids are very rare, although two or more species often grow together. These two were growing with the parents in central Turkey. They have grown well in cultivation, increasing fast by bulbils, and hybrids have been made between (h) and *F. aurea*. Source (h) Rix 1602; (i) Rix 1601.

(j) **Fritillaria pinardii** Boiss. (*Liliaceae*) (see pp.81 (d) and 89 (a)). This form is found scattered across central Turkey, and is usually rather small and delicate with pronounced 'shoulders' to the narrow flower. It is called *F. fleischeri* by Boissier in *Flora Orientalis*. Source Turkey, between Malatya and Kayseri, 2000m, on rocky steppe, Rix 1600.

Fritillaria latifolia

Fritillaria latifolia Willd., syn. *F. nobilis* Baker (*Liliaceae*). Native of the Caucasus and north-east Turkey, growing in alpine meadows and on stony hillsides by late snow patches from 1800 to 3000m, flowering from May to July. Similar to *F. tubiformis* from the Alps (p.99 (c)), but has shining green, not glaucous, leaves and the flowers are smaller, not greyish outside. Turkish collections have not grown well, but recent collections from the Caucasus, where it is more robust, may do better. Should do best in rich peaty soil outside. Photographed in NE Turkey between Yalnizçam and Ardanuç, in May 1970.

life size Photographed 21 March

(a), (c) **Fritillaria crassifolia** Boiss. & Huet subsp. **kurdica** (Boiss. & Noë) Rix, syn. *F. karadaghensis* Turrill (*Liliaceae*). Native of SE Turkey, NW Iran and S Transcaucasia, growing on stony alpine steppes and on rocks from 1500 to 3500m, flowering from April to July. Nectary linear, 8–10mm long. One form shown here was named *F. grossheimiana* A. Los. Better grown in a bulb frame, in rich loose and very gritty soil. Source (a) NW Iran, Kuh-i-Sahand, Furse 2923; (c) SE Turkey, Hakkari, Yukşekova, 2150m, Rix 1936.

(b) **Fritillaria straussii** Bornm. Native of SE Turkey and NW Iran, growing among oak scrub and large herbs at 1500–2500m, flowering in May and June. Flowers dark purple, or green going purple with age; nectary linear. Cultivation as (a). Source Iran, Sanandaj to Marivan, P. Furse 3397.

(d) **Fritillaria michailovskyi** Fomine. Native of NE Turkey from Erzurum to Kars growing on screes and earthy slopes from 2000 to 3000m, flowering in May and June. The dead petals remain around the seed capsule. Cultivation as for (a). Source Kars, subalpine meadow in clearings among pine trees, 2100m, Albury, Cheese & Watson 1617.

(e) **Fritillaria graeca** Boiss. & Spruner. Native of S Greece, growing in rocky places among garrigue and *Abies* forest from 700 to 1800m, flowering from March to May. Shown here a rather stout, robust form which was called *F. guicciardii* Held & Sart. Cultivation as for (a). Source Greece, Athens, Mount Parnis, Rix 568.

(f) **Fritillaria davisii** Turrill. Native of the Peloponnese growing at low altitudes in scrub, olive groves and cornfields, flowering in March. Very close to *F. graeca*, differing mainly in habit, with the lowest leaves flat, at ground level, and in having a purple flower without a clear green central stripe. Cultivation as for (a). Source Greece, S Peloponnese, S of Githion, A. A. M. Batchelor.

(g) **Fritillaria crassifolia** subsp. **poluninii** Rix (*Liliaceae*). Native of NE Iraq, growing on limestone screes from 2200 to 2400m, flowering from April to June, often by late snow patches. Source NE Iraq near Suleimaniya, 2400m, Polunin 5063.

(h) **Fritillaria crassifolia** Boiss. & Huet, subsp. **crassifolia** syn. *F. ophioglossifolia* Freyn & Sint. Native of Turkey, scattered from the SW to the NE, usually growing on limestone screes, from 1500 to 2600m, flowering in May and June. Source Turkey, Erzurm, Kop Dağ, 2600m, Rix 1710. See p.105 (c).

(i) **Fritillaria crassifolia** subsp. **hakkarensis** Rix. Native of SE Turkey and NE Iraq, growing by late snow patches from 1500 to 3500m, flowering from May to July. Close to subsp. *kurdica*, but has dark green shining leaves, and a smaller, more open flower. Source Turkey, Hakkari, Şemdinli, T. Baytop, ISTE 21620.

Fritillaria alburyana Rix, syn. *F. erzurumica* Kasapigil. Native of NE Turkey, growing in screes and in peaty soil among tussocks of grass, flowering in late May and June by late snow patches at 2000–3000m. Named after Sidney Albury, who died plant collecting in the Himalayas in 1970. This species has proved very difficult to flower well in cultivation, probably because it does not get a long enough cold period in lowland Europe. Photographed in Turkey, south of Erzurum, in May 1970.

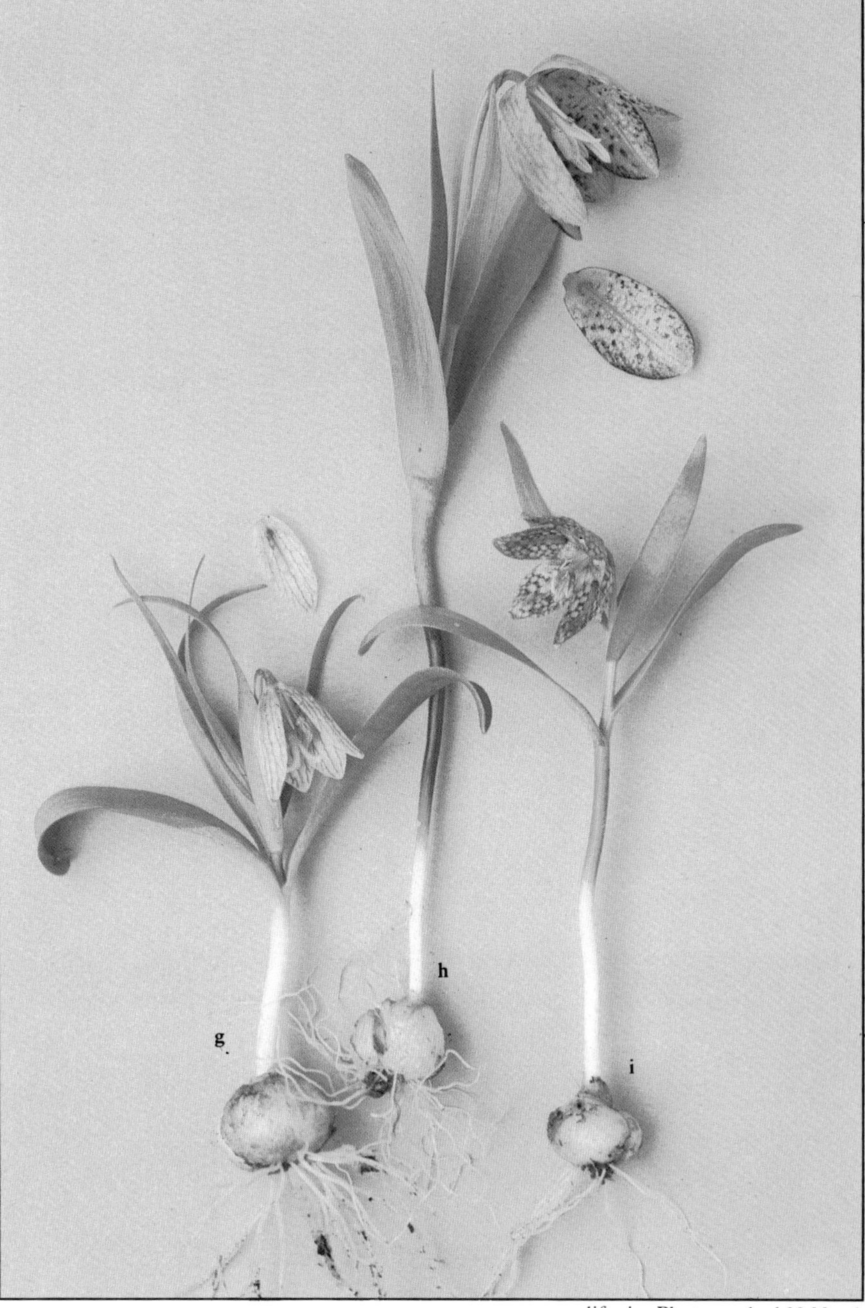

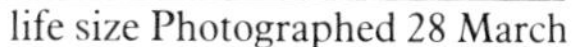
life size Photographed 28 March

¼ life size Photographed 28 March

Fritillaria alburyana

½ life size Photographed 14 April

⅓ life size Photographed 28 March

⅓ life size Photographed 2 April

(a) **Fritillaria sibthorpiana** (Sibth. & Sm.) Baker (*Liliaceae*). Native of SW Turkey, near Marmaris, where it grows in open pine forest on limestone at c.400m, flowering in April. Characterised by its small yellow flower, and two large ovate-lanceolate stem leaves. Easy to grow in a bulb frame or in a pot in the alpine house; increase by seed. Source Turkey, near Marmaris, Brickell & Mathew 8306.

(b) **Fritillaria alfredae** subsp. **glaucoviridis** (Turrill) Rix, syn. *F. haradjianii* Briq. (*Liliaceae*). Native of S Turkey, especially the northern Amanus mountains, growing in oak scrub and beech forest, at 500–1500m, flowering in April and May. Stem 10–36cm; capsule winged. Cultivation as for (a). Slow to increase, but will set seed if pollinated. Source Turkey, Amanus, Nurdağ pass, Rix 1357.

(c) **Fritillaria alfredae** subsp. **platyptera** (Samuelsson) Rix (*Liliaceae*). Native of S Turkey, and Syria in the southern Amanus mountains, growing in oak scrub from 500 to 800m, flowering in April and May. Close to subsp. *glaucoviridis*, but is more slender, with longer upper leaves and narrower lower leaves. Sub-species *alfredae*, a very rare plant from Lebanon, is still slenderer and more delicate. Source S Turkey, near Yayladağ, Rix 1360.

(d) **Fritillaria bithynica** Baker, syn. *F. citrina* Baker, *F. schliemannii* Sint.,*F. pineticola* Schwarz (*Liliaceae*). Native of western Turkey, Samos and Chios, growing in open pine forest or oak scrub from 100 to 1200m, flowering from March to May. Characterised by its green flowers, yellowish inside, occasionally with purple markings, and slender, undivided style. Cultivation as for (a). Source S Turkey, hills south of Muğla, Rix 1298.

(e) **Fritillaria ehrhartii** Boiss. & Orph. (*Liliaceae*). Native of the Aegean islands of Euboea, Skiros, Andros and Siros, growing in garrigue and among schistose rocks, from 180 to 800m, flowering from February to April. Differs from *F. bithynica* in its purple flowers, with a yellow point to each petal; cf. *F. zagrica* (p.89 (b)). Cultivation as for (a). Source Greece, Euboea, near Karystos, Rix 2167.

(f) **Fritillaria minuta** Boiss. & Noë, syn. *F. carduchorum* Rix (*Liliaceae*). Native of eastern Turkey and NW Iran, growing on earthy hillsides and among oak scrub from 1000 to 3500m, flowering from April to July, usually by late snow patches. Distinguished by its small narrow brick red flower, and deeply trifid smooth style. Easy to grow in a bulb frame or pot in the alpine house. Source Turkey, Bitlis, towards Tatvan, 2300m, Rix 779.

(g) **Fritillaria severtzovii** Regel, syn. *Korolkovia severtzovii* (Regel) Regel (*Liliaceae*). Native of Central Asia, especially the Tien Shan and the Pamir Alai, growing on cliff ledges, among scrub and on steep earthy slopes from 1000 to 3000m, flowering from March to July. The bulb is similar to many *Fritillaria*, and the branching roots are similar to *F. imperialis*. The petal shape and the nectary are closer to *Lilium*. Easy to grow in a bulb frame or pot in the alpine house, kept dry in summer. Source C Asia, mountains south of Ferghana, Chamsabad, 2000m, Rix 2781.

(h) **Fritillaria collina** Adams, syn. *F. lutea* M. Bieb. (*Liliaceae*). Native of the Caucasus, where it grows in alpine meadows and birch scrub at 2000–4500m, flowering in May and June. Close to *F. aurea* Schott, but flowers larger and paler, and inner petals with finely toothed edges. Has grown well in peaty soil in a bulb frame, but should also grow happily in well drained soil outside. Source USSR, N Caucasus, Dombai, coll. D. Schlummel.

Fritillaria severtzovii green form, in the Chimgan valley, central Asia

Fritillaria obliqua

Fritillaria hermonis subsp. **amana**

Fritillaria grandiflora Grossheim. (*Liliaceae*). Native of Soviet Azerbaijan, in the Talysh mountains above Lerik, in rocky woods and scrub and north facing cliffs, flowering in May. This interesting species falls somewhat between *F. latifolia* and the Iranian *F. kotschyana*, and also resembles a large broad-leaved form of *F. orientalis*. It has proved easy to grow and increases well by bulbils. Source: Moscow Botanic Garden.

Fritillaria orientalis Adams, syn. *F. tenella* M. Bieb. (*Liliaceae*). Native of the North Caucasus, in limestone gorges and rocky woods, growing in humus-filled rock crevices, flowering in April. Stems c.15cm tall. Leaves linear, often opposite or the upper in a whorl of 3. Style deeply divided. Requires cool and not too dry conditions in summer. Source: Fiakdon valley: collected by V. Pilous.

Fritillaria severtzovii Regel (*Liliaceae*). The form shown on p.95 (g), is the dwarfer of the two forms commonly cultivated. The taller form, from the Tien Shan mountains, north-east of Tashkent, has stems up to 50cm high, and flowers usually rich chocolate-brown inside, greenish outside, but all purple and all green individuals were also seen. Photographed near Tashkent in the Chimgan valley.

Fritillaria lusitanica Wikstrom (*Liliaceae*). Native of Spain and Portugal from near sea level to c.3000m in the mountains of SE Spain. The specimen shown on p.81 (g) is a tall one from near the coast in Portugal. Alpine and subalpine forms, which are more common in Spain and recorded from the Sierra de Guadarrama southwards, have shorter stems and numerous longer narrower leaves. Photographed in S Spain near Ronda, on limestone screes.

Fritillaria obliqua Ker-Gawl (*Liliaceae*). Native of Greece, around Athens in scrub and pine woods flowering in March and April. Stems usually c.15cm tall. Rather similar to *F. tuntasia* (p.98) but with fewer broader leaves and larger flowers. This is one of the rarest of all Fritillaries, as many of its habitats have been overrun by the suburbs of Athens. Fortunately it was collected recently by Ole Sonderhousen near Marathon and will be preserved in his nursery, from which the specimen shown here was obtained.

Fritillaria hermonis Fenzl. subsp. **amana** Rix. Native of the Amanus mountains from near Maraş southwards to the Lebanon and Anti-Lebanon, flowering in April to May. It is found among rocks and screes and in pine and cedar forest and abandoned terraces at 1400–2200m, flowering in April to June. A variable species, of which several clones are in cultivation: specimens from Lebanon have glaucous leaves; specimens from Turkey usually green leaves and in one clone (Horton & Stevens 2333) very yellow flowers; in another E. K. Balls 1034 collected in 1934, the flowers are long, rich green marked with brown. Photographed by Ken Aslet at the Cedars of Lebanon.

Fritillaria acmopetala Boiss. subsp. **wendelboi** Rix. Native of SW Turkey from Antalya to Içel growing in cedar forest and rocky places on limestone at 1600–2000m, flowering in April to June. This subspecies has broader leaves and a squarer flower than typical *F. acmopetala* and is found at higher altitudes. It often produces large numbers of bulbils and does not seem difficult to grow in a bulb frame. Source: above Akseki: collected A. Attila.

Fritillaria orientalis

Fritillaria lusitanica near Ronda

Fritillaria grandiflora

Fritillaria acmopetala subsp. **wendel boi**

½ life size Photographed 14 April

Fritillaria bucharica

Fritillaria walujewii

Fritillaria thunbergii

(a) **Fritillaria minima** Rix (*Liliaceae*). Native of SE Turkey, where it grows on steep slopes among limestone rocks at 2900–3000m, flowering in June and July by melting snow patches. Has proved unsatisfactory in cultivation, as the flowers open before the stem has elongated. It has grown in a sunny bulb frame, in a peaty alkaline soil. Source Turkey, Van, above Gevaş, Rix 735a.

(b) **Fritillaria montana** Hoppe (*Liliaceae*). Native of SE France, Italy and the Balkans south to northern Greece, where it grows on limestone pavements, and on rocky slopes, at from 50 to 1600m, flowering from March to May. Easy to grow in a bulb frame or a raised bed outside, kept rather dry in summer. Source Yugoslavia, near Kičevo, 1250m, rocky limestone area in wood, J. R. Marr 3429.

(c) **Fritillaria tubiformis** Gren. & Godron, syn. *F. delphinensis* Gren. & Godron (*Liliaceae*). Native of SE France, and NW Italy, growing in alpine meadows from 1500 to 2000m, flowering in May and June. Subsp. *moggridgei* Boiss. & Reut. ex Rix has yellow flowers and longer nectaries. Easy to grow in peaty soil in a slightly shaded bulb frame or raised bed. Should not become absolutely dry in summer. Source France, near Gap, Col de Glaize, Rix s.n.

(d) **Fritillaria tuntasia** Heldr. ex Halacsy (*Liliaceae*). Native of Greece, especially the islands of Serifos and Kithnos, growing in rocky places and scrub, flowering in March and April. Cultivation as for (b).

(e) **Fritillaria reuteri** Boiss. (*Liliaceae*). Native of SW Iran, north and west of Esfahan, growing in wet rocky meadows at 2500–3000m, often in huge numbers, flowering in May and June. Flower colour and nectary rather similar to *F. michailovskyi* (p.93 (d)), but taller and more slender, and has two small bracts at the base of each pedicel. Not very robust in cultivation, but will grow in a pot in the alpine house, or in a sunny bulb frame. Source Iran, near Esfahan, F. Baxter.

(f) **Fritillaria bucharica** Regel (*Liliaceae*). Native of NE Afghanistan and Central Asia, especially the Pamir Alai, growing on cliffs and rocky slopes, at 1000–2400m, flowering from March to May. Easy to grow in a bulb frame or

Fritillaria amabilis

pot in the alpine house, kept dry in summer. Source Afghanistan, Faizabad district, 1000m, P. Furse 6240. Photographed in Central Asia, Dushanbe, Varsob gorge, 1400m, 11 April 1979.

(g) **Fritillaria elwesii** Boiss. (*Liliaceae*). Native of southern Turkey, growing in fields, scrub and open pine woods along the coast at 500–1200m, flowering from March to May. Very close to *F. assyriaca* Baker (p.89 (c)), but usually taller, with a lobed style, and increasing well by numerous bulbils. Source Turkey, Içel above Mersin, 1200m, Davis 26500.

Fritillaria walujewii Regel, syn. *F. ferganensis* A. Los. (*Liliaceae*). Native of Central Asia, expecially the Dzungarian Ala Tau, the Tien Shan and the Pamir Alai, growing on cliffs and among Juniper scrub, at c.2000m, flowering in April and May. Nectary lanceolate. Only recently introduced into cultivation. In the wild growing in loose peaty soil, over limestone, often growing up through moss. Source Central Asia, mountains south of Ferghana, Chamsabad, 2000m, Rix 2780.

Fritillaria amabilis Koidzumi (*Liliaceae*). Native of S Japan, on the islands of Kyushu, Shikoku and SW Honshu, growing at

Fritillaria cirrhosa

600–800m, in woods in deep peaty soil, flowering at the end of March. Very difficult to grow, but has flowered grown in a pot in leafy soil, kept rather shaded and not allowed to dry out in summer.

Fritillaria cirrhosa D. Don. (*Liliaceae*). Native of the Himalayas from Nepal eastwards, growing in subalpine and alpine meadows and in scrub from 3000 to 4500m, flowering from May to July. Very variable. In the west this merges into *F. roylei* Hooker. Not easy to grow, but has thrived for many years outside in a sunny stony bed at Keillour Castle in Perthshire. Photographed in Nepal, trail to Annapurna, by Sir Colville Barclay.

Fritillaria thunbergii Miq. (*Liliaceae*). Native of eastern China, in bamboo forest, and naturalised in Japan, where it is used in cough medicine. Often confused with *F. verticillata* Willd., from the Altai mountains in central Asia, which has much larger flowers. Grows best in moist peaty soil in the open garden. Photographed in the Wild Garden at Wisley, Surrey.

Fritillaria persica c.v. 'Adiyaman' 1/3 life size Photographed 14 April

Fritillaria persica L., syn. *F. libanotica* (Boiss.) Baker, *F. eggeri* Bornm. (*Liliaceae*). Native of S Turkey, Syria, Lebanon, Israel, Jordan, Iraq and W Iran, growing on rocky slopes, in scrub and at the edges of cornfields, from 700 to 2800m, flowering from April to May. Shown here is c.v. 'Adiyaman', which probably originated in S Turkey. The distinction between the Mediterranean *F. libanotica* and *F. persica* from the Zagros in W Iran is not clear. *F. arabica* Gandoger, from cliffs near Petra in E Jordan, is more striking in its very broad leaves and obovate petals. All require deep rich soil, either in a bulb frame, or in a very warm sunny place outside, such as a bed under a south wall.

Fritillaria imperialis L. (*Liliaceae*). Crown Imperial. Native of Turkey, especially the south-east, and W Iran, and found also in Afghanistan, Pakistan and Kashmir, growing on cliffs, rocky slopes and among scrub, from 1000 to 3000m, flowering in April and May. Easily grown in good well-drained soil in sun or in the shade of deciduous trees or shrubs. Cultivated in Europe since the sixteenth century, when it was brought from Constantinople to Vienna and thence to Holland and England. It is called in Persian 'Tears of Mary' because of the great drops of nectar at the base of each petal. Christian tradition tells that of all the flowers, only the proud Crown Imperial refused to bow its head at the Crucifixion; it has bowed and wept ever since.

Fritillaria eduardii Regel (*Liliaceae*). Native of Central Asia, especially Tadzikistan where it grows in scrub and rocky places in the mountains, at c.2000m, flowering in April. Intermediate between *F. raddeana* (p.89) and *F. imperialis*. Photographed in Central Asia, E of Dushanbe, 2500m, in April 1979.

Fritillaria eduardii

Fritillaria eduardii

Fritillaria imperialis ½ life size Photographed 14 April

½ life size Photographed 14 April

(a) **Fritillaria messanensis** subsp. **gracilis** (Ebel) Rix, syn. *F. neglecta* Parl. (*Liliaceae*). Native of S Yugoslavia and N Albania, growing in rocky woods and on screes on limestone from 250 to 2000m, flowering from March to June. Distinguished from subsp. *messanensis* by having the flowers usually not tessellated, and the upper leaves not in a whorl of three. Easy to grow in a bulb frame, or in a rather dry place in half-shade under shrubs. Source S Yugoslavia, above Budva, c.900m, Marr 3130 and M.J.C./M. 33.

(b) **Fritillaria messanensis** var. **atlantica** Maire, syn. *F. oranensis* hort. (*Liliaceae*). Native of N Africa, growing in cedar forest and scrub from c.1200 to 3000m, flowering from March to June. The lowland fritillaries in N Africa seem inseparable from *F. messanensis*, but the subalpine and alpine forms have shorter broader leaves and a squat dark flower, and grow especially in the Middle Atlas, the Rif, and the High Atlas. Easy to grow in a dry bulb frame, or pot in the alpine house, but slow to increase. Source Morocco, High Atlas, A. Hamilton.

(c), (f)–(h) **Fritillaria graeca** Boiss. & Spurner, subsp. **thessala** (Boiss.) Rix, syn. *F. ionica* Halacsy (*Liliaceae*). Native of S Albania, S Yugoslavia and NW Greece as far south as Mt Parnassos, where it merges into subsp. *graeca* (see p.93 (e)). Leaves in a whorl of three at the top of the stem, flowers mostly green. Easy to grow in a bulb frame or a dry half-shady place outside. Source (c) Greece, near Meteora, W. K. Aslet; (f) Ziria, H. & M. Crook 3229; (g) origin not known, probably from Katara pass; (h) between Konitsa and Joannina, Marr 3213.

(d), (e) **Fritillaria graeca** Boiss. & Spruner subsp. **graeca** (*Liliaceae*). (See p.93 (e)). The forms shown here are from: (d) Peloponnese, Mt Chelmos, Polunin & Chater 13017; (e) Athens, Hymettos, 700m, Rix 572.

(i) **Fritillaria thunbergii** Miq. (see p.99).

(j) **Fritillaria messanensis** Rafin, syn. *F. oranensis* Pomel (*Liliaceae*). Native of Sicily, Italy, Greece, Crete and N Africa, growing in scrub and in open pine and oak woods, flowering from January to May. The leaves are narrow with a whorl of three below the flower; the nectary is large 6–10cm long, and oval. *F. sphaciotica* Gandoger from Crete is similar, but slightly more delicate than the Greek form shown here. Easy to grow in a bulb frame, and would probably do outside in a dry sunny spot. Source Greece, lower slopes of Mt Olympus, c.800m, Rix 630.

(k) **Fritillaria pyrenaica** L. (*Liliaceae*). Native of the Pyrenees and NW Spain, growing in subalpine meadows, from 450 to 2000m, flowering from April to June. Distinguished by its short alternate leaves, and very dark flowers rather square at the base. There is also a beautiful pale yellow semi-albino form which grows among the normal form in some places (p.105 (i)). Easy to grow in well-drained soil and will do well in thin grass.

Fritillaria pallidiflora Schrenk (*Liliaceae*). Native of Central Asia, especially the mountains on the Sino-Soviet border, the Dzungarian Ala Tau, and the Tien Shan, flowering in May and June on subalpine slopes. The broad glaucous leaves and pale yellowish flowers are characteristic. Easy to grow in rich peaty soil in half-shade, and one of the best species for the open garden.

½ life size Photographed 22 April

⅓ life size Photographed 17 April

(a) **Fritillaria latakiensis** Rix (*Liliaceae*). Native of southern Turkey, Lebanon and Syria, growing in scrub and open pine forest at up to 1000m, flowering in April. Easy to grow in a bulb frame, and possibly also outside. Source S Turkey, V. Horton.

(b) **Fritillaria drenovskii** Degen & Stoyanoff. Native of S Bulgaria and NE Greece, growing in hazel scrub from 300 to 1000m, flowering in May and June. Similar to *F. armena* (p.89 (g)) in flower, but with narrower, glaucous leaves. Cultivation as for (a).

(c) **Fritillaria crassifolia** Boiss. & Huet subsp. **crassifolia** (see p.93 (h)). Source Turkey, Denizli, Honaz Dağ, limestone screes, 1750m, C.M.W. 2556 (the westernmost locality of the species).

(d) **Fritillaria acmopetala** Boiss., syn. *F. lycia* Boiss. Native of SW Turkey along the coast to Lebanon, and Cyprus, growing in open pine woods, scrub, and corn fields, at 20–2000m, flowering from March to May. Easy to grow in any good well-drained soil.

(e) **Fritillaria pontica** Wahl. Native of Bulgaria, Albania, S Yugoslavia, N Greece and NW Turkey, growing in woods and scrub, from 30 to 1000m, flowering in April and May. Capsule with narrow wings. Cultivation as for (d). Source Turkey, Bursa, Ulu Dağ, Rix 1207.

(f) **Fritillaria gussichiae** (Degen & Dörfler) Rix, syn. *F. graeca* var. *gussichiae* Degen & Dörfler. Native of S Bulgaria, S Yugoslavia and N Greece, growing in woods, on shady rocks and alpine pastures from 500 to 1500m, flowering from April to June. There may be up to six flowers in robust specimens; the capsules are narrowly winged. Cultivation as for (d).

(g) **Fritillaria whittallii** Baker. Native of SW Turkey, growing on limestone screes, or in cedar forest, from 1500 to 2000m, flowering from April to June. The leaves are usually narrower than in the specimen shown here. Cultivation as for (a). Source Turkey, Isparta, Dedegöl Da, 1600m, Sorger 66-46-42.

(h) **Fritillaria involucrata** Allioni. Native of S France and NW Italy, in the foothills of the Alpes Maritimes, growing in scrub and woods at c.1000m, flowering in April and May. Cultivation as for (d). Source S France, near Caussols, 1000m, Rix s.n.

(i) **Fritillaria pyrenaica** L. (see p.103 (k)). This pale yellow form of *F. pyrenaica* is easy to grow.

(j) **Fritillaria olivieri** Baker. Native of the northern Zagros mountains in Iran, where it grows in damp meadows by streams, from 1800 to 4000m, flowering in May and June. Up to 40cm in the wild, flowers usually not tessellated. Source Iran, Hamadan, Kuh-i-Alwand, BSBE 1666.

(k) **Fritillaria grayana** Rchb. fil. & Baker, syn. *F. roderickii* Knight, *F. biflora* var. *ineziana* Jepson. Native of California, especially Mendocino and San Mateo counties, growing in clay soil on open grassy slopes, usually near the coast. One of the easier American species in cultivation in Europe, growing well in good soil in a bulb frame. Source California, Mendocino Co., W. Roderick.

(l) **Fritillaria pontica** var. **substipelata** Candargy (see also (e)). This variety of *F. pontica* is from the island of Lesbos, off the west coast of Turkey. Coll. I. B. Barton.

½ life size Photographed 2 May

$^{1}/_{3}$ life size Photographed 17 April

Fritillaria liliacea

Fritillaria purdyi

(a) **Fritillaria affinis** (Schult.) Sealy, syn. *F. lanceolata* Pursch (*Liliaceae*). Native of western N America from British Columbia south to central California and east to Idaho, growing in scrub and among oaks and pines, at up to 1000m, flowering from February to May. Grows best in a half-shaded bulb frame in stony, leafy soil, kept rather dry in summer. Source California, Sonamono Co., R. Macfarlane.

(b) **Fritillaria gentneri** Gilky. Native of Oregon where it grows in Jackson and Josephine counties, flowering in April and May. The style is divided in half, more deeply than *F. recurva*. Cultivation as for (a).

(c) **Fritillaria biflora** Lindl. subsp. **agrestis** (Greene) Macfarlane, syn. *F. agrestis* Greene. Native of California, especially the inner coast ranges, the Sacramento and San Joaquin valleys and the foothills of the Sierra Nevada, growing in grassland, flowering in February and March. The plant shown here is unusually small. Cultivation as for (a).

(d) **Fritillaria liliacea** Lindley. Native of central California, formerly common around San Francisco Bay but now almost extinct, growing in grassy places in heavy adobe soil on serpentine, on hills near the coast, flowering from February to April. The flowers are pale creamy white with green nectaries; the leaves shining green. Height 15–35cm. Grows best in rather heavy rich soil in a pot or bulb frame, not allowed to become very hot in summer. The leaves which emerge very early, are susceptible to damage by frost. Photographed in California by Roger Macfarlane.

Fritillaria pluriflora in Bear Valley, California

Fritillaria recurva

Fritillaria atropurpurea

Fritillaria pluriflora

Fritillaria striata

(e) **Fritillaria pudica** (Pursh) Sprengel. Native of western N America, from British Columbia east to Wyoming and south to New Mexico, growing in sandy or gritty soil between 400 and 2000m, flowering by melting snow patches, from March to June. In flower and leaf remarkably similar to *F. minima* or some of the yellow west asiatic species, but very different in bulb, which is covered with bulbils. Not easy to grow, but has lasted for many years in a bulb frame, kept dry in summer.

Fritillaria purdyi Eastwood. Native of California, especially the inner coast ranges, from Humboldt Co. to Napa Co., growing in heavy stony soil on serpentine, from 600 to 2000m, flowering from February to June. Height 10–40cm. Distinguished by its primarily basal leaves, mottled flowers and divided style. Not easy to grow, but has been cultivated well in a pot in the alpine house, kept dry in summer. Photographed in California by Roger Macfarlane.

Fritillaria striata Eastwood. Native to California, found only in the foothills of the Greenhorn Mts in Kern and Tulane counties, growing in heavy adobe clay at c.600m, flowering in March. Related to *F. pluriflora*, but nectary elliptical to ovate, not linear, and petals recurved at their tips. Height 20–40cm. Probably difficult to grow, requiring a hot dry summer, and not now cultivated in Europe. Photographed in California, 4 March 1967, by Roger Macfarlane.

Fritillaria pluriflora Torrey ex Benth. Native of northern California in the foothills bordering the upper Sacramento valley, growing in adobe clay in open fields, flowering in March. Stem up to 40cm high with one to four, rarely as many as twelve flowers. Nectary linear. Brian Mathew recommends a pot in the alpine house, but very difficult to cultivate successfully; the fields where it grows are very wet in winter and spring, baked hard in summer. Photographed in California, Colusa Co., Bear Valley, on 17 March 1979 by Roger Macfarlane.

Fritillaria recurva Benth. Native of S Oregon and N California, especially in the inner Coast Ranges, and Sierra Nevada foothills, growing on dry hillsides, in scrub and open forest, from 700 to 2000m, flowering from April to July. Can be recognised at once by its whorled leaves and scarlet tubular flowers which are pollinated by humming birds. Not difficult to grow in a bulb frame or in a pot in the alpine house, kept dry in summer. Photographed in California, Mendocino pass, on 4 May 1966 by Roger Macfarlane.

Fritillaria atropurpurea Nuttall. Native of N America from Oregon and California east to the Dakotas and Nebraska, and south to New Mexico, growing in scrub and coniferous forest from 1500 to 3000m, flowering from May to July. Stem up to 50cm, with as many as fifteen flowers. Variable in habit, from the robust form named *F. adamantina* Peck to the delicate *F. gracillima* Smiley. Not easy to grow in spite of its wide distribution, requiring much moisture up to flowering and drought thereafter. Photographed in California by Roger Macfarlane.

Fritillaria falcata

Fritillaria falcata

Fritillaria micrantha

Fritillaria glauca at Black Butte in north California

Fritillaria affinis var. **tristulis**

Fritillaria purdyi at Black Butte, in north California

Fritillaria delavayi on limestone scree in Lijiang, south west China

Fritillaria japonica

Fritillaria cirrhosa

Fritillaria cirrhosa D. Don (*Liliaceae*). A very widespread and variable species from Nepal east to Yunnan and Sichuan. Most plants have curled tips to the upper leaves, but that shown here had the upper leaves without curled tips and is probably var. *ecirrhosa* Franch. Photographed in NW Yunnan, growing on rocky limestone screes in the Lijiang mountains at 3500m, in early June, by Chris Grey-Wilson.

Fritillaria affinis (Schult.) Sealy var. **tristulis** (Grant), syn. *F. lanceolata* Pursh var. *tristulis* Grant. Native of California, this variety is found in grassy places on cliff tops by the sea. It is a triploid and exceptionally large-flowered and robust, as well as being easily cultivated, kept moist in winter and spring, rather dry in summer and autumn. Source: collected by L. Moret in California.

Fritillaria micrantha Heller. Native of California, in the W foothills of the central Sierra Nevada at 300–1800m, in dry open coniferous woods flowering in April to June. Stems 30–90cm. Flowers 3–20, about 2cm across. Leaves in whorls of 3–5. Requires water in late winter and spring, otherwise kept dry. Photographed in California by R. Macfarlane.

Fritillaria japonica Miq. (*Liliaceae*). Native of Japan in S Honshu and Shikoku growing in damp woods, flowering in April. A dwarf species to 15–20cm high, usually less. Flowers 15–18cm long. *F. koidzumiana* is somewhat larger with very fimbriate margin to the petals. All the Japanese species (except *F. camschatcensis*) have proved very difficult to cultivate in Europe. They require warm, wet summers, and cool rather dry winters, in leafy soil. Source: cultivated by K. Dryden.

Fritillaria delavayi Franch. (*Liliaceae*). Native of SE Tibet eastwards to Yunnan and W Sichuan, on screes and moraines at 3900–5500m, flowering in May to July. Stems to 15cm tall. Flowers to 10cm long, the petals remaining attached even when the capsule is ripe. The bulbs of this species are embedded deep in mobile scree or other very rocky soil, moist throughout the summer, frozen in winter. Photographed in the Likiang mountains in NW Yunnan by Chris Grey-Wilson.

Fritillaria purdyi Eastwood (*Liliaceae*). See p.106. Shown here is a semi-albino form, growing on stony schistose slopes at 1800m on Black Butte, Glenn Co., California, in early June.

Fritillaria falcata (Jeps.) Beetle (*Liliaceae*). Native of San Benito Co. and Santa Monica Co. in California, growing on serpentine screes at 300–1400m, flowering in April and May. Similar in general appearance to *F. glauca* but with flowers close to *F. pinetorum*. A rare plant in the wild, and very difficult to grow successfully in cultivation. Photographed in California by R. Macfarlane.

Fritillaria glauca Greene (*Liliaceae*). Native of California and southern Oregon, from Lake Co. north to the Siskyou mountains, growing on rocky hillsides and screes, often on serpentine at 1000–2000m, flowering in April to July. A dwarf species up to 10cm tall, with rather large flowers 1–2cm long, usually yellow but sometimes brownish. Difficult to cultivate, requiring deep stony soil, moist in spring, rather dry in summer and autumn. Photographed in California, Black Butte, Glenn Co.

½ life size Photographed 17 April

Erythronium revolutum near Toledo, Oregon

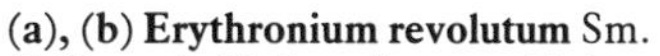

(a), (b) **Erythronium revolutum** Sm. (*Liliaceae*). Native of western N America from Vancouver Island south to N California, where it grows near the coast in redwood forest and in mixed evergreen forest, on the edges of bogs and along wooded streams, up to 1000m, flowering from March till June. Distinguished by its pink flowers, swollen anther filaments and mottled leaves. Two colour forms are shown here. The darkest pink forms have been called var. *johnsonii*. Grows best in sandy peaty soil, damp in spring and in semi-shade. Naturalised in the Wild Garden at Wisley.

(c) **Erythronium 'Pagoda'** (*Liliaceae*). A hybrid between *E. tuolumnense* (p.115 (c)) and one of the white flowered species. Very vigorous and growing easily in rich leafy soil under the shade of deciduous trees.

(d) **Erythronium americanum** Ker-Gawler (*Liliaceae*). Native of eastern N America, from New Brunswick to Ontario and Minnesota, south to Long Island, Tennessee, Arkansas and Oklahoma, growing in rich woods, valley bottoms and meadows, flowering from late March to June. Distinguished by its small size, mottled leaves and yellow flowers which only open in warm sun. The flowers are brownish-orange in the form *castaneum* L. B. Smith. Shy flowering in cultivation, but growing well in moist sandy soil under deciduous trees. Photographed in cultivation by Brinsley Burbidge.

(e) **Erythronium 'White Beauty'** (*Liliaceae*). This may be a hybrid between two of the white-flowered species, or a very vigorous form of *E. oregonum*. It is very strong growing and easy, increasing fast in leafy soil under deciduous trees or in half-shade.

Erythronium revolutum Sm. Photographed in Oregon, on the Pioneer Mountain road, E of Toledo, on 19 April 1980 by Roger Macfarlane.

Erythronium americanum

½ life size Photographed 22 April

Erythronium californicum

Erythronium oregonum

Erythronium montanum

Erythronium hendersonii

(a) **Erythronium californicum** Purdy (*Liliaceae*). Native of northern California, especially the coast ranges, growing in chaparral scrub, pine and evergreen woods, and mixed coniferous forest usually on north-facing slopes at up to 1000m, flowering in March and April. Very similar to *E. oregonum* (below), but has thin not swollen filaments, and usually white anthers. Easy to grow in shade, or semi-shade, in leafy well-drained soil. Photographed in California, between Boonville and Manchester, 14 April 1979 by Roger Macfarlane.

(b), (e), (f) **Erythronium oregonum** Appleg. (*Liliaceae*). Native of Vancouver Island southwards to Oregon and northwest California, growing in open fields, moist woods and in mixed evergreen forest at around 200m. Very similar to *E. californicum* Purdy (above), but has the filaments dilated at their base. Anthers usually yellow, but white in subsp. *leucandrum* Appleg., two forms of which are shown here. See also 'White Beauty' (p.111). Easy to grow in half-shade in well-drained leafy soil. Photographed in Oregon, west of Philomath, on 19 April 1980 by Roger Macfarlane.

(c) **Erythronium helenae** Appleg. (*Liliaceae*). Native of NW California in the area of Mt St Helena, growing in woods and scrub from 500 to 600m, in moist volcanic soil, flowering from March to May. Close to *E. oregonum*, but has narrow or only slightly expanded anther filaments. Grows best in very well drained leafy soil on sand as it resents too much wet in winter.

(d) **Erythronium 'Jeanette Brickell'** (*Liliaceae*). A very beautiful hybrid raised by E. B. Anderson at Porlock, and named after the wife of C. D. Brickell, Director of the RHS Gardens, Wisley, by Mrs K. Dryden. The crimson style and anthers suggest that *E. hendersonii* was one parent, possibly crossed with 'White Beauty' or some other white-flowered species, Hybrids between *hendersonii* and *oregonum* are reported to occur in the wild.

Erythronium hendersonii Watson (*Liliaceae*). Native of SW Oregon and N California, growing in glades in pine forest at 400–1500m, flowering from April to July. Distinct in its dark green leaves, pinkish lilac flowers with a purple centre, and purple anthers. Requires a rather well drained spot in partial shade. B. Mathew records that it grew well among the roots of a beech tree, wet in winter and spring, dry in summer. Photographed in California by Roger Macfarlane.

Erythronium montanum Watson (*Liliaceae*). Avalanche Lily. Native of western N America from Vancouver Island, south to the Olympic mountains and Cascades to N Oregon, growing in subalpine to alpine forest, and in alpine meadows, flowering from late June to September, according to altitude, near melting snow. Very difficult to grow successfully, like so many late-flowering snow patch plants. Photographed in Washington, on Mt Rainier, near Tipsoo Lake, by Roger Macfarlane.

$^{2}/_{3}$ life size Photographed 2 April

Erythronium grandiflorum in Washington

Erythronium grandiflorum

Erythronium dens-canis

(a) **Erythronium albidum** Nutt. var. **mesochorium** (Knerr) Rickett (*Lilaceae*). Native of N America from Iowa and Nebraska to Missouri, Oklahoma and Texas, growing in woods, thickets and meadows, flowering from March to May. In var. *mesochorium* the leaves are narrow and folded, the flowers are pinkish to bluish-white. In var. *albidum*, which grows mostly to the north-east, the flowers are white, the leaves mottled. Rather unsatisfactory in cultivation in Europe because it emerges very early and the flowers probably require more heat to open properly.

(b) **Erythronium dens-canis** L. (*Liliaceae*). Dog's-tooth Violet. Native of Europe from Spain and Portugal to Austria, Romania, Bulgaria and Turkey, growing in scrub, in deciduous woods and rocky places and meadows up to 1700m, on the south side of the Alps, flowering from April to June. The amount of spotting on the leaves is very variable, and some forms from Italy have especially beautiful leaves. Easy to grow in leafy soil or in thin grass in half-shade. Photographed near Serrat, Andorra, by Brinsley Burbidge.

(c) **Erythronium tuolumnense** Appleg. (*Liliaceae*). Native of central California, especially the foothills of the Sierra Nevada in Tuolumne and Stanislaus counties, growing in open pine and evergreen oak woods at 300–600m, flowering from March to May. The plain green leaves and the small deep yellow flowers are characteristic of this species. The stigma is undivided. Grows best in a well-drained peaty soil in partial shade, but does not increase as quickly as some other species or its hybrid 'Pagoda' (p.96 (c)), and can be shy-flowering.

(d) **Erythronium japonicum** Dcne. (*Liliaceae*). Native of Japan, on the islands of Hokkaido, Honshu and Shikoku, growing in woods in the lowlands and on low mountains, flowering in April. Best grown in a shady spot in peaty or leafy soil. Often damaged by slugs.

Erythronium grandiflorum Pursh (*Liliaceae*). Native of western N America from S British Columbia to N California, eastwards to Alberta, Wyoming and Colorado, growing in sagebrush and montane forest up to near the tree line (c.2000m), flowering from March to August. Leaves unmarked. Flowers cream to golden, larger than *E. tuolumnense* (c); anthers white to yellow, red or purple. Stigma lobed. Not easy to grow, and probably best in well-drained soil, wet in spring and rather dry in summer. Photographed in Washington, July 1974, by Brinsley Burbidge.

½ life size Photographed 22 April

(a) **Trillium erectum** L. (*Liliaceae*). Native of eastern N America, from Quebec to Ontario and Michigan, south to Pennsylvania, Georgia and Tennessee, growing in rich woods, often in large numbers, flowering from April to early June. Very variable, and subject to mutation; and green, white and yellow-flowered forms have been described (see (g) and p.121). Easily grown in loose leafy soil in the shade of deciduous trees. Source Ohio, Madison, in woods, T. Brotzman.

(b) **Trillium grandiflorum** (Michx.) Salisb. (*Liliaceae*). Native of eastern N America, from Maine and S Quebec, east to Ontario and Minnesota, south to Georgia and Arkansas, growing in woods and thickets, often in huge numbers, usually on limestone, flowering from April to June. Very variable, and particularly subject to mutation. The double forms in cultivation are much sought after. Petals obovate to oblanceolate or suborbicular, rarely pinkish. Easily grown in leafy soil in shade or half-shade. Source Ohio, Madison, in woods, T. Brotzman.

(c) **Trillium ovatum** Pursh (*Liliaceae*). Native of western N America from central California, north to British Columbia and Montana, growing in redwood forest and mixed evergreen forest, flowering from February to April. Close to *T. grandiflorum* from the eastern States, but the flowers are usually smaller, with petals 2.5–5.5cm long, ovate, tapering from a broad base. Grows best in well-drained leafy soil in the shade of deciduous trees.

(d) **Trillium rivale** Wats. (*Liliaceae*). Native of western N America from Del Norte and Siskiyou counties in N California to SW Oregon, growing in rocky places by streams, in the yellow pine forest from 400–1200m, flowering in March and April. Easily recognised by its long-stalked leaves and flowers, which become pendulous as they mature. Flowers white to pink. Grows best in well-drained leafy soil in half-shade or in a pot kept plunged in a shady frame.

(e) **Trillium undulatum** Willd. (*Liliaceae*). Painted Trillium. Native of eastern N America, from Nova Scotia and Quebec to Manitoba, south to the hills of Georgia and Tennessee, growing in acid woods and bogs, flowering from April to June, after *T. erectum*. Distinguished by the shortly stalked leaves and white petals marked with red. The specimen shown here is unusually small; stem usually c.30cm high. Grows best in a moist peaty soil in shade. Rarely seen in cultivation, so probably not easy.

(f) **Trillium sessile** L. (*Liliaceae*). Native of eastern N America from Virginia and New York to Ohio and Missouri and south to Georgia and Arkansas, growing in rich woods, flowering from April to early June. Easily grown in rich leafy soil in shade or half shade.

(g) **Trillium erectum** L. forma **albiflorum** R. Hoffm. A particularly beautiful form of *T. erectum*. The plant shown here is unusually small.

(h) **Trillium luteum** (Muhl.) Harbison. Very similar to *T. sessile*, but with yellowish or greenish flowers. The plant shown here is unusually small. Grows in woods from Kentucky and Missouri south to Alabama and Arkansas.

½ life size Photographed 2 May

Trillium chloropetalum in north west California

Trillium cernuum at Kew

Paris incompleta

Trillium 'Olive Shore'

Trillium chloropetalum (Torr.) Howell (*Liliaceae*). Native of California from San Mateo and Placer Cos, northwards in the Coast ranges and the Sierras to Washington west of the Cascades, growing in woods and scrub at up to 1500m, flowering in April to June. A very variable and complex species with much variation in size and flower colour. To the north of San Francisco the flowers are usually white or green, and yellowish forms are found, especially in Marin Co. In the south part of the range and in the San Francisco Bay area the flowers are usually pink, deep red or purple. See p.121. Photographed in N California in Glenn Co.

Trillium cernuum L. Native of SE Canada and Illinois, south to Maryland and in the mountains to Georgia, growing in woodlands, usually on calcareous soil, flowering in May and June. Stem c.20cm. Leaves very short-stalked; flower stalk bent down below the leaves; flowers with white or pale pink petals, and purple anthers and ovary. Easily grown in woodland soil. *T. flexipes* Raf. is similar, but has yellow or cream anthers, a whitish ovary with recurved stigmas and stalkless leaves.

Trillium 'Olive Shore'. A hybrid between *T. cernuum* and *T. erectum* which arose in the woodland garden at Kew in c.1980, and was named by Tony Hall. Similar hybrids have been reported in the wild, but not substantiated. Although they often grow together, the species are usually separated by flowering at different times, *T. cernuum* several weeks later than *T. erectum*.

Paris incompleta M. Bieb. (*Liliaceae*). Native of NE Turkey from Ordu eastwards, and of the Caucasus, growing in beech, spruce and birch woods and *Rhododendron* scrub, at 460–2000m, flowering in May and June. Leaves 6–9, 6–9.5cm long. Easily grown in woodland soil in part shade.

Zantedeschia aethiopica 'Crowborough' at the Savill Garden, Windsor

Arum conophalloides var. **syriacum**

Arum korolkovii

Eminium rauwolffii

Arum conophalloides Kotschy ex Schott var. **caudatum** Engler (*Araceae*). Native of C and E Turkey, as far east as Trabzon and Mardin, in oak and conifer woods and among rocks and old walls at 1300–2060m, flowering in May and June. Var. *caudatum* has a purplish spathe, 34–38mm long, and the end of the spadix purple or brownish. Var. *virescens* (Stapf) Engler, from N Iran, the C Tauros and near Lake Van, has a greenish or white spathe and yellowish spadix; it is illustrated on p.193.

Arum dioscoridis Sibth. & Sm. var. **syriacum** (Blume) Engler. Native of W Syria and S Turkey, among rocks and under old walls, flowering in March to May. In this variety the spathe is green, with few blotches only on the lower third. Collected in the Amanus mountains and photographed in cultivation by Norman Stevens. Var. *spectabile* (Schott) Engler differs in having a purple spathe with large blotches coalescing in the lower part. This variety is endemic to S. Turkey.

Arum korolkovii Regel. Native of C Asia, in the Tien Shan, Pamir Alai and Kopet Dağ, on rocky hills among scrub and in shady rock crevices, flowering in April to June. Stem to 30cm; leaves produced in spring. A very hardy species. Source: Tashkent, Chimgan Valley.

Eminium rauwolffii (Blume) Schott (*Araceae*). Native of E and S Turkey and the Syrian desert, on rocky limestone hills and in cornfields, at 350–1750m, flowering in March to May. Stem 5–20cm; spathe 8–16cm long. The white-spotted leaves are sporadic, but most common in N E Turkey. Close to *E. intortum* (p.179), but differing in its thickened scape below the spadix and in the leaf veins which run parallel in the lower part of the leaf before entering the petiole, not diverging at the base of the lamina. Collected near Sivas and photographed by Norman Stevens.

Zantedeschia aethiopica (L.) Sprengel **'Crowborough'**. This clone was found in a garden in Crowborough, Sussex by Graham Thomas, and chosen for its hardiness. It is a fine plant, shown here growing in shallow water at the Savill Garden, Windsor, where it is completely hardy. It will flower in cultivation from July until November, and will also thrive in a reasonably moist border. It is best in full sun. Mr Thomas advises covering it in winter with bracken or dry peat as an insurance against exceptional frosts. In the cold parts of E North America and N Europe it would be wise to bring it indoors for the winter, kept cold, but away from frost. 'Green Goddess', a large variety with a green spathe, is said to be equally hardy.

Arum discoridis var. **spectabile**

½ life size Photographed 17 April

(a) **Narcissus pseudonarcissus 'Princeps'**, syn. *N. gayi* Jord. (*Amaryllidaceae*). An old garden variety.
(b) **Narcissus 'Carlton'** (2Y-Y). Raised by P. D. Williams at Lanarth, Cornwall, in 1927. Much grown for cutting and forcing.
(c) **Narcissus 'King Alfred'** (1Y-Y). Raised by J. Kendall from *N. pseudonarcissus* subsp. *major* (Curtis) Baker (syn. *N. hispanicus* Gouan), in about 1890.
(d) **Narcissus 'Telemoneus Plenus'**, syn. 'Van Sion', 'Vincent Sion'. A double *Narcissus pseudonarcissus*, introduced into England from Florence c.1620.
(e) **Narcissus 'Beersheba'**. Raised by the Rev. G. H. Engleheart of Andover and Salisbury, England, in 1923. One of the earliest Large White Trumpets, derived from selfing of pale forms of *N. pseudonarcissus*.
(f) **Narcissus 'Emperor'**. Raised by William Backhouse of Wolsingham, Co. Durham, c.1865. A hybrid of *N. pseudonarcissus* subsp. *pseudonarcissus* and *N. bicolor* L., a native of the Pyrenees in France and Spain.
(g) **Narcissus × medioluteus** Miller (*N. poeticus × N. tazetta*). The form shown here is close to 'Cragford', raised by P. D. Williams in 1930.
(h) **Narcissus poeticus 'Actaea'**. Raised by G. Lubbe & Son, Oegstgeest, Holland, in 1927.
(i) **Narcissus 'Butter and Eggs'**, syn. *N. × incomparabilis* var. *plenus*, 'Golden Phoenix', 'Yellow Phoenix', 'Incomparable' and '*aurantius* var. *plenus*'. An old double form of *N. × incomparabilis*, grown in gardens since the seventeenth century.
(j) **Narcissus 'Sweetness'**. Raised by R. V. Favell in 1939. A hybrid of *N. jonquilla* L., other parent not known.
(k) **Narcissus tazetta** subsp. **italicus** (Ker-Gawler) Baker, syn. *N. canaliculatus* hort; *N. tazetta* subsp. *lacticolor* (Haw.) Baker. Native of the N and E Mediterranean.
(l) **Narcissus** cf. 'Dick Wellband' raised by Mrs Backhouse A.M. 1937
(m) **Narcissus × incomparabilis** Miller. A hybrid between *N. pseudonarcissus* and *N. poeticus*, and found wild where the parents grow together, especially in the Pyrenees. Also common in old gardens.
(n) **Narcissus 'Cheerfulness'**. A sport from *N. 'Elvira'* which appeared in 1923. The doubling is caused by the stamens becoming petaloid, the perianth and corona are unaffected.
(o) **Narcissus poeticus** L. Native of the mountains of central and southern Europe, growing in damp meadows, often in huge numbers, flowering from April to June. Easy to grow in moist soil, doing well in grass, but sometimes shy-flowering.

Trillium tschonoskii Maxim. (*Liliaceae*). Native of Japan especially Honshu and Shikoku, and Korea, growing in mountain woods, flowering from April to June. The petals are usually white, but may be purplish or pinkish in forma *violaceum* Makino. Photographed in Japan, Honshu, Oze-numa reserve, 1500m, in June 1978 by Peter Barnes.

Trillium chloropetalum (*Liliaceae*). (p.118) Photographed in the RHS Gardens, Wisley.

Paris polyphylla Smith (*Liliaceae*). Native of Afghanistan and the Himalayas, from Kashmir to central China and Formosa, and from Manipur to N Thailand, growing in forests from 1700 to 3500m, flowering from March to June. Very variable; leaves stalked, fruits splitting open to reveal a spectacular mass of fleshy red seeds. Easily grown in moist peaty soil in half-shade. Photographed in N India, Tunglu above Darjeeling, by Oleg Polunin.

Trillium chloropetalum var. **giganteum** at Wisley

Paris polyphylla

Trillium tschonoskii

¾ life size Photographed 25 February

(a) **Narcissus hedraeanthus** (Webb & Held.) Colmeiro (*Amaryllidaceae*). Native of south-east Spain, especially the Sierra de Cazorla, growing in stony places above 1500m, flowering in May as the snow melts. Distinguished by its very small size, long exserted stamens, and curving flower stalk. This is the most distinct of the 'hoop petticoat' daffodils. Easily grown in a bulb frame or pot in the alpine house, and would require a sunny place outside. Source Spain, Sierra de Cazorla, Tucker.

(b), (f) Narcissus romieuxii Br. Bl. & Maire (*Amaryllidaceae*). Native of Morocco, where it grows in cedar and oak forest, at 1700–2000m, usually on limestone or basalt, flowering in winter and early spring. Distinguished from *N. bulbocodium*, of which it is often considered to be only a subspecies, by its creamy sulphur-yellow flowers, and exserted stamens. The corona also appears to be wider at the mouth. Best cultivated in a bulb frame because it flowers so early, but will grow in a sunny well-drained place outside.

(c) **Narcissus asturiensis** (Jordan) Pugsley, syn. *N. minimus* hort. (*Amaryllidaceae*). Native of N Portugal, NW and NC Spain, growing at up to 2000m, in rocky meadows, flowering from March to May. Distinguished by its very small flowers 14–25mm long, and greenish spathe. Stem 7–10cm. Very early flowering in cultivation, often appearing in January, and should be protected from slugs. Grows best in sandy peaty soil, not drying out in summer.

(d) **Narcissus minor** L., syn. *N. pumilus* Pugsley (*Amaryllidaceae*). Native of the Pyrenees and N Spain, growing in mountain meadows and scrub, very close to *N. asturiensis*, but larger with stem 8–25cm, and flowers 25–40mm long. The form shown here flowers in midwinter, often starting in November and continuing until February. It has been named *N. minor* 'Cedric Morris', from whose garden it was distributed.

(e) **Narcissus cantabricus** DC. subsp. **monophyllus** (Dur.) A. Fernandes (*Amaryllidaceae*). Native of N Morocco and Algeria, growing in similar places to subsp. *cantabricus* (h). Distinguished by its white flowers with included stamens, and the single narrow leaf per bulb. Best grown in a pot or in a bulb frame, kept dry in summer.

(g) **Narcissus bulbocodium** L. (*Amaryllidaceae*). Native of Algeria, Morocco, Spain, Portugal and SW France, growing in scrub, rocky ground and peaty moorland, flowering from January to July. Very variable in size and in flower colour, from pale lemon yellow to golden; anthers not exserted. This species is particularly good for naturalising in grass on sandy soils; the lemon-yellow form is beautiful in Windsor Great Park, the darker yellow at Wisley. The early-flowering form shown here probably originated in Morocco.

(h) **Narcissus cantabricus** DC. (*Amaryllidaceae*). Native of S Spain, and Morocco, growing in oak and pine woods on limestone, flowering in early spring. Distinguished from *N. bulbocodium* by its white flowers. Stamens always included in the corona, not projecting. Grows best in a pot or bulb frame or in a very sunny place outside where it is dry in summer.

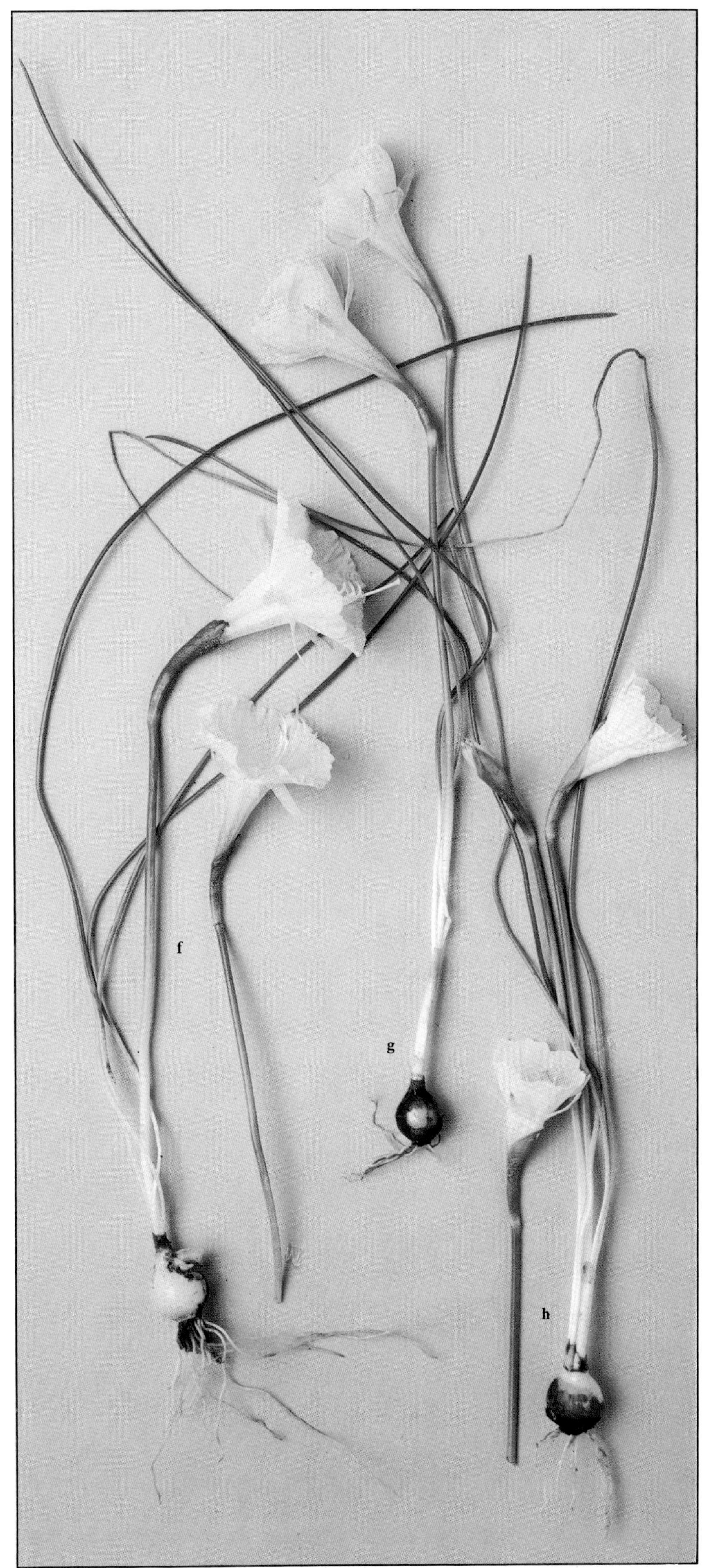

¾ life size Photographed 13 February

²/₃ life size Photographed 14 April

(a) **Narcissus rupicola** Dufour (*Amaryllidaceae*). Native of central Spain and N Portugal, growing in rocky places and in stony mountain pastures at c.2000m, usually on acid rock, flowering from March to May. Height here 10cm. Easy to grow in a bulb frame, a pot in the alpine house, or a dry sunny place outside; does not require acid soil. Source C Spain, Rascafria, Sierra de Guaderrama, c.200m, Rix. s.n.

(b) **Narcissus cuatrecasasii** Casas, Lainz & Ruiz Rejón, syn. *N. rupicola* subsp. *pedunculatus* (Cuatrec.) Lainz ex Meikle (*Amaryllidaceae*). Native of central Spain, growing in rocky and stony places in the mountains, usually on limestone. Like a slightly larger darker flowered *N. rupicola* with a long (9–12mm) stalk to the ovary. Cultivation as for (a). Source SC Spain, Sierra de Cazorla, Rix. s.n.

(c) **Narcissus watieri** Maine (*Amaryllidaceae*). Native of Morocco, growing in the Atlas Mountains from 1800 to 2600m, in forest and grassy places flowering in May and June. Not difficult in a pot in the alpine house, but slow to increase. The other North African species in this group, *N. marvieri* Johand. & Maire, is closer to *N. rupicola* with a paler yellow flower.

(d) **Narcissus requienii** M. J. Roemer, syn. *N. juncifolius* auct. (*Amaryllidaceae*). Native of S France, E and S Spain, growing on rocky hillsides, often on limestone, flowering in April. The plant shown here is rather larger than usual. Flowers normally one or two per stem. Leaves 1–2mm wide. *N. jonquilla* L. is similar, but larger in all its parts, with leaves 2–4mm wide. Both are very sweet-smelling. Easily grown in a dry sunny place. Source S Spain, Sierra Morena, c.500m, C. Quest-Ritson, s.n.

(e) **Narcissus 'Hawera'** (*Amaryllidaceae*). This beautiful plant is a hybrid between *N. triandrus* (g) and *Narcissus jonquilla* L. Raised in New Zealand by Dr W. M. Thompson in the 1930s.

(f), (g) **Narcissus triandrus** L. (*Amaryllidaceae*). Native of Brittany, Spain and Portugal, growing in scrub, woods and rocky hillsides, flowering from February to April. (f) subsp. *pallidulus* (Graells) D. A. Webb, syn. *N. concolor* (Haw.) Link, has flowers yellow to cream, a shorter corona and tube, with petals 10–18mm about equalling the tube. Found in Portugal, central, S and E Spain. (g) subsp. *triandrus*, syn. *N. cernuus* Salisb., has flowers white to cream, larger, with petals 15–30mm, and a longer corona. Found in N Portugal and N Spain. *N. triandrus* will grow well on a peat bank or in thin grass on sandy soil in a sunny place. Good drainage is important. Photographed in the RHS Gardens, Wisley.

(h) **Narcissus gaditanus** Boiss. & Reut. Native of S Spain and S Portugal, growing in rocky places, flowering in March. *N. scaberulus* Henriq. is very similar, but has leaves with two keels and rough edges. Cultivation as (a). Source S Spain, Granada near Almunecar, 1000m, C. Quest-Ritson, s.n.

Narcissus cyclamineus DC. (*Amaryllidaceae*). Native of NW Portugal and NW Spain, where it grows on river banks and damp mountain pastures, flowering in March. Grows best in damp sandy peaty soil at the edge of water: some very fine clumps grow in the roots of *Osmunda* by the waterside at Wisley. Photographed in the RHS Gardens, Wisley, by Roger Phillips.

Narcissus bulbocodium L. (*Amaryllidaceae*) (see p.107 (g)). Photographed in C Spain, Sierra de Urbion, c.2000m, 4 June 1967.

Narcissus cyclamineus in the wild garden at Wisley

Narcissus triandrus

Narcissus bulbocodium

¾ life size Photographed 21 March

(a) Narcissus 'February Silver' (*Amaryllidaceae*). A hybrid between *N. cyclamineus* and probably a pale form of *N. pseudonarcissus* raised by de Graaf in 1949 in Holland. Outside it does not usually flower until late March, even in S England.

(b) Narcissus pseudonarcissus L. Daffodil. Native of Western Europe from England and Holland to France, Switzerland, Spain and Portugal, growing in woods, meadows and rocky hillsides, flowering from March to May. Very variable in flower colour, from white to deep yellow, and in the shape and posture of the flower, and in *Flora Europaea* divided into seven subspecies. For cultivation see p.131. Shown here is a pale form of subsp. *pseudonarcissus*.

(c) Narcissus 'Tosca'. Raised by Alec Gray and introduced by Broadleigh Gardens in 1969.

(d) Narcissus cyclamineus DC. (see p.125). *N. cyclamineus* crosses easily with forms of *pseudonarcissus*, and various combinations are common in gardens where the parents are allowed to seed. They show the influence of *cyclamineus* in their early flowering, narrow trumpets and recurved petals.

(e) Narcissus 'March Sunshine'. A hybrid between *N. cyclamineus* and *N. pseudonarcissus* raised by de Graaf in Holland in 1923.

(f) Narcissus 'February Gold'. A hybrid between *N. cyclamineus* and *N. pseudonarcissus* raised by de Graaf in Holland in 1923. Good for forcing, but usually March flowering outside in England.

(g) Narcissus 'Tête à Tête'. Raised by Mr Alec Gray of Camborne, Cornwall, in 1949. The result of crossing *N. cyclamineus* with *N. tazetta* 'Soleil d'Or' was the doubtfully hardy *N. 'Cyclataz'*, and 'Tête à Tête' is an improved and hardy form.

(h), (i), (j) Ipheion uniflorum (R. C. Graham) Rafin., syn. *Triteleia uniflora* (*Liliaceae*). Native of Argentina and Uruguay, where it is widespread. Three colour forms are shown here: **(h) 'Froyle Mill'** a dark-flowered form which appeared in a garden of that name in Hampshire. It is not as strong growing as the other forms; **(i) 'Wisley Blue'**, named after the RHS Gardens at Wisley, Surrey; **(j)**, a strong-growing pure white form. The commonest form in cultivation is smaller than 'Wisley Blue', and is a pale silvery lilac colour. Easy to grow in a sunny place, kept dry in summer. The crushed leaves smell faintly of onion, the flowers of soap.

(k) Bulbocodium vernum L. (*Liliaceae*). Native of the Pyrenees, the western and central Alps, and one locality in Austria, growing in alpine meadows, and flowering from April to June. *Bulbocodium* is superficially similar to *Colchicum* and *Merendera*, but the styles are trifid only at the apex (in *Colchicum* and *Merendera* they are divided to the base), and the petals fall apart as the flower ages. *Bulbocodium versicolor* (Ker-Gawler) Sprengel, from eastern Europe and Western Asia, has smaller flowers and narrower leaves, and is found in dry grassland. Should be grown in good well-drained soil, and replanted frequently, if it is to increase.

¾ life size Photographed 13 March

The text is on page 131 ⅔ life size Photographed 22 April

The text is on page 131 ⅔ life size Photographed 22 April

½ life size Photographed 17 April

Modern Daffodil Hybrids

The name is the name of the raiser; the date that of registration. All daffodils are easily grown in good soil in full sun or half-shade. It is important not to cut off the leaves until they begin to turn yellow (about six weeks after flowering), and better not to tie them in a bunch. On poor soil a tomato fertiliser applied in early spring will help growth and flowers for the following year.

Illustrated on the previous spread (pp. 112-113):

(a)	'Arctic Gold'	J. L. Richardson 1951
(b)	'Golden Aura'	J. L. Richardson 1964
(c)	'Ormeau'	W. J. Dunlop 1949
(d)	'Langwith'	Mrs J. Abel Smith 1969
(e)	'Dunmurry'	W. J. Dunlop 1958
(f)	'Grand Prospect'	Mrs J. Abel Smith 1974
(g)	'Irish Minstrel'	J. L. Richardson 1958
(h)	'Pipe Major'	F. E. Board, 1965
(i)	'Toreador'	J. L. Richardson 1961
(j)	'Rockall'	J. L. Richardson 1955
(k)	'Emily'	Mrs J. Abel Smith 1974
(l)	'Leonaine'	G. E. Mitsch 1959
(m)	'Knightwick'	J. L. Richardson 1963
(n)	'Farnsfield'	Mrs J. Abel Smith 1979
(o)	'Rufford'	Mrs J. Abel Smith 1975
(p)	'Langford Grove'	Mrs J. Abel Smith 1979
(q)	'Jewel Song'	Mrs Richardson 1967
(r)	'Aircastle'	G. E. Mitsch 1958
(s)	'Birchill'	Mrs J. Abel Smith 1974
(t)	'Suilven'	J. S. B. Lea 1956
(u)	'Tutankhamun'	Mrs J. Abel Smith 1972
(v)	'Vigil'	G. L. Williams 1947

Illustrated on this spread (pp. 114-115):

(aa)	'Devon Loch'	J. L. Richardson 1956
(bb)	'Patagonia'	J. L. Richardson 1956
(cc)	'Crocus'	P. D. Williams 1927
(dd)	'Chester'	Barr & Sons 1945
(ee)	'Binkie'	W. Wolfhagen 1938
(ff)	'Golden Ducat'	sport from 'King Alfred'
(gg)	'Polindra'	P. D. Williams 1927
(hh)	'Salome'	J. L. Richardson 1958
(ii)	'Spellbinder'	G. L. Wilson 1944
(jj)	'Brunswick'	P. D. Williams 1931
(kk)	'Dunlewey'	G. L. Wilson 1934
(ll)	'Blaris'	G. L. Wilson 1960
(mm)	'Knowehead'	G. L. Wilson 1954
(nn)	'Passionale'	G. L. Wilson 1956
(oo)	'Penvose'	P. D. Williams 1937
(pp)	'White Lion'	Le Graef-Gerharda 1949

(qq), (rr) Narcissus minor L. (see p.123 (d)).

(ss) Narcissus pseudonarcissus subsp. **moschatus** (L.) Baker. Native of the Pyrenees and Cantabrian mountains of N Spain, in mountain meadows and open pine woods at c.1800m.

(tt) Narcissus pseudonarcissus subsp. **pallidiflorus** (Pugsley) A. Fernandes. Distribution as (ss).

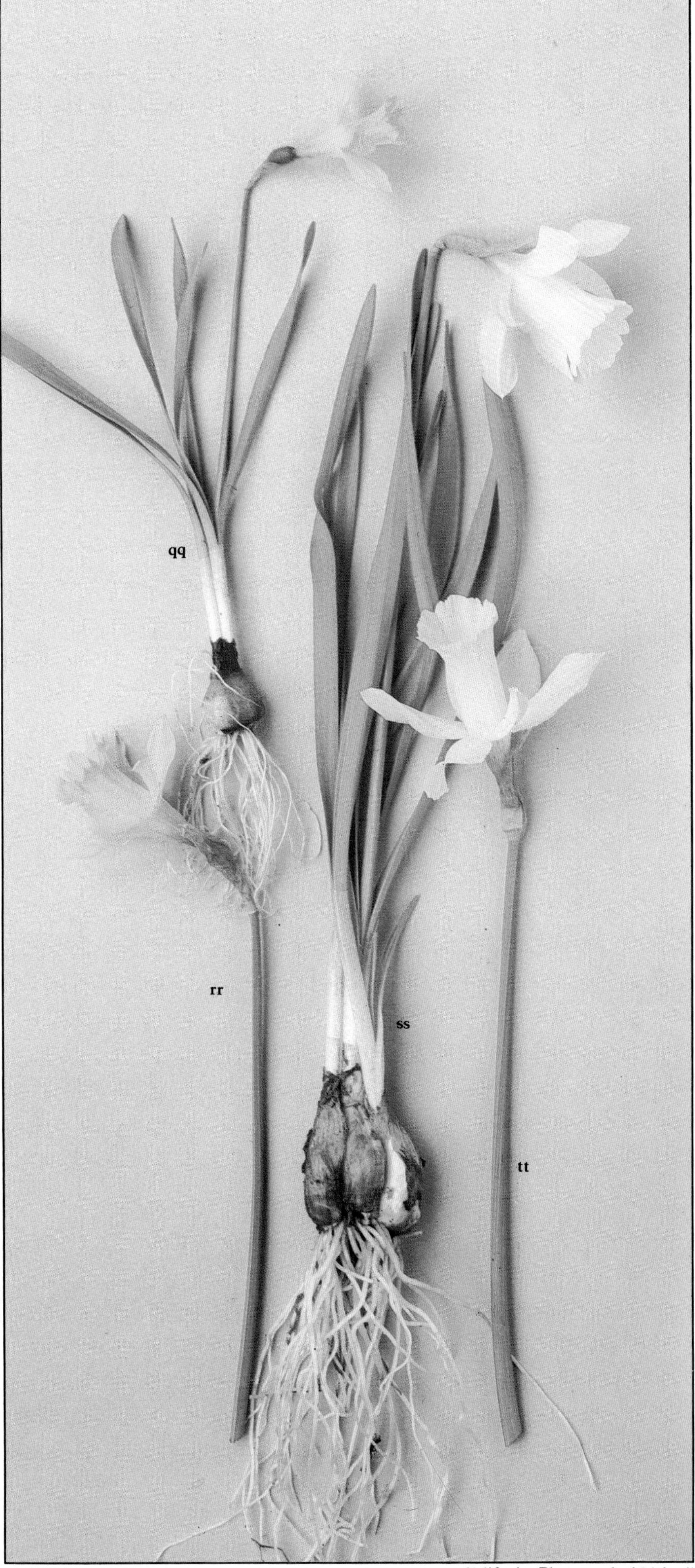

⅔ life size Photographed 14 April

½ life size photographed 10 April

Narcissus 'Eystettensis'

Small Narcissus cultivars. These are mainly only 15–20cm high, and have originated from *N. pseudonarcissus* or *N. poeticus* crossed with one of the dwarf species. The dates given are those on which the cultivar was registered.

(a) Narcissus 'Segovia'. Raised by Mrs F. M. Gray in 1962. A *poeticus* hybrid.

(b) Narcissus 'Dove Wings'. Raised by C. F. Coleman and introduced by Mrs C. R. Wotton in 1949. A *cyclamineus* hybrid.

(c) Narcissus 'Jack Snipe'. Raised by M. P. Will in 1951. A *cyclamineus* hybrid.

(d) Narcissus 'Sundial'. Raised by A. Gray in 1955. A *jonquilla* group hybrid.

(e) Narcissus 'Cobweb'. Raised by A. Gray in 1938. A *triandrus* hybrid.

(f) Narcissus 'Sugar Bush'. Raised by A. Gray in 1954. A *jonquilla* group hybrid.

(g) Narcissus 'Rikki'. Raised by A. Gray in 1962. A *jonquilla* group hybrid.

(h) Narcissus 'Thoughtful'. Raised by A. Gray in 1951. A *triandrus* hybrid.

(i) Narcissus 'Rippling Waters'. Raised by Barr & Sons in 1932. A *triandrus* hybrid.

(j) Narcissus 'Beryl'. Raised by P. D. Williams in 1907. A hybrid between *N. cyclamineus* and *N. poeticus*.

(k) Narcissus 'Clare'. Raised by A. Gray and introduced by Broadleigh Gardens in 1968. A *jonquilla* group hybrid.

(l) Narcissus minor L. var. **pumilus** (Salisb.) Fernandes **'Plenus'** syn. 'Rip van Winkle'. An old double form of *N. minor*, see pp.122, 131.

(m) Narcissus × odorus L. **'Plenus'** syn. *N.* 'Campernellii Plenus'. A double form of the hybrid between *N. pseudonarcissus* and *N. jonquilla*. Scented.

Narcissus 'Eystettensis' synonym 'Queen Anne's Double Daffodil', 'Capax Plenus'. An ancient variety of unknown origin grown widely since 1601, and said to be a hybrid of *N. triandrus*. A dwarf elegant plant with regular overlapping rows of petals.

Narcissus 'Jenny'. A hybrid of *N. cyclamineus*, raised by C. F. Coleman in 1943. A beautiful variety like a white version of the better-known 'February Gold'.

Narcissus 'W. P. Milner'. A dwarf pale trumpet daffodil raised by William Backhouse in 1884. A good grower, close to stronger forms of subsp. *moschatus* (c.f. 131 ss).

Narcissus 'Thalia'. A hybrid of *N. triandrus* raised in Holland by M. van Waveren & Sons at Hillegom in 1916. An excellent plant for drier or hotter climates than England, but doing well on warm soils there. Flowers scented; stems to 40cm.

Narcissus pseudonarcissus L. subsp. **moschatus** (L.) Baker. This is the smallest palest form of this subspecies, formerly known as *N. alpestris* Pugsley. It is native of the C Pyrennees, growing in alpine meadows and is now very rare in the wild due to over collecting. It is slow to increase and worth protecting in a moist peaty soil in partial shade.

Narcissus 'Jenny'

Narcissus pseudonarcissus subsp. **moschatus**

The spring garden at Sissinghurst, Kent, April

Narcissus 'W. P. Milner'

Narcissus 'Thalia'

The Tien Shan mountains above Frunze in Kirghizia, Central Asia. In the foreground *Tulipa dasystemon* Regel and *Gagea* spp.

Tulipa dasystemon Regel (*Liliaceae*). Native of Central Asia, especially the Tien Shan and the Pamir Alai, growing in stony places and subalpine meadows at above 2000m, flowering in May and June. *T. dasystemonoides* is similar, but was described as having tunics with wool all over the inside, not only at the top of the bulb. *T. tarda* Stapf has a hairless tunic and three to seven leaves. Would probably grow best in a peaty sandy soil, kept dry but not baked in summer. Photographed in Central Asia, above Frunze, in May 1980.

Amana edulis (Miq.) Honda, syn. *Tulipa edulis* (Miq.) Baker (*Liliaceae*). Native of Japan and China, growing in meadows along rivers at low altitudes, flowering in March and April. *Amana* is close to *Tulipa*, but has an elongated style, and a pair of small leaves below the flower. Var. *latifolia* Makino, with broader and shorter leaves is found on wooded hills on Honshu. Easy to grow in a well-drained sunny position. Dormant in summer, but should not need protection from rain.

Tulipa heterophylla (Regel) Baker, syn. *Eduardoregelia heterophylla* (Rgl.) M. Popov (*Liliaceae*). Native of Central Asia, especially the Tien Shan, growing on stony slopes and in alpine meadows above 2500m, flowering in June and July. Between *Amana* and *Tulipa* with an elongated style, and two small leaves. The inner petals are much broader than the outer. Probably requires a light peaty soil, dry but not baked in summer. Photographed in C Asia, above Alma Ata, in June 1980.

Tulipa turkestanica Regel (*Liliaceae*). Native of Central Asia, especially the Tien Shan and the Pamir Alai, and NW China, growing in stony slopes, by streams and on rock ledges from 1800 to 2500m, flowering from March to May. *T. bifloriformis* Vved. is said to differ in its bulb tunics which are woolly all over the inside. *T. biflora* L. is smaller with glabrous stems. Easily grown in well-drained soil in full sun, kept dry in summer. Photographed in C Asia near Samarkand.

Tulipa turkestanica

Amana edulis ⅔ life size Photographed 23 February

Tulipa heterophylla in the Tien Shan mountains above Alma Ata

Tulipa dasystemon

½ life size Photographed 2 April

(a) **Tulipa praestans** Hoog (*Liliaceae*). Native of Central Asia, especially Tadzikistan in the southern Pamir Alai, growing on steep earthy slopes and in light woodland, flowering from April and May. Distinguished by its plain orange-red petals without a basal blotch and hairy stems which may have up to four flowers in cultivation. Shown here is 'Van Tubergen's Variety' with large orange-scarlet flowers (see also pp.141 and 143). Easily grown in well-drained good soil in a sunny place. A good species for the rock garden.

(b) **Tulipa kolpakowskiana** Regel (*Liliaceae*). Native of Central Asia, especially the northern Tien Shan and the southern Ala Tau, growing on rocky slopes and in scrub at up to 2000m, flowering in May. Flower stem curved, with orange-yellow petals shaded reddish and greyish-violet on the back. Easily grown in well-drained soil in a sunny position.

(c) **Tulipa turkestanica** Regel (*Liliaceae*) (see p.135). This plant, from commercial stock, shows the dark anthers supposed to be a character of *T. bifloriformis* Vved.

(d), (e) **Tulipa humilis** Herbert, syn. *T. pulchella* Fenzl, *T. violacea* Boiss. & Buhse (*Liliaceae*). Native of E Turkey, N Iraq and NW Iran, growing on stony hillsides, flowering from April to June. The flowers vary in colour from palest pink to crimson and almost purple, the central blotch may be yellow or black, as may the anthers (see pp.143 and 145). Easily grown in good well-drained soil. The flowers may abort if it is kept too dry in spring while the bud is developing. Source (d) commercial stock; (e) Iran, Mianeh, Tabriz–Tehran road, 1500m, BSBE 1310.

(f) **Tulipa kurdica** Wendelbo (*Liliaceae*). Native of NE Iraq, growing on stony slopes by melting snow from 2400 to 3000m, flowering in May and June. Very similar to *T. humilis*, but has bright brick-red to orange-red flowers, a colour not seen elsewhere in *T. humilis*. The small black basal blotch is also characteristic. The bulb here shows a 'dropper' forming, behaviour typical of Tulips if planted too shallow. A shoot descends several inches downwards and a new bulb is formed at its end. Cultivation as for *T. humilis*.

(g) **Tulipa kaufmanniana** Regel (*Liliaceae*). Native of Central Asia, especially the western Tien Shan, E of Tashkent, growing on stony slopes in the mountains, flowering in April and May (see p.139).

(h) **Tulipa biflora** Pallas, syn. *T. polychroma* Stapf (*Liliaceae*). Native of SE Russia, the Crimea, S Yugoslavia, the Caucasus, E Turkey and N Iran to Afghanistan and extending into Siberia, growing on steppes and stony and rocky hillsides, flowering in April and May. Very similar to *T. turkestanica* but usually smaller, and supposed to have a glabrous rather than pubescent stem; *T. biflora* is supposed to be diploid, *T. turkestanica* tetraploid. Easy to grow in well-drained stony soil, kept dry in summer.

½ life size Photographed 28 March

Tulips in the Chimgan valley, near Tashkent, Uzbekistan

Tulipa dubia

Tulipa kolpakowskiana

Tulipa ferganica

Tulipa kaufmanniana

Tulipa tschimganica

Tulipa tschimganica Z. Botsch. (*Liliaceae*). Native of Central Asia, especially the Chimgan valley NE of Tashkent, growing in rocky places at c.2000m, flowering in May. Characterised by its yellow flowers with a startling blotch of red inside each petal. This is variable in size and can be almost lacking or covering most of the petal. *T. dubia* and *T. kaufmanniana* also grow here, and *T. greigii* (p.143) is also recorded. Intermediates are common, and *T. tschimganica* has probably arisen by hybridisation. Photographed in the Chimgan valley on 13 May 1980.

Tulipa dubia Vved. (*Liliaceae*). Native of Central Asia, especially the western Tien Shan, growing on earthy and stony slopes above 1800m, flowering in May and June. Leaves two to four, spreading and with wavy edges; flower yellow, tinged violet outside; bulb tunics papery, hair all over inner surface. Photographed in the Chimgan valley, NE of Tashkent, in May 1980.

Tulipa kolpakowskiana Regel (*Liliaceae*). (See p.137.) Reported in *Flora of the USSR* to hybridise with the red-flowered *T. ostrovskiana* Regel, but in this locality no red-flowered tulips or possible hybrids were found. Photographed in C Asia, above Alma Ata, near Medeo, at c.1800m, in May 1980, growing exclusively on rocky bluffs.

Tulipa kaufmanniana Regel (*Liliaceae*). (See p.137.) Distinguished by its anthers which twist as they dehisce from the top downwards. Hybridising in the wild with *T. greigii*, *T. dubia* and *T. tschimganica* (p.139). Many colour forms have been produced in cultivation, in various combinations of red, pink, yellow or white. Easy to grow in well-drained sandy soil, kept dry in summer. Photographed in Central Asia, Chimgan valley, NE of Tashkent, in May 1980.

Tulipa ferganica Vved. (*Liliaceae*). Native of Central Asia, especially the Alai, Fergana and Chatkal ranges, growing on stony slopes at c.1800m, flowering in April and May. Very close to *T. dubia*, but differs in its dark leathery bulb tunic, less hairy inside. Photographed in C Asia, mountains S of Fergana, in April 1979.

½ life size Photographed 14 April

(a) **Tulipa sosnowskyi** Achverd. & Mirzoeva (*Liliaceae*). Native of Soviet Armenia, growing on open stony hillsides, flowering in May. Characterised by often having more than one flower, and by the narrowly pointed petals with a black basal blotch and a large greyish blotch in the centre of each petal. Height here 36cm. Easily grown in a sunny place in well-drained soil, kept dry or lifted in summer. Source Soviet Armenia, Meghri near Artzvaherd, E Gabrielian s.n.

(b) **Tulipa sylvestris** L. subsp. **sylvestris** (*Liliaceae*). Native of Italy, Sicily and Sardinia, and widely naturalised further north in Europe, including England and Holland, growing in meadows and open woods, flowering in April and May. Distinguished from subsp. *australis* (p.125) by the thicker stem, over 2.5mm in diameter, larger flowers with petals 36–63mm against 20–35mm long, greenish not reddish outside, and by the broader lowest leaf, over 1–2cm wide. Easily grown and will naturalise in grass on well-drained soil. Similar plants are found in N Iran, and are in commerce under the name 'Tabriz'. Subsp. *sylvestris* is variously reported as triploid or tetraploid, subsp. *australis* as diploid.

(c) **Tulipa fosterana** Irv. (*Liliaceae*). Native of Central Asia, especially the mountains S of Samarkand, growing in deep soil among limestone rocks at c.1700m, flowering in April. Distinguished by its usually shining green leaves and large red flowers which open out wide in the sun. Petals up to 12.5cm long, rounded. Many garden forms and hybrids are cultivated; shown here is c.v. 'Cantata' (see p.143 for wild form). Cultivation as for (a).

(d) **Tulipa cretica** Boiss & Held. (*Liliaceae*). Native of the mountains of Crete, especially in the 'hedgehog' scrub zone, flowering in April. Flowers pale pink or white, opening into stars; leaves usually two, shining green. Increasing greatly by stolons. Bulb tunic with few straight hairs inside, leathery. Grow in a bulb frame or very sunny place outside in stony soil, kept dry in summer.

(e) **Tulipa praestans** Hoog, c.v. **'Fusilier'**. A fine form with very glaucous hairy leaves and up to five rather small flowers. Cultivation as for (a). See pp.137 (a), 143.

(f) **Tulipa batalinii** Regel (*Liliaceae*). This is a pale yellow colour form of *T. maximoviczii*. Intermediates between the two forms in various shades of bronze are found in cultivation. Height here 30cm.

(g) **Tulipa maximoviczii** Regel. (*Liliaceae*). Native of Central Asia, especially the Pamir Alai, growing on rocky hillsides, flowering from April to June. Very close to *T. linifolia* Regel which is said to have a large black blotch at the base of each petal. Cultivation as for (a).

(h), (i) **Tulipa julia** C. Koch (*Liliaceae*). Native of E Turkey, W Iran and the southern Transcaucasus, growing on stony hillsides, flowering from April to June. Bulb tunic very shaggy inside; leaves rather narrow. Outer petals longer than inner. Cultivation as for (a). Source (h) Turkey, near Agri, 2000m, Rix 869; (i) Turkey, Erzurum, Çakmak Da, 2250m, Rix 859.

½ life size Photographed 28 April

½ life size Photographed 22 April

Tulipa humilis

Tulipa praestans Hoog

Tulipa fosterana

Tulipa hoogiana

Tulipa systola

(a) **Tulipa greigii** Regel (*Liliaceae*). Native of Central Asia, especially the Tien Shan, and the Syr Darya valley, growing on earthy slopes, flowering in April. Flowers usually orange-red, sometimes yellow; petals 3–10cm long. Leaves always marked with purple. The form shown here is c.v. 'Red Riding Hood', one of the many hybrids, raised in 1953. Easily grown in well-drained rich soil in full sun, either kept dry in summer or dug up and ripened under cover.

(b) **Tulipa vvedenskyi** Z. Botsch. Native of Central Asia, especially the western Tien Shan, SE of Tashkent, flowering in June. Characterised by its large orange-red flowers with a yellow basal blotch, and narrow glaucous leaves. Cultivate as for (a).

(c) **Tulipa cuspidata** Regel. Native of the Aures Mts in NW Algeria; close to *T. sylvestris* subsp. *australis* but flowers white. Cultivation as for (a).

(d) **Tulipa orphanidea** Boiss. ex Heldr., syn. *T. whittallii* A. D. Hall, *T. hageri* Heldr. Native of Greece, Crete, Bulgaria and W Turkey, growing in cornfields and stony places, flowering in April. Flowers may be orange or red. Easy in good soil outside.

(e) **Tulipa urumiensis** Stapf. Probably native of W Iran, but not known in the wild. Common in cultivation, dwarf, many-flowered with green leaves.

(f) **Tulipa sylvestris** subsp. **australis** (Link) Pamp. Native of most of S Europe, N Africa, the Caucasus and N Iran, growing in scrub, stony hillsides, steppe and subalpine meadows, flowering in April and May (see p.141). Source Greece, Mt Hymettus, near Athens, Rix 574.

(g) **Tulipa armena** Boiss., var. **armena**. Native of NE Turkey and NW Iran, growing on stony hillsides, from 1300 to 2800m, flowering in May and June. The flowers are sometimes yellow. Bulb tunic with long silky hairs. Source Turkey, pass between Erzurum and Çat, Rix 1683.

(h) **Tulipa confusa** Gabrielian. Native of Soviet Armenia, in the Karabagh range, growing in steppe at c.1500m, flowering in May. Cultivate as for (a).

Tulipa systola Stapf. Native of N Iraq and W Iran, growing in fields and rocky places, from 200 to 3000m, flowering in March and April. Petals always acuminate, leaves wavy edged; bulb tunics very woolly. Photographed in NE Iraq, near Piramagrun, by Oleg Polunin.

Tulipa fosterana Irv. (see p.141). Photographed in Central Asia, S of Samarkand, Amankutan valley, on 13 April 1979.

Tulipa praestans Hoog (see p.137). Photographed in Central Asia, Tadjikistan, valley of Sorbo river, E of Dushanbe, 2000m, on 9 April 1979.

Tulipa humilis Herbert (see p.137). Photographed in SE Turkey, Hakkari, near Yukşekova, in May 1972.

Tulipa hoogiana B. Fedsch. Native of Central Asia, especially the Kopet Dağ, growing on stony slopes, flowering in April and May. Leaves very glaucous; petals with a black, yellow edged blotch. Cultivate as for (a). Photographed in Tashkent Botanic Garden.

½ life size Photographed 17 April

(a) **Tulipa tarda** Stapf (*Liliaceae*). Native of Central Asia, especially the Tien Shan, growing on stony and rocky slopes flowering in April and May. Flowers one to eight; bulb tunics glabrous. Easily grown in good well-drained soil, kept dry in summer, or lifted and ripened under cover.

(b) **Tulipa eichleri** Regel (*Liliaceae*). Native of south-east Transcaucasia and NW Iran, growing on dry slopes and in cornfields, flowering in April and May. Bulb tunic leathery, hairy inside. Petals with a small black blotch at the base, margined with yellow, up to 7cm long. Leaves glaucous, not striped. Easily grown in a sunny place outside, kept dry in summer.

(c) **Tulipa saxatilis** Sieber, syn. *T. bakeri* A. D. Hall (*Liliaceae*). Native of Crete, growing in fields and rocky places, flowering in April, Like a very large *T. cretica* (p.141). Increasing greatly by stolons, but often not flowering very freely. Requires a well-drained soil and a very warm sunny position. The shining green leaves appear in early winter. The plant known as *T. bakeri* has rather darker flowers.

(d) **Tulipa aucheriana** Baker (*Liliaceae*). Native of western Iran, but like *T. urumiensis* better known in cultivation than in the wild. Now considered a form of *T. humilis* with smaller more starry flowers, pink with a yellow centre. Easy to grow in well-drained soil in a sunny position, not requiring lifting in summer.

Tulip cultivars

(e) **'Pink Beauty'** (Single Early). Raised by Baars & Dibbits 1889.

(f) **'Big Chief'** (Darwin hybrid). Raised by A. Frijlink & Sons Ltd 1959.

(g) **'Gudoshnik'** (Darwin hybrid). Raised by D. W. Lefeber & Co. 1952.

(h) **'Apeldoorn'** (Darwin hybrid). Raised by Lefeber & Co. 1951.

(i) **'Diana'** (Single Early). Raised by A. van den Berg Gzn 1909.

(j) **Mr van der Hoef** (Early double). Sport of Murillo before 1911.

½ life size Photographed 17 April

½ life size Photographed 2 May

Tulip cultivars

(a) **'Maureen'** (Cottage). Raised by Segers Bros Ltd 1950.

(b) **'Big Chief'** (Darwin hybrid). Raised by A. Frijlink & Sons Ltd 1959.

(c) **'Purple Star'** (Triumph). Raised by S. J. Zandvoort 1952.

(d) **'Kansas'** (Triumph). Raised by Zocher & Co. before 1930.

(e) **'Lefeber's Favourite'** (Darwin hybrid). Raised by D. W. Lefeber & Co. 1942.

(f) **'Aristocrat'** (Darwin). Raised by Segers Bros Ltd 1935.

(g) **'Oranjezon'** (Darwin hybrid). Raised by C. V. Hybrida 1947.

(h) **'La Tulipe Noire'** (Darwin). Raised by E. H. Krelage & Son 1891.

(i) **'Copland's Magenta'** (Darwin). Sport of 'William Copland' raised by E. H. Krelage & Son 1891.

(j) **'White Triumphator'** (Lily-flowered). Raised by Van Tubergen Ltd 1942.

(k) **'West Point'** (Lily-flowered). Raised by de Mol-Nieuwenhuis 1943.

(l) **'Apeldoorn'** (Darwin hybrid). Raised by D. W. Lefeber & Co. 1951.

(m) **'Bellona'** (Single Early). Raised by H. de Graaff & Sons Ltd 1944.

(n) **'Vuurbaak'** (Double Early). Raised by C. Alkemade Azn 1980.

(o) **'Van der Neer'** (Single Early). Raised by G. Leembruggen 1860.

(p) **'Marechal Neil'** (Double Early). Sport of 'Murillo' 1930.

½ life size Photographed 28 April

½ life size Photographed 2 May

Tulip cultivars

(a) **'May Wonder'** (Double Late). Raised by C. V. Hybrida 1951.

(b) **'Eros'** (Double Late). Raised by Zocher & Co. 1937.

(c) **'Ibis'** (Single Early). Sport of White Hawk 1910.

(d) **'Keizerskroon'** (Single Early). Raiser not recorded, 1750.

(e) **'Garden Party'** (Triumph). Raised by P. Hopman & Sons Ltd 1944.

(f) **'Mount Tacoma'** (Double Late). Raised by Polman Mooy before 1926.

(g) **'Rosy Dawn'** (Cottage). Raised by de Graaf Bros Ltd 1946.

(h) **'Ossi Oswalda'** (Darwin). Raised by J. J. Grullemans & Sons Ltd before 1939.

(i) **'K. & M.'s Triumph'.** Flamed flower from red original Triumph.

(j) **'Gudoshnik'** (Darwin hybrid). Raised by D. W. Lefeber & Co. 1952. The original is yellow, spotted and flamed red, but this flower shows more red flaming than normal (see p.145).

(k) **'Dreaming Maid'.** Flamed flower from violet-pink, white-edged original Triumph (see p.151).

(l) **'Artist'** (Green-flowered Cottage). Raised by Captain Bros 1947.

(m) **'Van der Neer'.** Flamed flower from purple original. Single Early (see p.147).

(n) **'Prins Carnaval'** 1930. Sport of Prince of Austria (see p.151).

(o) **'Garden Party'.** White sport of white, deep pink edged original Triumph.

The 'breaking' of plain coloured tulip flowers into stripes and 'flames' of different colours is caused by infection with Tulip-breaking virus, which can be spread by aphids. For this reason the 'broken' varieties, often called 'Rembrandt Tulips', should be grown well away from other tulips. The appearance of different colours by 'sporting' is also a common phenomenon, and has been the source of many new varieties.

½ life size Photographed 2 May

½ life size Photographed 2 May

Tulip cultivars

(a) **'Dreaming Maid'** (Triumph). Raised by J. J. Kerbert 1934.

(b) **'Flying Dutchman'** (Darwin). Raised by Wamaar & Co. Ltd 1956.

(c) **'Orange Wonder'** (Triumph). Raised by A. Sabelis 1940.

(d) **'Clara Butt'** (Darwin). Raised by E. H. Krelage & Son 1889.

(e) **'Rosy Wings'** (Cottage). Raised by Van Tubergen Ltd 1944.

(f) **'Mrs John T. Scheepers'** (Cottage). Raised by Van Tubergen Ltd before 1930.

(g) **'Prince of Austria'** (Single Early). Raiser not recorded, 1860.

(h) **'Couleur Cardinal'** (Single Early). Raiser not recorded, 1845.

(i) **'China Pink'** (Lily-flowered). Raised by de Mol-Nieuwenhuis 1944.

(j) **'Blue Parrot'** (Parrot) Sport of 'Bleu Aimable' before 1935.

(k) **'Fantasy'** (Parrot) Sport of Clara Butt 1910.

(l) **'Firebird'** (Parrot) Sport of 'Fantasy' before 1939.

(m) **Narcissus poeticus** L. var. **recurvus** (Haw.) Fernandes (*Amaryllidaceae*). An old garden variety of *N. poeticus*, very late flowering, usually after all other Narcissus have finished. Easy to grow, but in some seasons flowers more freely than others. Very sweet-scented.

⅓ life size Photographed 6 May

½ life size Photographed 29 May

(a) **Zigadenus micranthus** Eastwood (*Liliaceae*). Native of northern California and Oregon, growing on dry slopes and valleys below 1000m, flowering in May and June. Petals 4–5mm long, about equalling the stamens. Easy to grow in a well-drained sunny position.

(b) **Tulipa sprengeri** Baker (*Liliaceae*). Native of NW Turkey, near Amasya, but not seen recently in the wild, though well known in cultivation. Very late flowering, usually 35–45cm high. Brian Mathew records that it has grown well in south-facing borders in full sun, at the foot of north-facing peat banks, and in grass under trees. Easy from seed.

(c) **Pancratium illyricum** L. (*Amaryllidaceae*). Native of Corsica, Sardinia, Capri and neighbouring islands, growing on rocks at low altitudes, flowering in May. The bulb is large with black tunics. Easily grown and flowering freely at the foot of a south-facing wall, but slow to increase. Source Corsica, near Porto Vecchio.

(d) **Calochortus nuttallii** Torr. (*Liliaceae*). Native of eastern California, Oregon and Montana to Colorado and New Mexico, growing on dry slopes with grass and scrub at 1500–2800m, flowering from May to August. The colour varies from white to deep yellow. Grow in a bulb frame, kept dry in summer.

(e) **Brimeura amethystina** (L.) Chouard, syn. *Hyacinthus amethystinus* L. (*Liliaceae*). Native of the Pyrenees and mountains of north-east Spain, and north-west Yugoslavia, in mountain meadows up to the subalpine region, usually on limestone, flowering in May and June. The flowers vary in colour from white to deep blue or violet. Cultivation as for (a).

(f) **Calochortus pulchellus** Dougl. ex Benth. (*Liliaceae*). Native of central California where it is frequent on wooded and bushy slopes in chaparral and pine and oak forest above 200m, flowering from April to June. One of the easier species of the group. Grows well in good very gritty soil in a bulb frame in sun or half-shade.

(g) **Calochortus amoenus** Greene (*Liliaceae*). Native of central and S California, in the western foothills of the Sierras to the Greenhorn Mts, growing in leafy loam in partial shade, and on grassy slopes from 500 to 1400m, flowering from April to June. Cultivation as for (f).

(h) **Calochortus albus** Dougl. ex Benth. (*Liliaceae*). Native of central California, especially the coast ranges and the foothills of the Sierras, growing in shaded and often rocky places in evergreen oak and pine forest, and in chaparral scrub, below 1500m. Cultivation as for (f). Photographed in California, Butt Co., by Roger Macfarlane.

(i) **Calochortus caeruleus** (Kell.) Watson, (*Liliaceae*). Native of northern California in the western Sierra Nevada, growing in open stony places in montane coniferous forest from 1000 to 2200m, flowering from May to July. Cultivation as for (f).

(j) **Calochortus monophyllus** (Lindl.) Lem. (*Liliaceae*). Native of the foothills of the Sierras in northern California on wooded slopes from 400 to 1100m, flowering in April and May.

Hyacinthella pallens Schur. syn. *H. dalmatica* (Baker) Chouard (*Liliaceae*). Native of western Yugoslavia, growing in grassy places among limestone rocks. Cultivation as for (a). Photographed in Yugoslavia, near Dubrovnik, by Brian Mathew.

½ life size Photographed 28 April

Calochortus albus

Hyacinthella pallens

Erythronium purpurascens in north California

Erythronium purpurascens

Calochortus clavatus near Bakersfield, California

Erythronium purpurascens Watson (*Liliaceae*). Native of the Sierra Nevada in northern and central California, growing in shady or grassy places by rocks and cliffs in coniferous forest at 1300–1500m, flowering by late snow patches in May to August. Stems to 20cm tall; leaves not spotted. Stigma undivided. Flowers opening white, becoming purplish as they fade. Photographed in N California near Mount Shasta.

Calochortus elegans Pursh var. **nanus** Wood. Native of NE California and Oregon to C Idaho, in open coniferous woods at 1500–2800m, flowering in May to July. Stems to 15cm, usually unbranched, with 1–3 flowers. Needs well-drained soil, dry in late summer. Photographed in NE California near Burney Falls.

Calochortus nuttallii var. **panamintensis** Ownby. Native of California, in the Panamint mountains to the west of Death Valley, at 2200–3000m, growing among Pinyon pines and Junipers in dry shady soil, flowering in June and July. Stems up to 60cm. Petals with no spot above the nectary. Photographed near Wild Rose Canyon, California.

Calochortus albus Douglas ex Benth. var. **rubellus** Greene. Native of California in the southern coast ranges from Santa Lucia to Santa Cruz mountains on shaded rocks in woods and scrub, flowering in April to June. This has proved hardy and a good grower in a bulb frame, easy to raise from seed. Source: from Santa Lucia mountains near San Antonio.

Calochortus clavatus Wats (*Liliaceae*). Native of S California in the foothills of the Sierra Nevada and in the coast ranges on rocky slopes at up to 1200m, flowering in April to June, and usually found on serpentine soils. Stems robust to 50cm. Needs deep soil, moist in spring; hot and dry in summer, needing no water before early winter. Photographed in S California, in the coast ranges.

Calochortus elegans var. **nanus**

Calochortus nuttallii var. **panamintensis**

Calochortus albus var. **rubellus**

Calochortus lyallii

Calochortus macrocarpus

Moraea loubseri

Calochortus lyallii Baker (*Liliaceae*). Native of S British Columbia to Washington, along the E slope of the Cascades, and on Badger mountain, in open coniferous forests, flowering in May to July. Stems 10–50cm, with 1–4, or rarely to 9 flowers. Petals sometimes tinged purple, triangular-lanceolate, with long wavy hairs on the margin. For well-drained soil, dry in summer.

Calochortus macrocarpus Douglas (*Liliaceae*). Native of N California to British Columbia and Montana, growing in sagebrush scrub and open conifer forest at up to 2000m, flowering in July and August. Stem to 50cm high. Distinct in its purple flowers with pointed sepals longer than the petals. Photographed by R. Macfarlane.

Moraea loubseri Goldblatt (*Iridaceae*). Native of S Africa, known only from a single granite hilltop near Langebaan in the SW Cape. Stems 15–20cm, from a corm with a coarsely netted tunic. Outer petals 20–24mm long, 14–20mm wide. Although so rare in the wild, this species has proved easy to grow and raise from seed. Hardy to −3°C, perhaps, so needing alpine house treatment in all but the mildest climates; shown here in cultivation in California, where it flowers in February.

½ life size Photographed 6 June

Calochortus luteus

Calochortus venustus

Calochortus kennedyi

Calochortus amabilis

(a) **Triteleia ixioides** (Ait. fil.) Greene, syn. *Brodiaea lutea* (Lindl.) Mort. (*Liliaceae*). Native of central California, growing in sandy soil in pine and pine-oak forest up to 1500m, flowering from May to August. Easily grown in a bulb frame or warm sunny place outside. The stamens have a long tooth either side of the anther, which distinguishes it from *T. crocea* and *Bloomeria crocea* (Torr.) Cav.

(b), (c) **Calochortus venustus** Dougl. ex Benth. (*Liliaceae*). Native of central and S California, especially the Sierra Nevada and southern coast ranges, growing in grassland and in open evergreen oak and pine forest, in light sandy soil, usually decomposed granite, from 300 to 2600m, flowering from May to July. The flowers vary from white to yellow, pink, dark red or purple. Grows in well-drained sandy soil, kept rather dry in winter and watered until flowering, and so best in a pot in the alpine house, or in a bulb frame. Photographed in the Greenhorn Mts by Roger Macfarlane.

(d) **Calochortus luteus** Doug. ex Lindl. (*Liliaceae*). Native of central California in the Sierra Nevada and the coast ranges, growing in heavy soils in open grassland, and in pine, evergreen oak and mixed coniferous woodland, below 650m, flowering from April till June. Close to *C. venustus* (p.156), but always clear yellow in colour. Nectary curved. Cultivation as for (b). Photographed in California, near Chico, by Roger Macfarlane.

(e) **Dichelostemma ida-maia** (Wood) Greene, syn. *Brodiaea ida-maia* (Wood) Greene (*Liliaceae*). Native of northern California and Oregon, growing in the redwood and mixed evergreen forest zone in open grassy places from 300 to 1200m, flowering from May to July. The leaves which are usually withered at flowering are normally three, 30–50cm by 4–8mm; flowering stem up to 90cm. Easily grown in a pot in the alpine house, a bulb frame or a very sheltered warm place outside.

(f) **Triteleia hyacinthina** (Lindl.) Greene (*Liliaceae*). Native of northern California north to Vancouver Is., and Idaho, growing in wet places, meadows and slopes up to 1800m, flowering from May to August, the large white-fld form from wet places, the smaller forms from drier slopes. Cultivation as (e).

(g) **Allium caeruleum** Pallas, syn. *A. azureum* Ledebour (*Liliaceae*). Native of the far east of Europe north of the Caspian, and Central Asia south to the Pamir and the Tien Shan, in steppes and salt marshes, flowering May to July. Leaves withered by flowering time, triangular in section. Easily cultivated in a dry place.

Calochortus amabilis Purdy (*Liliaceae*). Native of NW California, especially the coast ranges, where it grows in loamy or rocky soil on dry slopes in chaparral, scrub or evergreen mixed forest up to 1000m, flowering from April to June. Photographed in California, Lake Co., 23 April 1966, Roger Macfarlane.

Calochortus kennedyi Porter (*Liliaceae*). Native of S California, Nevada and Arizona, growing in heavy soil on open plains or on dry rocky or scrubby slopes, usually in desert conditions, at altitudes of 600–2000m, flowering from April till June. Variable in colour, being usually scarlet, but orange in the E Mojave desert and yellow at high altitudes. Has not proved amenable in cultivation in England. Photographed in California, near China Lake, M. Williams.

Camassia leichtlinii subsp. **leichtlinii**

Camassia quamash

Camassia quamash (Pursh) Greene (*Liliaceae*). Native of Washington State south to California and east to Montana and Utah, growing in marshy meadows in coniferous forest at up to 2300m (subsp. *breviflora*) flowering in May to July. Stems up to 80cm tall. Flowers with the lowest petal rather separate from the others. Capsules appressed to the stem. Easily grown in rich or moist soil. Photographed in North California in Six Rivers National Forest, in early June.

Camassia leichtlinii (Baker) Wats. subsp **leichtlinii** (*Liliaceae*). Native of Oregon in mountain meadows (with the blue-flowered subsp. *saksdorfii* (Greenman) Gould) from British Columbia to S California, flowering in May to August. Stems to 130cm tall. Flowers regular, often pale greenish. Capsules not appressed to stem. Easily grown in rich or moist soil. Seen here with *Viola cornuta* f. *alba*, a most pleasing combination. A double-flowered form, commonly cultivated, is rather ugly.

Brodiaea elegans Hoover (*Liliaceae*), Harvest Brodiaea. Native of Oregon and N California to Monterey and rarely further south, in wet or dry grassland or open woods at up to 2000m, flowering from April to July. Stems 10–40cm tall. Flowers 35–60mm long. Staminodes erect, rounded at apex. Photographed in Mendocino Co., California, in June.

Bloomeria crocea (Torr.) Cov. (*Liliaceae*) Golden Stars. Native of S California in the southern coast ranges south to Kern Co. and in Baja California, in grassland and chaparral at up to 1800m, flowering in April to June. Distinguished from *Brodiaea lutea* (syn. *Triteleia ixioides*) by its very narrow-petalled starry flowers, with filiform stamen filaments, in an expanded not crowded umbel. Photographed in the Sierra Madre mountains in June.

Dichelostemma multiflorum (Benth.) Heller, syn. *Brodiaea multiflora* Benth. Native of S Oregon and NW California south to Mariposa Co. along the Sierra Nevada in grassy places, open woods and scrub, below 1500m, flowering in May and June. Recognised by its umbel of flowers with pedicels 3–15mm, entire and not forked staminodes, and inflated perianth tube. Height 30–80cm. Flowers 15–20mm across. Easily grown in soils which become rather warm and dry in summer. Photographed in Mendocino Co. in June.

Dichelostemma volubile (Moriere) Heller, syn. *Brodiaea volubilis* (Moriere) Bajer. Snake Lily. Native of central California, in the foothills of the Sierra Nevada, and in the coast ranges of N California, growing in scrub below 1000m, flowering in May and June. One of the few bulbous *Liliaceae* with a twining stem; this usually seems to grow up through branches of poison oak which no doubt give it added protection from grazing animals. Photographed in Tehama Co. in early June.

Dichelostemma congestum (J. E. Smith) Kunth., syn. *Brodiaea congesta* Sm. Native of Washington south to central California, in grassy places and scrub, flowering in April to June. Recognised by its umbel of flowers with very short pedicels only 1–6mm long, an only slightly inflated perianth tube and forked staminodes. Height 40–100cm. Flowers 15–20mm across. Photographed in Mendocino Co. in June.

Dichelostemma ida-maia (Wood) Greene. See also p.157 (e). This unusual looking species is a typical humming-bird flower with its tubular red perianth. Compare with *Fritillaria recurva* p.107. Photographed in N California, in Mendocino Co. flowering in early June.

Dichelostemma multiflorum

Dichelostemma congestum

Dichelostemma multiflorum

Bloomeria crocea

Dichelostemma volubile

Dichelostemma ida-maia in the Salmon Mountains, north California

Brodiaea elegans

½ life size Photographed 2 May

(a) Allium circinatum Sieber (*Liliaceae*). Found only on Crete, on dry rocky hillsides, where it flowers in March and April. Unusual in its coiled leaves covered with long silky hairs, and hairy stem. Best cultivated in a bulb frame or pot, kept dry in summer.

(b) Allium neapolitanum Cyr. Native of the Mediterranean region from Spain to Turkey and Egypt, growing in grassy places and fields, flowering from March to May. Anthers dark, filaments flattened. Easily grown in sunny places, but said to be rather frost-tender. Source Spain, J. Pym s.n.

(c) Allium ursinum L., Ramsons. Native of most of Europe from Scotland and Finland to Spain and Greece, and east to the Caucasus. Found in damp woods, often in great quantity, flowering from April to June.

(d) Allium trifoliatum Cyr. Native of the Mediterranean region from France to Sicily, Crete and Israel, growing on stony hillsides, flowering in April and May. Like *A. subhirsutum*, but has flowers tinged with pink, yellow not brown anthers, pedicels 15–20mm as opposed to 25–40mm. Forms a dense clump.

(e) Allium roseum L. Native of the Mediterranean region from Spain and Portugal to Turkey and N Africa, growing in rocky places, dry open woods, and cultivated ground, flowering from April to June. The bulb tunic is hard and brittle; the leaves 1–14mm wide. Some forms have bulbils in the inflorescence. Cultivation as (b). Source Spain, coll. Linzee Gordon.

(f) Allium zebdanense Boiss. & Noë. Native of the eastern Mediterranean region from Syria to Israel, growing in rocky places in the mountains, flowering in May and June. Umbel short-stalked; stamens with wide-based filaments. Leaves glabrous. Cultivation as (b).

(g) Allium triquetrum L. Native of the western Mediterranean region from Italy to France and N Africa, where it grows in damp shady places, often by streams. Naturalised in Britain. Stem triangular. Easily grown in cool leafy soil.

(h) Leucojum nicaeense Ardoino (*Amaryllidaceae*). Native of SE France east of Nice, and possibly Italy, growing on rocky hills, flowering in spring. Dislikes disturbance, so best sown thinly and carefully potted on.

(i) Notholirion thomsonianum (Royle) Stapf (*Liliaceae*). Native of the western Himalayas from Afghanistan to Kumaon, growing in scrub and rocky places at 1600–2300m, flowering in March and April. Grow in well-drained rich soil, kept dry in summer to ripen the bulbs and encourage flowering.

(j) Tulipa clusiana DC. (*Liliaceae*). Native of Iran, near Shiraz eastwards to the Himalayas and Tibet, and naturalised in S Europe. It grows on stony mountain sides, flowering from April to June. The ground colour is usually white, with pink on the outer petals. Shown here is c.v. 'Cynthia' raised by Van Tubergen in 1959.

(k) Ixiolirion tartaricum (Pall.) Herbert, syn. *I. montanum* (La Bill.) Herb., *I. pallasii* Fisch. & Meyer (*Amaryllidaceae*). Native of western Asia from Turkey and Egypt eastwards to western Siberia and Songaria, growing in fields and on hillsides from 200 to 2700m, flowering from April to June. Requires a hot dry summer.

(l) Allium longisepalum Bertol. see p.169 (e).

½ life size Photographed 2 May

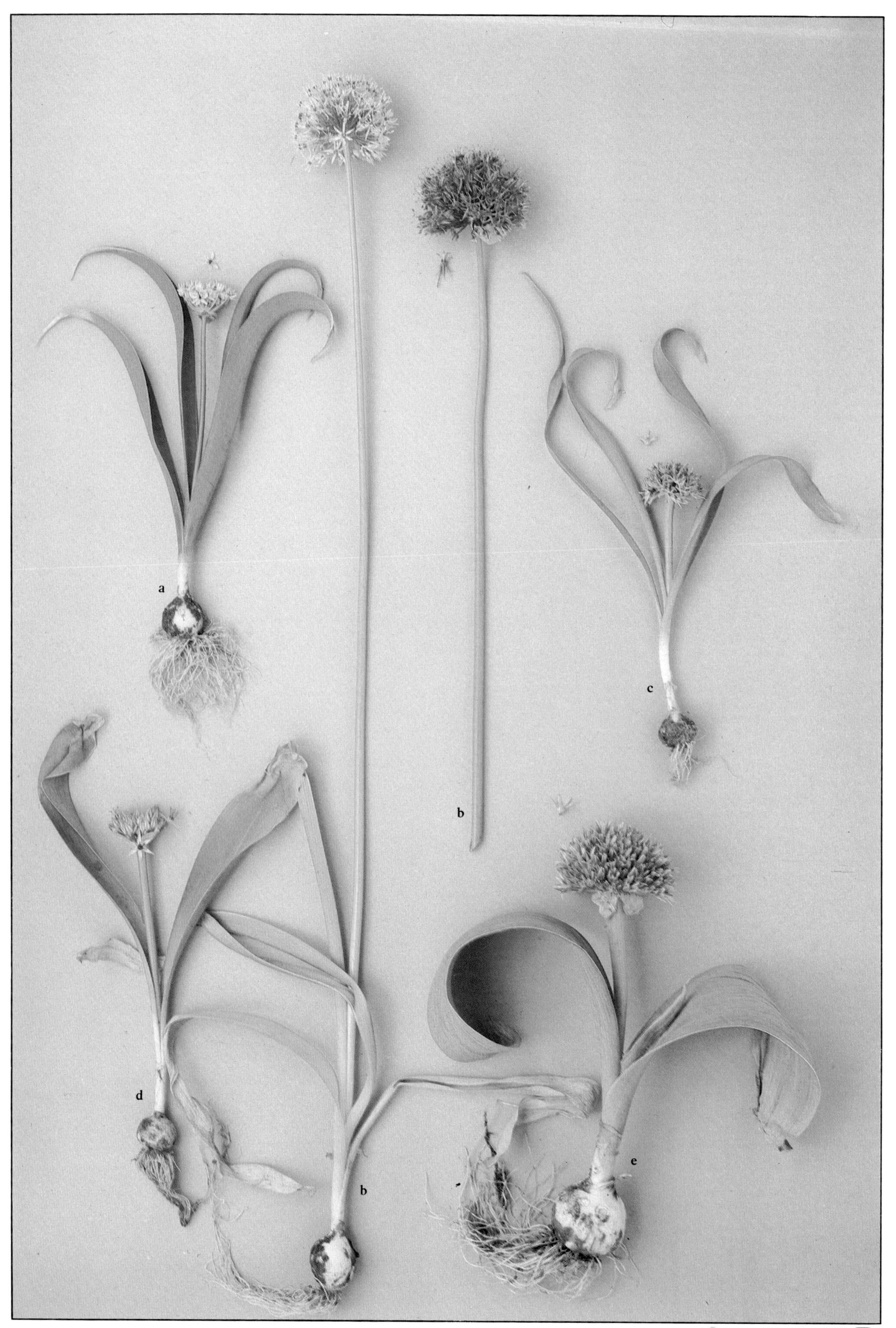

⅓ life size Photographed 6 May

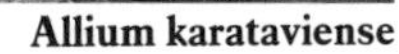

Allium karataviense

Allium protensum

Allium akaka in the mountains southeast of Lake Van

Allium sphaerocephalon

(a) **Allium kharputense** Freyn & Sint. (*Liliaceae*). Native of Turkey and W Iran, growing on stony hillsides from 1500 to 2500m. The obtuse petals and dark ovary are characteristic. Height here 24cm. Source Turkey, Adiyaman, Kahta, towards Nemrut Dağ, Linzee Gordon 5163.

(b) **Allium hirtifolium** Stapf (*Liliaceae*). Native of the Zagros Mts in west and south-west Iran, on rocky hillsides up to 3200m. Flowering stem up to 150cm. Leaves hairy beneath. Very similar to *A. stipitatum* Regel from Afghanistan and Central Asia, but has a smooth not ribbed flower stem, and less tapered petals. Easily grown in a bulb frame or in the open. Both the white and pink forms were collected by Brian Mathew on the Bowles Scholarship Botanical Expedition to Iran in 1963. Source Iran, SW of Arak, BSBE 1840.

(c) **Allium breviscapum** Stapf (*Liliaceae*). Native of Iran, where it is confined to the area of Isfahan. Differs from *A. akaka* in its narrower leaves which are four to six in number and hairy beneath. Easily grown in a bulb frame. Source Iran, Kuh-i-Alwand, P. Furse 1986.

(d) **Allium ellisii** Hooker (*Liliaceae*). Native of Iran, especially the Elburz mountains. Characterised by its scabrid leaf margin and starry shining flowers like *A. christophii* (p.167), but stems are always much shorter. Cultivation as for (c). Source P. Furse 2571.

(e) **Allium akaka** Gmelin, syn. *A. latifolium* Jaub. & Spach. (*Liliaceae*). Native of E Turkey, Transcaucasia, NW Iran and N Iraq, growing on screes and loose stony slopes in the mountains from 1600 to 3000m, flowering from June to August. Distinguished by its one or two broad glaucous leaves and short stem with a spherical head of pale pink flowers. Cultivation as for (c). Source SE Turkey, Pelli Da., S side of Lake Van, Rix 714. Photographed at 3000m on Artos Dağ, south of Van, in June 1968.

Allium protensum Wendelbo (*Liliaceae*). Native of Central Asia from the Kizil Kum desert to the Pamir-Alai, and northern Afghanistan, from 300 to 3000m, flowering in May and June. This species was for a long time confused with *A. schubertii* Zucc. from Israel, Syria and Libya, but differs in its shorter stem, and brown rather than purplish flowers. Whereas *A. schubertii* is frost tender, *A. protensum* should be quite hardy provided that it is kept rather dry. Photographed in Tashkent Botanic Garden.

Allium karataviense Regel (*Liliaceae*). Native of Central Asia especially the Alai and western Tien Shan, growing in loose limestone scree, flowering in April and May. Leaves grey-purple. Petals recurved and twisted after flowering. Easily grown in well-drained soil in full sun. See p.184.

Allium sphaerocephalon L. (*Liliaceae*). Native of most of Europe, from England and Belgium to the Caucasus, and N Africa to Israel, growing in dry places and in fields, flowering from June to August. Flowers sometimes replaced by bulbils. Spathe shorter than the pedicels, two-valved; leaves up to 30cm, 1–4mm wide, sheathing the stem. Easily grown in well-drained soil in full sun. Photographed in Greece near Kastoria by Oleg Polunin.

⅓ life size Photographed 6 June

(a) **Allium neapolitanum** Cyr. (*Liliaceae*) (see p.161 (b)). Height here 40cm. Source between Tunis and Tabarka, 50m, Linzee Gordon 465.

(b) **Scilla peruviana** L. (*Liliaceae*). Native of the western Mediterranean region from Italy and Sicily westwards, growing in damp grassy places, flowering from April to June. Very variable in size and flower colour, from white to dark purple or pale brown in N Africa. The form shown here is probably *S. hughii* Tin. ex Guss. from Isole Egadi. Plant shallow, in a warm sunny place.

(c) **Allium regelii** Trautr. (*Liliaceae*). Native of Central Asia, especially the Kara Kum desert, Kopet Dağ and Badgis north of Herat, Afghanistan, especially the Hindu Kush, and NE Iran. It grows on sandy deserts and rocky slopes in the mountains from 800 to 3000m, flowering in May and June. It is unique in its candelabra-like inflorescence, which may have up to six whorls of flowers in a robust specimen. The flowers are either pink, as shown here, or deep purple. Easily grown but probably safer in a bulb frame where it can be kept dry in summer. Source Afghanistan, Hindu Kush, Salang pass, P. Furse 6614.

(d) **Allium subhirsutum** L. (*Liliaceae*). Native of the Mediterranean region from Spain to Greece, growing on rocky and sandy places, flowering from March to May. Close to *A. trifoliatum* and *A. neapolitanum* (p.161) but *A. subhirsutum* has ciliate leaves and slender not flattened stamen filaments. Easily grown in warm sunny places. Source Greece, Cephalonia.

(e) **Allium nigrum** Boiss. & Reut. (*Liliaceae*). Native of S Europe eastwards to Iran, growing in fields and among limestone rocks, at 100–200m, flowering from April to June. With its purple anthers and purplish petals the plant shown here approaches *A. atropurpureum* Waldst. & Kit. *A. nigrum* usually has yellowish anthers and white or pink, green-veined petals. Easily grown in a well-drained sunny place. Source W Turkey, between Denizli and Budur, Linzee Gordon 504.

(f) **Allium moly** L. (*Liliaceae*). Native of E Spain and SW France where it grows on shady rocks and screes in the mountains, and flowers in May. Cultivation as for (e).

(g) **Allium schoenoprasum** L. Chives (*Liliaceae*). Native of most of Europe, and usually found in damp meadows in the mountains, forming dense clumps. It is very variable in the wild, and many different forms are grown in gardens for use in cooking and salads. Flowers sometimes white. *A. sibiricum* L., from Kamschatka and Siberia to Japan and across N America, is a more robust tetraploid form.

(h) **Allium oreophilum** C. A. Meyer, syn. *A. ostrovskianum* Regel (*Liliaceae*). Native of Central Asia, especially the Tien Shan, the Pamir Alai and the Ala Tau, and of eastern Turkey and the Caucasus, growing on stony slopes at 3000–3800m, flowering in July and August. Flowers pinkish, darker in the c.v. 'Zwanenburg' shown here. Easily grown in a sunny place.

(i) **Nothoscordum inodorum** (Aiton) Nicholson, syn. *Allium fragrans* Vent. (*Liliaceae*). Native of South America, but widely naturalised in Europe and California. *Nothoscordum* differs from *Allium* in its lack of the onion-like smell, and in the petals which are united at the base. Cf. p.167 (i).

½ life size Photographed 29 May

⅓ life size Photographed 16 July

(a) **Allium tuberosum** Rottler ex Sprengel, syn. *A. odorum* L. pro parte (*Liliaceae*). Chinese Chives. Widely cultivated in E Asia. Flowers open, starry, capsule obovate, emarginate. Flowers July to October in S England. Grows well in tropical or temperate climates, and appears hardy.

(b) **Ornithogalum narbonense** L. (*Liliaceae*). Native of S Europe, growing in grassy places and waste ground, flowering from May to July. Easily grown and will survive in grass.

(c) **Allium christophii** Trautv., syn. *A. albopilosum* Wright (*Liliaceae*). Native in northern Iran in the central Elburz and N Khorassan, and in the Kopet Dağ in Soviet Central Asia, growing on rocky slopes from 900 to 2250m. Leaves silky hairy when young, withered by flowering time. Height here 56cm. Easy to grow in hot sunny places.

(d) **Allium ramosum** L., syn. *A. odorum* L. pro parte (*Liliaceae*). Native of Siberia, growing in meadows and on grassy slopes. Flowers not opening flat; petals with a reddish line outside. Ovary ovate, emarginate. Flowers in S England during June and July. Cultivation as (a).

(e) **Allium scorodoprasum** L. subsp. **jajlae** (Vved.) Stearn, syn. *A. jajlae* Vved. Native of the Crimea and the Caucasus, growing on mountain slopes, flowering in June and July.

(f) **Allium cernuum** (*Liliaceae*). Native of North America from New York State to British Columbia southwards to Georgia and Arizona, growing in gravelly and rocky places in the mountains, flowering in July and August. Flowers may be white, pink or purple. Cultivation as (e). Source Columbia River Gorge, Wyoming.

(g) **Allium obliquum** L. (*Liliaceae*). Native of Romania to Siberia and north-western China, growing in meadows, scrub and cliffs, flowering from April to July. Filaments subulate. Cultivation as (e).

(h) **Allium nutans** L. (*Liliaceae*). Native of Siberia and Central Asia, growing in steppes, meadows and stony slopes, flowering in June and July. Inner petals longer than outer. Cultivation as (e).

(i) **Caloscordum neriniflorum** Herbert, syn. *Allium neriniflorum* (Herbert) Baker (*Liliaceae*). Native of E Siberia, Mongolia and China, growing on dry slopes, flowering in July and August. Close to *Allium*, but the stamen filaments are fused to the petals.

(j) **Brodiaea stellaris** Wats. (*Liliaceae*). Native of northern California, from Humboldt to Sonomona counties, on rocky slopes below 1000m, flowering from May to July. Grow in a bulb frame or a warm place outside.

(k) **Triteleia hyacinthina** (Lindl.) Greene (see p.157).

(l) **Triteleia laxa** Benth., syn. *Brodiaea laxa* (Benth.) Wats. Native of western California and S Oregon, growing in heavy soils up to 1200m, flowering from April to June. Flowers deep blue to white. Cultivation as for (j).

(m) **Dichelostemma pulchella** (Salisb.) Heller, syn. *Brodiaea pulchella* Greene (*Liliaceae*). Native of western California and S Oregon, commoner in the west, growing on plains and hillsides, up to c.1800m, flowering from March to May. Cultivation as for (j).

½ life size Photographed 4 August

½ life size Photographed 16 July

(a) **Allium paniculatum** L. subsp. **paniculatum** (*Liliaceae*). Native of southern Europe northwards to central France, on dry grassy slopes at up to 1000m. Flowering in late summer. Very variable in flower colour. Easily grown in dry sunny places.

(b) **Allium cyathophorum** var. **farreri** (Stearn) Stearn (*Liliaceae*). Native of north-western China, especially Kansu, where it grows on grassy slopes between 3000 and 3300m. The stamens are fused into a tube at their base. Easily grown in well-drained peaty soil in full sun, kept moist throughout the summer, flowering in late summer.

(c) **Allium flavum** L. (*Liliaceae*). Native of southern Europe from France to Greece, growing on dry hills and flowering in July. Many dwarf mountain forms have been named, e.g. *A. flavum* var. *minus* Boiss. Easy to grow in sunny places.

(d) **Allium stamineum** Boiss. (*Liliaceae*). Native of Greece, Turkey and the S Caucasus to Iraq, Arabia and Jordan, growing in steppe, scrub and desert from 100 to 2000m, flowering from May to September. Height up to 30cm. Stamens and style exserted. Easily grown in a bulb frame or pot in the alpine house.

(e) **Allium longisepalum** Bertol., syn. *A. eriophyllum* Boiss. (*Liliaceae*). Native of E Turkey, N Syria, Iraq, S and W Iran, growing in stony fields and hillsides from 150 to 1000m, flowering in May and June (see also p.161). Very variable. Cultivation as for (l). Source Iran, coll. Ann Ala.

(f) **Allium amabile** Stapf (*Liliaceae*). Native of SW China, growing in stony alpine meadows at up to 4200m, flowering from July to September. Flowers pink to magenta. Cultivation as for (b).

(g) **Allium huber-morathii** Kollman, N. Özhatay & Koyuncu (*Liliaceae*). Native of western Turkey, growing on screes at 1–2000m. Cultivation as for (a).

(h) **Allium cyaneum** Regel (*Liliaceae*). Native of NW China from Kansu to Szechuan, growing in open grassland from 2400 to 2700m, flowering from August to October. Suitable for a ledge on the rock garden. Cultivation as for (b).

(i) **Allium algirdense** Blakelock (*Liliaceae*). Native of high mountains in N Iraq and SE Turkey, where it grows on open stony slopes between 2500 and 3800m, flowering in August and September. The leaves are tubular, up to 10cm long and withered by flowering time. Cultivation as for (d). Source Hakkari, Sat Da., 3000m, Rix 161A.

(j) **Allium insubricum** Boiss. & Reut. (*Liliaceae*). Native of limestone hills between Lake Como and Lake Garda in N Italy, at c.1800m, flowering in June and July. The closely related *A. narcissiflorum* Vill., from the SW Alps, differs in its fibrous bulb sheath. Cultivation as for (b).

(k) **Allium callidyctyon** C. A. Meyer (*Liliaceae*). Native of central Turkey, Caucasia, Iraq and Iran, growing in dense tufts in rocks and in fields, from 500 to 800m, flowering in August. The leaves which are withered by flowering time appear in autumn and are narrowly tubular, covered with short dense white hairs. The bulbs have a fine woven tunic. Has grown easily in a bulb frame, but is likely to be susceptible to winter damp if planted outside. Source Turkey, Kayseri, south of Pinarbaşi, Rix 1398.

⅓ life size Photographed 6 June

(l) **Allium crispum** Greene (*Liliaceae*). Native of central California in the inner coast ranges, Santa Barbara and the Sierra Nevada foothills, growing in heavy soil on rolling hills below 800m, flowering from March to May. Height here 20cm, but may be up to 30cm. Grows in good soil in a sunny position, and probably better if protected in summer from too much wet, and in winter from hard frost.

(m) **Ornithogalum montanum** Cyr. (*Liliaceae*). Native of SE Europe, from Italy to Greece, and Turkey, growing on rocky and grassy slopes, flowering in April and May. Very variable. Leaves glabrous, 8–20mm wide. *O. narbonense* L. is similar, but has a more elongated inflorescence. Easily cultivated in a sunny position or in thin grass. Source W Turkey, Eğredir to Beyşehir, Linzee Gordon 5066.

(n) **Ornithogalum sphaerocarpum** A. Kerner (*Liliaceae*). Native of south and eastern Europe from France to Czechoslovakia southwards, growing in meadows and scrub, flowering in May and June. Close to *O. pyrenaicum* L., but flowers greenish white not yellowish, and ovary subglobose. Cultivation as (b).

(o) **Allium unifolium** Kellogg (*Liliaceae*). Native of N California and S Oregon in the coast ranges, growing in moist soils in pine or mixed evergreen forest below 1200m, flowering from May till July. The bulb is very unusual, reforming each year on a short stalk at the side of last year's bulb which has shrunk to almost nothing by flowering time. Grows in good well-drained soil in a sunny position.

(p) **Scilla litardieri** Breitstr. syn. *S. amethystina* Vis., *S. pratensis* Waldst. & Kit. (*Liliaceae*). Native of W Yugoslavia, growing in meadows and among limestone rocks. The rather similar *S. hyacinthoides* L. has eight to twelve leaves, a taller stem with a laxer 40–150 flowered inflorescence of purplish flowers. Cultivation as for (o).

Allium platycaule in north California

Allium cernuum 'Major'

Allium platycaule

Allium obtusum

Allium bodianum Regel (*Liliaceae*). Native of N Iran in Gorgan and Khorassan, and in Kopet Dağ in Soviet Turkmenistan, growing on stony slopes at 1600–2300m, flowering in May to August. Leaves 3–5cm across; umbel c.12cm in diameter; petals 12mm long. A striking plant, easily raised from seed, and increasing slowly by division of the bulbs. The fruiting head becomes detached and acts as a tumbleweed, the seeds being retained in the open capsule for some time. Source: collected by Ann Ala south of Karadj.

Allium cernuum Roth. **'Major'**. This is a much finer garden plant than the form illustrated on p.166. It is similar to *A. allegheniense* Small. Stems to 45cm. Umbel to 4cm in diameter. Easily grown in good garden soil, flowering in summer.

Allium obtusum Lemmon. Native of California in the W Sierra Nevada at 2000–4000m, in Juniper scrub or bare gravelly areas in the mountains, flowering in May to July. A dwarf stemless onion with flowers 5–8mm long. Leaves up to 5mm wide. Photographed on the Donner Pass near Truckee.

Allium narcissiflorum Vill. Native of the Alpes Maritimes and Dauphiné and reported once from NW Portugal, growing on limestone screes, flowering in July. Stems 15–35cm. Leaves 2–6mm wide; flowers 10–15mm long. Distinguished from the similar *A. insubricum* (p.68) by the presence of parallel fibres around the narrow bulbs. Easily grown in well-drained soil in a sunny position. Photographed in the rock garden at Wisley.

Allium beesianum W. W. Smith. Native of W China, in NW Yunnan, especially Lijiang, and neighbouring Sichuan, growing in stony meadows at 3100–4200m, flowering in August and September. Stems 25–50cm. Leaves 4–10mm wide. Flowers 1.1–1.7cm long, 6–12 in an umbel. Easily grown in well-drained soil, moist and cool in summer.

Allium platycaule Wats. Native of S Oregon, W Nevada and N California south to Placer Co., growing on dry screes and gravelly hills at 1200–3000m, flowering in May to August. Recognised by its flat, falcate leaves, 8–15mm wide, flattened stem, and very narrow petals which first enclose the ovary and then spread like bristles. Photographed in N California in Lassen Co. in June.

Allium parciflorum Viv. Native of Corsica and Sardinia, on rocks by the sea among garrigue, flowering in July to September. Stems to 30cm, usually c.10cm. Leaves to 1mm wide, emerging in early winter. Spathe 2-valved. Flowering stem forming in spring, like *A. callimischon*. Close to *A. cupanii* which has fibrous, not thin and papery outer tunics, and a 1-valved spathe. Easily grown in a bulb frame, kept dry in summer.

Allium carolinianum DC. Native of Afghanistan to C Nepal, growing on stony slopes and screes at 3300–4800m, flowering in July and August. Stems 10–30cm. Leaves flattened, 8–12mm wide. For well-drained soil, moist in summer.

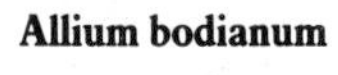

Allium bodianum

Allium narcissiflorum

Allium parciflorum

Allium carolinianum

Allium beesianum

Eremurus regelii in the Aktaş valley near Tashkent

Eremurus lactiflorus in the Chimgan valley

Eremurus lactiflorus

Eremurus olgae

Eremurus M. Bieb. (*Liliaceae*). The genus is found from Turkey (two spp.) eastwards to the Himalayas, with one species in China and the main concentration (forty-one spp.) in Central Asia. They usually grow on dry, stony, heavily grazed hillsides. The leaves. which are linear and triangular in section, appear in spring; they are not grazed, and so the plants often occur in huge numbers. The roots are long, thick and fleshy, spreading out from a central stock. In cultivation in northern Europe the plants should be grown in sandy soil and protected against late frosts and slugs. A pile of sharp sand or ash over the crowns will help them to survive the wet of winter. In summer after flowering they should be kept as dry as possible. Full sun is important while the leaves are green.

Eremurus cristatus Vved. Native of the western and central Tien Shan, flowering in May. One of the shortest species, about 60cm high in good conditions. Photographed in Tashkent Botanic Garden in April 1979.

Eremurus olgae Regel. Native of N Iran, N Afghanistan and Central Asia especially Tadjikistan, growing on stony hills at 1200–2500m, flowering from May to August. Height 70–100cm. Hybrids with other species are common in the wild, and the 'Shelford hybrids' often cultivated, were derived from *E. olgae* × *stenophyllus*. Photographed in Afghanistan by C. Grey-Wilson, G.-W. & Hewer 1251.

Eremurus stenophyllus (Boiss. & Buhse) Baker, syn. *E. bungei* Baker. Native of Central Asia, especially the Kopet Dağ, Iran (subsp. *stenophyllus*), Afghanistan, W Pakistan and the Pamir Alai (subsp. *aurantiacus* (Baker) Wendelbo), growing on stony slopes at c.2500m, flowering in June and July. Stem up to 150cm. Photographed in N Afghanistan, Hindu Kush, north of Kenjan, by C. Grey-Wilson.

Eremurus regelii Vved. Native of Central Asia, especially the western Tien Shan, and the western Pamir Alai, growing on earthy hillsides and rocky places at c.1000m, flowering in April and May. Height up to 180cm. Photographed NE of Tashkent, near Aktaş, in May 1980.

Eremurus lactiflorus O. Fedtsch. Native of the western Tien Shan, growing on screes and steep slopes at 1000–2000m, flowering in April and May. Stem 50–100cm. Capsules strongly inflated, c.3.5cm in diameter. Photographed in the Chimgan valley NE of Tashkent, in May 1980.

Eremurus cristatus

Eremurus olgae in the Elburz Mts above Qazvin

Eremurus stenophyllus in the Hindu Kush

Iris iberica subsp. **elegantissima** in the foothills of Mount Ararat, like discarded handkerchiefs

Iris iberica subsp. elegantissima

Iris iberica subsp. **elegantissima:** form with heavily veined standards

Oncocyclus Irises. So-called because they have a fleshy aril on the seed, these irises are all native of the Middle East from the Negev desert northwards to Turkey, Iran and Soviet Georgia. Most of the species in Israel, Lebanon, Syria and Jordan are frost-tender and need greenhouse treatment in north-west Europe and north-east USA, but do well in California or the warm desert areas of the south-west and here a special society, the Aril Society (see p.251) has been formed, devoted to their culture and preservation. The species from Turkey and Iran are hardy, surviving temperatures down to −20°C without damage, as they mostly come from high mountain steppes above 1800m. In cultivation however they require protection from rain from midsummer until mid-autumn and through the winter. Root growth begins in autumn, but often in the wild the soil is still dry when the cold of winter begins. The major growth period is in the spring months. In early summer the leaves begin to die off, but the long unbranched roots which survive the summer droughts are being formed. These hardy species should therefore grow well in the higher inland areas of California, especially east of the Sierras. Full sun is essential. Soils in the wild vary from the heaviest, stickiest clay which becomes rock-like in summer, to light pumice-like volcanic sandy soils. In cultivation a good mixture has proved to consist of burnt alkaline soil mixed with perlag or perlite and a little leafmould or peat. Feeding weekly during the growing season with high potash tomato fertiliser is beneficial.

Regelia irises, shown on the following page, require similar treatment. Hybrids between the two sections, so-called Regeliocyclus have been popular in the past.

Iris iberica Hoffm. subsp. **elegantissima** (Sosn.) Takht. & Federov, (*Iridaceae*). Native of NE Turkey from Erzurum eastwards, NW Iran, and Soviet Armenia, growing on grassy steppes and clay hills, often in uncultivated areas between cornfields at 1100–2250m, flowering in May and June. Height to 30cm. Very striking and conspicuous on the dry hills around Mount Ararat where the flowers are pollinated with great violence by huge black bee-like flies. One of the easiest species to grow in northwest Europe and from its habitat one of

Iris sari large form

Iris sari small form

the hardiest.

Subsp. **lycotis** (Woron.) Takht. differs in having standards equally heavily veined and stippled, and more horizontal, less strongly deflexed falls. It is found in SE Turkey near Yukşekova, in S. Armenia and southwards in Iran as far as the hills west of Isfahan. It usually grows on rocky slopes and low hills at 1470–3000m. The variety illustrated is a heavily veined form of subsp. *elegantissima* from NE of Erzurum. Similar forms are found near Erevan.

Iris barnumae Baker & Foster. Native of E Turkey, NW Iran and N Iraq, on dry stony slopes at 1300–2600m, flowering in May and June. This species is usually purple in colour, but is yellow in f. *urumiensis* (Hoog) Mathew & Wendelbo which is found around Lake Urmia (Reziayeh) in NW Iran and in one locality in adjacent SE Turkey. In f. *protonyma* (Stapf) Mathew & Wendelbo, also from around Lake Reziayeh, the standards are darker, and the falls smaller, more pointed and recurved, with a fine black beard. Source: SE Turkey near Van, Linzee Gordon 7108; f. *urumiensis* photographed at Wisley; f. *protonyma*, photographed by Brian Mathew.

Iris gatesii Foster. Native of SE Turkey, and N Iraq, growing among limestone rocks at 1000–2000m, flowering from April to June. This is the largest flowered of the Turkish species and is probably less hardy than those from the Anatolian plateau. Source: SE Turkey, Siirt, Watson et al. 1230.

Iris sari Schott ex Baker. Native of central and E Turkey from Cankiri and Erzurum, south to Gaziantep and Van, on steppes, low hills, oak scrub, and earthy places in mountains at 900–2700m, flowering from April to June. A variable species, especially in height. Forms from the west of the range are smaller, up to 20cm high, with pale brownish flowers, and are usually found on bare, steppe-like hills. From around Adiyaman, eastwards and usually in more rocky habitats, the plants are often taller, 20–30cm tall, broader leaves and more heavily marked blackish flowers. Source: tall form Rix 713; small form Rix 1594.

Iris barnumae forma **urumiensis**

Iris barnumae forma **protonyma**

Iris barnumae

Iris gatesii

Iris hoogiana

Iris hookeriana in Kashmir

Iris korolkovii

Iris stolonifera

Iris acutiloba C. A. Meyer subsp. **lineolata** (Trautv.) Mathew & Wendelbo (section *Oncocyclus*). Native of Armenia, Azerbaijan, N Iran and the Kopet Dağ, in dry fields, hills and bare mountainsides at 1500–3000m, flowering in April and May. One of the easiest and most floriferous species with pointed standards and falls in various shades of brown, yellowish or grey. Subsp. *acutiloba* from north of the Kura river in Soviet Georgia, has two spots on the falls. Source: Rix 879, from near Tabriz.

Iris hookerana Foster (section *Pseudoregelia*). Native of N Pakistan and Kashmir, in subalpine meadows and earthy slopes at 2400–4400m, flowering in April to July. Stems 5–10cm. Leaves 3–5mm wide. Should grow best in a sunny border with well-drained rich soil, rather dry in summer. Section *Pseudoregelia* have seeds with an aril, and form quite large clumps of upright leaves. Most are found in the drier parts of the Himalayas.

Iris hoogiana Dykes (section *Regelia*). Native of Central Asia, in the Pamir Alai, especially the Varsob valley N of Dushanbe, flowering in June. Stems to 60cm. Flowers 7–10cm across, scented. This is one of the easiest species to grow, forming large clumps, and growing outside at Kew in a sunny border, where the picture was taken. Continuously in cultivation since 1913.

Iris stolonifera Maxim. (section *Regelia*). Native of Central Asia, in the Pamir Alai, especially the Saravshan and Gissar ranges between Samarkhand and Dushanbe, at 800–2200m, flowering in May and June. In the Amankutan valley near Samarkhand this iris grows in rich earthy meadows on low hills, in soil which is very damp in spring. Flowering stems to 60cm: rhizomes, as the name suggests, producing long stolons. Source: Amankutan: collected by Inge Baker.

Iris afghanica Wendelbo (section *Regelia*). Native of Afghanistan especially on the N side of the Salang pass and northwards at 1300–3000m, flowering in May to June. The habitat is described as among limestone or granite rocks among other drought-resistant bulbs and grass. This is one of the best and easiest of the group to cultivate either in pots or in a bulb frame. The flowering stems may reach 35cm high. It is easily raised from seed. Source: Salang pass, Furse 5319.

Iris korolkovii Regel (section *Regelia*). Native of NE Afghanistan, and Central Asia in the Pamir Alai and Tien Shan, growing in rich valleys and on rocky slopes in open Juniper forest at 1500–3800m, flowering in May to June. Stems to 60cm. Leaves 5–10mm wide. Flowers variable in colour, purplish or creamy white, variously veined, 2 per stem. Source: Chimgan valley NE of Tashkent.

Iris meda Stapf (section *Oncocyclus*). Native of Iran from Mianeh to Golpaigan on stony hills, steppes and the edges of fields at 1300–2200m, flowering in April and May. A slender species which is in my experience more difficult to grow than most others. Source: hills above Qazvin, with *Eremurus olgae* (p. 173), Rix 883.

Iris paradoxa Steven (section *Oncocyclus*). Native of Soviet Armenia and probably Azerbaijan, growing on dry hills, flowering in May. This is the original form with dark purplish standards. Height about 20cm. Source: Erevan Botanic Gardens.

Iris paradoxa Steven forma **choschab** (Hoog) Mathew & Wendelbo. Native of E Turkey, NW Iran and S Azerbaijan, growing on dry hills at 1750–3000m, flowering in May and June. This is characterised by its white-blue-veined standards and small very furry falls. Height to 25cm. Source: near the town of Hoşap (Guzelsu) R. Macfarlane.

Iris afghanica

Iris meda

Iris paradoxa

Iris acutiloba subsp. **lineolata**

Iris paradoxa forma **choschab**

⅓ life size Photographed 28 April

Arum creticum ⅓ life size Photographed 17 April

Gladiolus italicus

Gladiolus atroviolaceus

(a) **Triteleia ixioides** (Ait. fil.) Greene (see p.137). Pedicel length can vary from 1.5 to 7cm.

(b), (c) **Zigadenus fremontii**, Torr. (*Liliaceae*). Native of California and S Oregon, growing on dry grassy slopes or in scrub, below 1000m, flowering March to May. Very variable. Inflorescence racemose to paniculate, petals 10–12mm long, stamens 5–7mm.

Rhodohypoxis baurii Nel. (*Hypoxidaceae*). Native of southern Africa in Natal and Lesotho, in the Drakensberg mountains growing in grassy peaty soil often on seeping rocks at 1500–3000m, flowering from October to December. Varying in colour from white to deep red and in selected cultivated forms flowers may be 3cm in diameter. Best grown in pots, kept rather dry in winter and protected from hard frost, and watered well in spring until after flowering. Otherwise can be planted out into a sink each spring and brought in in winter, or left out and given some protection from wet and frost.

Gladiolus imbricatus L. (*Iridaceae*). Native of central and eastern Europe from Germany to Greece and the Caucasus, and of Turkey, growing in wet meadows and marshes, flowering from May to July. Distinguished by its dense four to twelve-flowered spike, and obtuse lowest leaf. Flowers sometimes deep purple (cf. *G. atroviolaceus*). Photographed in the N Caucasus, 2000m, June 1980.

Gladiolus atroviolaceus Boiss. (*Iridaceae*). Native of E Turkey, Iraq, Iran and Soviet Armenia, growing in cornfields on dry hillsides, flowering from May to July. The dark flowered species growing in wet meadows, usually at high altitudes, has been distinguished as *G. kotschyanus* Boiss, or as a variety of *G. imbricatus*. Grows happily in a bulb frame, kept dry in summer. Photographed near Erevan, on dry hills, in May 1978.

Gladiolus illyricus Koch (*Iridaceae*). Native of south and west Europe from England southwards, and of the Mediterranean region, growing on heaths, in scrub and open woods, flowering from April to August. Very close to *G. communis*, but usually shorter, up to 50cm,

Gladiolus imbricatus

Gladiolus italicus

Gladiolus illyricus

Rhodohypoxis baurii ½ life size Photographed 6 June

Gladiolus × colvillei

with three to ten flowers on a rarely branched spike. Will naturalise itself in grass in southern England. Photographed by Oleg Polunin.

Gladiolus communis L. (*Iridaceae*). Native of southern Europe from Spain and France to Greece, Turkey and Iran (?), growing in fields and scrub, flowering from April to August. Flowers not all facing one way, not crowded, usually with ten to twenty flowers on the often branched spike. Photographed in the Peloponnese by Roger Philips.

Arum creticum Boiss. & Held (*Araceae*). Native of SW Turkey and of the islands of Crete, Samos, Rhodes and Karpathos, where it grows on stony hillsides. The leaves appear in autumn and the flowering stem which may be up to 40cm high appears in spring. Not likely to be confused with any other *Arum* because of its very loosely folded often recurved spathe. The spadix may be yellow (as illustrated) or dark purple, and the spathe white, yellow or green. Sweetly scented unlike other species. Easily cultivated, but probably better in a pot, protected from severe frost in winter and kept rather dry in summer. (See also p.192).

Gladiolus italicus Miller, syn. *G. segetum* Ker-Gawler (*Iridaceae*). A weed of cultivated land from France southwards to N Africa, and eastwards to Romania, Central Asia and Iran, flowering from March to July. Distinguished from other species by having anthers longer than the filaments. Photographed in Turkey near Ankara in May 1972.

Gladiolus × colvillei Sweet (*G. tristis* × *cardinalis*), syn. *G. nanus* hort. (*Iridaceae*). Various coloured hybrids have been derived from these two South African species, in shades of white, pink, crimson and mauve. They are only hardy in the mildest gardens in southern and western Britain. Photographed at Knightshayes, Devonshire.

Eminium intortum

Eminium intortum (Banks & Sol.) O. Kuntze (*Araceae*). Native of southern Turkey and Syria, growing in dry fields and stony places, flowering from March to May. Tuber almost spherical, with a white waxy powder. Has survived, but not grown well in a bulb frame. Photographed in Turkey, near Gaziantep, in May 1970.

The Sani Pass in the Natal Drakensberg

Hesperantha scopulosa

Hesperantha baurii

Gladiolus longicollis

Hesperantha baurii Baker (*Iridaceae*). Native of the Transvaal, Swaziland, Natal, Orange Free State, Transkei and Lesotho, growing in moist grassland at up to 2450m, flowering in January and February. Stems to 60cm, usually c.30cm with 5–15 flowers, opening in the afternoon. This should grow well in moist peaty soil in full sun, and collections from high altitudes should be frost hardy. Photographed on the Sani pass in Natal in January, at 2000m.

Hesperantha scopulosa Hilliard & Burtt. Native of Natal, at 1500–2200m in the Drakensberg, growing in rock crevices and in shallow peaty soil on the tops of cliffs, usually in the shade, flowering in January and February. Stem 5–25cm. Flowers 43–63mm long, opening in the morning. A dwarf species for alpine house cultivation in sandy peaty soil, moist in summer, rather dry in winter. Photographed near Cathedral Peak in early February.

Gladiolus oppositifolius Herbert subsp. **salmoneus** (Baker) Oberm. Native of the NE Cape and S Natal, growing in moist, rocky, mountain grassland, at up to 2500m, flowering in January to March. A showy species with flowers up to 10cm long, on stems up to 1.5m tall. For ordinary garden soil, moist in summer. Photographed near Barkly Pass in NE Cape Province in late January.

Gladiolus longicollis Baker. Native of the NE Cape, Natal, the Orange Free State and Lesotho, growing on moist grassy slopes at up to 3300m, flowering in October to December, and at other times through the summer. Flowers scented in the evening, with a long tube up to 12cm; stems 40–80cm, with 1–3 flowers. Close to the more familiar, winter-flowering *G. tristis* L., but coming from much colder districts and being summer-growing, this species should be hardier.

Gladiolus crassifolius Baker (*Iridaceae*). Native of the E Cape, Natal, Orange Free State and Transvaal, as well as in Lesotho, Swaziland, and Zimbabwe, growing in grassland from near sea level to 2500m, flowering in February to April. A very variable species, with flowers from pink to purple or orange. The yellow lines on the

Gladiolus oppositifolius subsp. **salmoneus**

Gladiolus ecklonii subsp. **ecklonii**

Gladiolus crassifolius

leaves are characteristic, as is the bent flowering stem. For well-drained, rather dry but peaty soil. Photographed in the N Drakensberg near Witsieshoek at 2300m in February.

Gladiolus ecklonii Lehm. subsp. **ecklonii.** Native of the NE Cape north to E Transvaal, along the Drakensberg, on grassy slopes at up to 2300m, flowering in February and March. A short, stout species, up to 60cm, with leaves to 3cm broad, and flowers c.5cm long, white speckled with red or purple. Good, well-drained soil. The leaves are hardy to −4°C, the bulbs probably hardier if kept dry in winter. Photographed on the Sani Pass at c.1800m in February.

Gladiolus microcarpus Lewis. Native of Natal, in the high Drakensberg from Cathedral Peak to Mont-aux-Sources, growing in rock crevices and along the tops of cliffs at 1800–2700m, flowering in January and February. A beautiful species, described as recently as 1972, with long-tubed flowers with acuminate segments, and minute hairs on the nerves of the leaves. Should be one of the hardier species, for a well-drained crevice in peaty, sandy soil, wet in summer, dry in winter. Photographed near Witsieshoek in February.

Gladiolus callianthus W. Marais syn. *Acidanthera bicolor* Hoch., *A. murielae* Hoog (*Iridaceae*). Native of the mountains of East Africa from Ethiopia and Somalia to Tanzania and Malawi, growing in grassland, on wet rocks and cliffs, at 1200–2500m, flowering in December to April in the southern, in July to August in the northern hemisphere. Stems leaning or upright, to 2m. Flowers with tube up to 18cm long, often with a deep purple blotch in the throat, scented at night, and pollinated in the wild by long-tongued hawk moths. The corms are not hardy, but will survive outside in mild climates or if protected from freezing. Photographed on the Zomba plateau in Malawi in January. (In climates where deep frost is common, the corms can be lifted and stored for the winter, and the cormlets detached and grown on. During the growing season it requires plenty of warmth and water.)

Gladiolus microcarpus near Mont-aux-Sources, Natal

Gladiolus callianthus on Zomba mountain, Malawi

Dierama pulcherrimum at Mount Usher, Co. Wicklow, Ireland

Dierama pulcherrimum

Dierama reynoldsii

Dierama dracomontanum Hilliard & Burtt (*Iridaceae*). Native of South Africa in the Drakensberg from S Transvaal and Orange Free State, through Natal to NE Cape Province, in mountain grassland at up to 3000m, flowering in January and February. Plant forming low tufts with stems up to 50cm. Flowers usually reddish-pink, conic with petals curving outward from the base, c.2.5cm long. Easily grown in well-drained soil, and hardy to −10°C and lower. Photographed at c.2000m on the Sani Pass, Natal.

Dierama medium N.E.Br. Native of S Transvaal, Natal and Swaziland, growing in grassland at around 1500m, flowering in December and January. Stems 60–90cm, not densely tufted. Leaves very narrow. Flowers c.2.5cm long. For a warm, well-drained position in full sun. Hardy to −10°C, perhaps.

Dierama pulcherrimum (Hook. fil.) Baker. Native of E Cape Province, Natal and Transvaal, growing in rich damp meadows, flowering in September and October. Stems clump-forming, to 2m. Flowers purple to red, rarely white, about 3cm long. Hardy to −10°C, requiring well-drained but rich peaty soil. Even if the normally evergreen leaves are killed by frost, the corms, if planted deeply, will survive. In the wild, they would regularly be killed by bush fires in early spring, and soon regenerate. Photographed at Mount Usher, Co. Wicklow, Ireland.

'Plover' Leslie Slinger of Slieve Donard Nurseries, Co. Down, N Ireland, raised numerous named varieties in the 1950s, by selection of seedlings of *D. pulcherrimum*. These varied in colour from white to pale pink and purple, but apparently no other species were involved in their breeding. They were named after birds; sadly only a few of his varieties are still grown. Later a dwarfer race was produced, using a dwarf species, possibly *D. dracomontanum*: these were named after Shakespearean fairies. All these thrive in moist but well-drained soil in full sun, and are happiest in the warmer parts of the British Isles, and in damp climates where frosts are of short duration.

Dierama reynoldsii Verd. Native of Transkei, NE Cape Province and SW Natal, growing in grassland in heavy clay soil, at c.1800m, flowering in October to January. Stems to 1.75m, not tufted. Bracts very silvery. Flowers 2–4cm long, deep purplish. Hardy to −10°C, perhaps.

Dierama robustum N.E. Br. Native of the Drakensberg mountains in Natal and NE Cape Province, growing in moist peaty grassland and rocky places at 2000–3000m, flowering in January and February. Stems to 2m, forming large clumps. Flowers pale pink and mauve to white, c.4cm long. Photographed on Naude's Nek, NE Cape Province in February. From its habitat this should be one of the hardier species.

Dierama dracomontanum

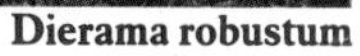

Dierama robustum

Dierama robustum

Dierama dracomontanum on the Sani Pass, Natal

Dierama medium on Ngeli Mountain, Natal

⅓ life size Photographed 29 May

(a) Gladiolus communis L. subsp. **byzantinus** (Miller) A. P. Hamilton (*Iridaceae*). Native of S Spain, Sicily and N Africa. A form of it with magenta-crimson flowers is commonly cultivated. It requires a very warm sunny position. Subsp. *communis* see p.179.

(b) Moraea huttonii (Baker) Obermeyer (*Iridaceae*). Native of S Africa, from the NE Cape, through the Drakensberg, where it is common, to the SE Transvaal, growing in clumps on rocks in the middle and on the edges of streams, at up to 2600m, flowering from October to December. Easily cultivated in well-drained, peaty soil: hardy, but the evergreen leaves are killed by frosts below −10°C. Distinguished from the similar *M. spathulata* (L. Fil.) Klatt (syn. *M. spathacea* Ker) by the purplish blotch on the style crests.

(c) Iris 'Wedgwood'. This is the commonest of the 'Dutch' Irises, and much used for forcing. Derived from crosses between *I. xiphium* L. and *I. tingitana* Boiss. & Reut. Colour ranges from purple and blue to white, yellow, bronze and apricot. Best lifted and dried after flowering, before replanting in early autumn.

(d), (e) Nectaroscordum siculum (Ucria) Lindley (*Liliaceae*). Native of southern Europe from France eastwards to Bulgaria and the Crimea and Turkey, growing in damp shady woods, flowering in May. The plants from Italy westwards have dull greenish-red flowers (subsp. *siculum*) (e), those in Turkey, Bulgaria eastwards (subsp. *bulgaricum* (Janka) Stearn) have whitish flowers shaded with green and pink (d). Both are easily grown in light soil in sun or half-shade.

(f) Allium karataviense Regel (see p. 163).

(g) Allium giganteum Regel (*Liliaceae*). Native of Iran, Afghanistan, and Central Asia in Turkomania and the Pamir Alai, growing on gentle slopes at low altitudes, up to 1200m, flowering in April and May. The leaves are glaucous, 5–10cm wide, and the obtuse petals are 5–6mm long. The very similar *A. macleanii* Baker (= *A. elatum* Regel) differs in its shining green leaves, rather shorter ridged stalk, small umbel and longer (6–7mm), subacute tepals. Easily grown in well-drained soil in full sun, and useful for the herbaceous border.

(h) Iris 'Professor Blaauw'. One of the darkest flowered of the 'Dutch' Irises, this variety was raised from *Iris tingitana* Boiss. & Reut. var. *fontanesii* (Gordon) Maire, collected in Morocco.

(i) Arum italicum Miller (*Araceae*). Found throughout south and west Europe and N Africa in hedges and rocky places, often among old walls. The leaves appear in autumn, the flowers in spring. Very variable and may be divided into four subspecies. Subsp. *italicum* shown here has beautifully white-veined leaves which make it a good garden plant; individuals can be found with even more marbling than shown here. This subspecies is often called 'Pictum' or *marmoratum*. The other subspecies do not have marbled leaves. Subsp. *neglectum*, native to southern England, at the foot of the chalk downs, and W Europe, has a flowering stem shorter than the leaves and a greenish-yellow spathe. Subsp. *albispathum* from the Crimea and SW Asia has a spathe pure white inside, and subsp. *byzantinum* from Greece, Turkey and Crete has taller flowering stem and a green spathe marked with purple. Easily grown in sun or dry shade.

⅓ life size Photographed 6 June

Iris latifolia, pale form

Iris latifolia (Miller) Voss, syn. *I. xiphioides* Ehrh., English Iris (section *xiphion*). Native of the Pyrenees and Cantabrian mountains of northern Spain, growing in damp meadows, flowering in June and July. Flowers larger than the other species of section *xiphion*, with longer falls, 60–75mm. Stem 25–50cm. Flowers in cultivation blue and violet to white. Grows well in any good garden soil. Photographed naturalised in long grass at Great Dixter, Sussex.

Iris latifolia

Watsonia latifolia at Hawkfall Nursery, Natal

Watsonia latifolia

Watsonia beatricis

Watsonia ardernei Sander (*Iridaceae*). Native of S Africa in Cape Province, at Roman River in the Tulbagh district, growing on wet sandy flats, flowering in September to November. Stems around 1m. Well-known in cultivation but found once only in the wild, growing among *W. wordsworthiana* Mathews & L. Bolus, but differing from that in other characters as well as colour. Hardy only to c. −5°C.

Watsonia beatricis Mathews & L. Bolus. Native of Cape Province in the Outeniqua Mts near Knysna, flowering in December and January. Stem to 1.2m, unbranched. Basal leaves to 3cm wide. Perianth tube c.5cm, lobes to 2.5cm. For moist but well-drained soil. Hardy to −10°C perhaps. Photographed at Mount Usher, Co. Wicklow, Ireland, in July.

Watsonia densiflora Baker. Native of Transvaal, Natal and the Orange Free State, growing on rocky, grassy, usually N-facing slopes at up to 2100m, flowering in January and February. Clump-forming, with stems to 1m. Flowers with tube 2.5cm, lobes c.1.8cm long. For a hot well-drained position. Hardy to −10°C.

Moraea robusta (Goldblatt) Goldblatt (*Iridaceae*). Native of the N Transkei, SE Lesotho, S Orange Free State and SE Transvaal, growing on moist grassy slopes in the mountains at 2000–2500m, flowering in October to November and occasionally to February. Distinguished by its pale yellow flowers, the inner petals with a spreading limb, 40mm long; outer petals 5.5–6.5cm long. Photographed below the Sentinel, near Mont-aux-Sources, C.D. & R. 269.

Watsonia socium Mathews & L. Bolus. Native of the Drakensberg and nearby mountains in Natal and the NE Cape, growing on rocky slopes, often in shallow soil on sandstone at up to 2400m, flowering in November to January. Plant tufted; stems to 50cm. Flowers c.5cm long. For well-drained soil, moist in summer. Hardy to −10°C, perhaps. Photographed on the Sani Pass, Natal: C.D. & R.62.

Watsonia species still unnamed. Native of the Drakensberg in Natal and nearby mountains, growing in damp grassland at up to 2400m, flowering in January to February. Stems to 70cm. Differs from *W. densiflora* which occurs in the same area, in its shorter stems, flower spikes only slightly longer than the leaves, and earlier flowering. Photographed in C Natal on Ngeli Mtn.

Watsonia latifolia Oberm. Native of SW Transvaal, N Natal and Swaziland, growing in grassland among rocks, flowering in February and March. Stem to 1.5m. Plant tufted; leaves 30–90 × 4–9cm. Flowers 6–8cm long. For rich, peaty soil. Deciduous in winter. Hardy to −10°C, perhaps. A very striking and elegant plant. Photographed at Hawkfall Nursery, Himeville, Natal.

Watsonia unnamed species

Watsonia ardernei at Logan Botanic Garden, Scotland

Watsonia socium

Moraea robusta

Watsonia densiflora near Nottingham Road, Natal

½ life size Photographed 29 May

Arisaema consanguineum

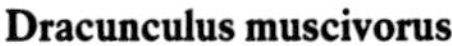

Dracunculus muscivorus

Arisaema consanguineum

Sauromattum venosum

(a), (c) **Arisaema triphyllum** (L.) Schott (*Araceae*). Native of most of eastern N America, west to Manitoba, growing in moist woods and bogs, flowering from mid May to early July. The flowers are followed by beautiful shining red berries in a cylindrical cluster. Shown here a small form from New Hampshire. Easily grown in moist leafy soil in shade.

(b) **Arisaema ringens** (Thunb.) Schott (*Araceae*). Native of China, S Korea and Japan especially the islands of Honshu, Shikoku and Kyushu where it grows in woods near the sea, flowering from March to May. The strange contorted spathe and the tapering tips of the tripartite leaves are characteristic of the species. Forma *praecox* T. Koyama has a plain greenish spathe, and forma *sieboldii* a plain purplish one. Probably one of the hardier species. Grown in leafy soil in shade, kept moist in summer.

Arisaema consanguineum Schott. (*Araceae*). Native of the Himalayas from NW India to Thailand, C China and Taiwan, in scrub and semi-deciduous forest at 1800–3000m, flowering in May to June. Stem to 100cm. Leaves with 11–20 very narrow leaflets, tapering to a hair-like point. Hardy to −10°C. Photographed near Lijiang, Yunnan in May, a green form, and in Baoxing, a striped form.

Dracunculus muscivorus (L. fil.) Parl. syn. *Helicodisceros crinitus* Schott (*Araceae*). Native of the Balearic Islands, Corsica and Sardinia, growing in scrub and grassy places near the sea, flowering in April to May. Stem 30–45cm. Leaves divided into around 10–15 segments; stems spotted. Smelling of bad meat. Probably hardy to −5°C only, and best in an alpine house or outside in a mild climate.

Sauromattum venosum (Aiton) Kunth syn. *S. guttatum* Schott (*Araceae*). Native of NW India to C Nepal and SE Tibet, on stony slopes in hot valleys at 1000–2300m, flowering in March to May. Spathe variable in the amount of blotching. A single leaf appears in late summer, with 9–11 unequal leaflets. This is sometimes sold as a wonder plant which will flower without soil or water if placed in a warm room or on an office desk. Hardy to −5°C perhaps.

Hedychium densiflorum 'Stephen'

Hedychium densiflorum

Oxalis pes-caprae

Hedychium spicatum

Hedychium densiflorum 'Assam Orange'

Cautleya spicata 'Robusta'

Hedychium densiflorum Wallich (*Zinziberaceae*). Native of the Himalayas from Nepal, east to Bhutan and Assam, growing on grassy slopes and in *Rhododendron* and evergreen oak forest at 2000–2750m, flowering in July to September. Stems to 1.5m. Flowers scented in spikes around 25cm long. '**Assam Orange**' was collected by Kingdon Ward in 1938, and has proved to be a good hardy clone. '**Stephen**' is a large clone with pale orange-yellow flowers, collected by Tony Schilling. Hardy to −10°C or thereabouts, with the rhizomes covered in winter.

Hedychium spicatum Smith (*Zinziberaceae*). Native of the Himalayas from NW India east to Yunnan, in open places in forest and in scrub at 1800–2800m, flowering in July and August. Clump forming with stems to 150cm. Flowers scented in a spike 15–25cm long. Some collections of this species are the hardiest of the hedychiums, and survive outside in most parts of S England and the warmer parts of the eastern United States without difficulty, especially if the rhizomes are covered with dry peat or leaves in autumn.

Cautleya spicata (Smith) Baker '**Robusta**' (*Zinziberaceae*). Native of the Himalayas from NE India to Sikkim, growing in scrub and among rocks, and sometimes even epiphytic, at 1800–2800m, flowering in July to September. Stems to 60cm, forming spreading clumps.

Oxalis depressa

Oxalis laciniata

Roscoea cautleyoides

Roscoea humeana

Roscoea alpina

Oxalis enneaphylla

Bracts red and flowers orange-yellow, not scented. The cultivar 'Robusta' is an extra large form, common in cultivation. Hardy to −10°C, and lower if the rhizomes are protected in winter.

Oxalis pes-caprae L. (*Oxalidaceae*). Native of the SW of Cape Province of S Africa, but naturalised as a weed in Australia, California, Mediterranean Europe and SW England, flowering in June to October in the southern, February to April in the northern hemisphere. Stems 10–18cm, with bulbils produced at the soil surface. Hardy only to about −5°C.

Roscoea alpina Royle (*Zingiberaceae*.) Native of the Himalayas from Kashmir to Sikkim up to 3500m, growing on rocky slopes, flowering in June and July. The flowers open one at a time and the plant is up to 20cm high. Photographed in Garhwal, near Pindari glacier, by Oleg Polunin.

Roscoea humeana Balfour fil. & W. W. Smith (*Zingiberaceae*). Native of China in Szechuan and Yunnan, growing on grassy slopes at up to 3800m, flowering from May to July. Stems up to 60cm. The roots are very fleshy and should be planted at least 15cm deep in well-drained, leafy or peaty soil. Photographed in cultivation by Valerie Finnis.

Roscoea cautleyoides Gagnep. (*Zingiberaceae*). Native of western China, especially the SW Yunnan. The flowers may be yellow or purple. The roots are very fleshy and should be planted about 15cm deep, in well-drained, leafy or peaty soil. Photographed in cultivation by Valerie Finnis.

Oxalis laciniata Cav. (*Oxalidaceae*). Native of Patagonia, growing on grassy screes. The flowers vary in colour from pale blue to deep reddish mauve. Rhizomes fleshy, worm-like. Grows best in light shade in peaty soil. There is an attractive hybrid between this species and *O. enneaphylla*. Photographed in cultivation by Valerie Finnis.

Oxalis enneaphylla Cav. (*Oxalidaceae*.) Native of the Falkland Isles and S. Chile, growing on heathland and sandy places especially near the sea. Flowers varying from pink to white. The rather similar *Oxalis adenophylla* has less deeply lobed leaflets and often two- or three-flowered stems. Easily grown in a sunny spot in sandy peaty soil. Photographed by Brinsley Burbridge.

Oxalis depressa Eckl. & Zeyh. syn. *O. inops* Eckl. & Zeyh. (*Oxalidaceae*). Native of S Africa, growing in sandy places near the sea, flowering from February to September. It has a small tuberous rootstock. Easy to grow in a sunny place, and reported to be hardy in southern England, but can become a weed. Photographed in cultivation by Valerie Finnis.

Arum palaestinum

¼ life size Photographed 12 July

Arisarum vulgare

Arum palaestinum Boiss. (*Araceae*). Native of Syria, Lebanon and Israel, growing on shady rocks and walls, flowering in April. Close to *A. dioscoridis*, but reputed to be sweet smelling, and spathe always unspotted. Probably requires protection from extremes of cold and wet. Photographed in Lebanon by Oleg Polunin.

Arisarum vulgare Targ-Tozz. (*Araceae*). Native of the Mediterranean region and Portugal, flowering from March to May, growing in rocky places. The leaves appear in autumn and are not very hardy, so the plant is better kept in the alpine house or in a warm frame. Photographed by Brinsley Burbidge.

(a) **Zantedeschia aethiopica** (L.) Sprengel (*Araceae*). Arum Lily. Native of South Africa from the Cape to the Drakensberg mountains, growing in wet marshy places flowering in spring. It varies greatly in its hardiness, but some forms, notably 'Crowborough' p.119, seem to be quite hardy in eastern England, especially if planted deep or below water level in which situation they flower in summer.

(b) **Arisaema tortuosum** (Wall.) Schott (*Araceae*). Native of the Himalayas from the Punjab to Sikkim, W China and Manipur, growing in forests at 1300–2900m, flowering from April to July, sometimes before the beginning of the rains.

Dracunculus vulgaris Schott (*Araceae*). Native of the Mediterranean region from Sardinia and Sicily eastwards to S Bulgaria, Greece and S Turkey, growing in scrub and rocky places, flowering in April. Naturalised in S France and Portugal; a most beautiful white form is found on Crete. *Dracunculus muscivorus* (L. fil.) Parl., see page 188, grows in Corsica, Sardinia and the Balearic Islands. Neither is reliably hardy in cold winters, but is easy to grow under a warm wall, and often produces numerous small tubers around the parent. Photographed in Crete by Brinsley Burbidge.

Dracunculus vulgaris

Arum conophalloides var. **virescens**

Arum dioscoridis var. liepoldtii

Eminium albertii

Arum conophalloides Kotschy var. **virescens** (Stapf) Engler (*Araceae*). Native of Turkey and N Iran, growing on rocky slopes at up to 2000m, flowering from April to June. This grew well in cultivation for a few years but then disappeared. Photographed in Turkey, Van, near Gevaş, in June 1968.

Arum dioscoridis Sibth. & Sm. var. **liepoldtii** (Schott) Engler (*Araceae*). Native of southern Turkey, from Chios and Rhodes south to Cyprus, Lebanon and Syria, where it grows in hedges and rocky places, flowering in April and May. Leaves emerging in winter from a large rounded tuber. The spathe may vary in colour from almost black as shown here, to yellowish spotted with black at the base. Smells like bad meat. Easy to cultivate under a warm wall or in a bulb frame. Photographed in Lebanon by Oleg Polunin.

Eminium albertii Regel (*Araceae*). Native of Central Asia, especially the Tien Shan and the Pamir Alai, growing on earthy and rocky slopes, flowering from April to June. Will probably grow best in a bulb frame, kept dry in summer. Photographed in Tashkent Botanic Garden in May 1980.

A view of the Himalayas in Sikkim; in the foreground *Rhododendron falconeri*

Lilium polyphyllum

Arisaema concinnum

Arisaema griffithii

Arisaema jacquemontii

Arisaema speciosum

Arisaema propinquum

Arisaema candidissimum

Lilium polyphyllum Royle (*Liliaceae*). Native of the western Himalayas, from Kumaon and Kashmir to Afghanistan, growing on steep grassy slopes and cliffs and forest from 2000 to 4000m, flowering in June and July. Not easy to grow, although quite common in the wild. Photographed in Kashmir near Trunkal by Oleg Polunin.

Arisaema concinnum Schott (*Araceae*). Native of the central and eastern Himalayas from Nepal to Bhutan, growing in clearings in forest from 2400 to 2700m, flowering in April and May. Hardy if well protected by snow or loose leaves. Photographed in Sikkim near Bakhim by Oleg Polunin.

Arisaema speciosum (Wall.) Mart. (*Araceae*) Native of the eastern Himalaya from Nepal to NE India, N Assam and W China, growing in forest at 2300–3500m, flowering from April to June. Photographed in Sikkim near Pemayangtse by Oleg Polunin.

Arisaema jacquemontii Blume (*Araceae*). Native of the Himalayas from Afghanistan to Bhutan, N Assam and SE Tibet, growing on grassy slopes and in open forest from 2700 to 4000m, flowering in June. Probably the hardiest of the Himalayan species. Photographed near Gagaria by Oleg Polunin.

Arisaema griffithii Schott. Native of the eastern Himalayas, growing in forests at around 2500m, flowering in April and May. Photographed in Sikkim by Oleg Polunin.

Arisaema propinquum Schott, (*Araceae*). Native of the Himalayas from Kashmir to Bhutan and S Tibet, growing at 2500–3800m, flowering in May and June. Hardy if well protected by dry leaves in winter. Photograhed in Sikkim by Oleg Polunin.

Arisaema candidissimum W. W. Smith (*Araceae*). Native of western China, especially NW Yunnan and SW Szechuan, growing on steep shady slopes or in open pine forest, flowering in June. The spathe may be pink or white. Although the habitat appears dry, the soil is always wet underneath, and summer drought is probably very harmful to this species. Grows best in leafy soil in shade or half-shade. Photographed in cultivation by Valerie Finnis.

(a) **Arisarum proboscoideum** (L.) Savi, 'Mouse Plant' (*Araceae*). Native of southern Italy and south-west Spain where it grows in woods and shady places. Forms dense patches of leaves under which the mouse-like inflorescences are hidden. Hardy and easy to grow in shade.

(b) **Fritillaria camschatcensis** (L.) Ker-Gawler (*Liliaceae*). Native of western N America from Washington northwards to Alaska, along the Kurile Islands and into Kamschatka and northern Japan, growing in moist open woods, in subalpine meadows up to 1800m (in Japan) and grassy places near the sea, flowering in June and July. Very variable in size, and flower colour from purplish to green and black. Grows best in moist peaty soil and a partial shade, never allowed to become dry.

(c) **Arisaema sikokianum** Fr. & Savi (*Araceae*). Native of Japan, especially the islands of Honshu, Sikoku and Kyushu, growing in woods, flowering in May and June. The very blunt club-shaped spadix and three to five parted leaves are characteristic. Said to be hardy and easily grown, but although introduced in 1938 is very rarely seen in English gardens. A loose leafy soil in shade would be suitable.

½ life size Photographed 14 May

Lilium bakerianum var. **delavayanum** near Lijiang, Yunnan

Lilium lophophorum near Lijiang, Yunnan

Lilium souliei

Lilium souliei Franch. syn. *Nomocharis souliei* (Franch.) W.W. Sm. & Evans. Native of W China in SE Xizang and NW Yunnan, in wet alpine meadows and in scrub at 3000–4300m, flowering in June and July. Stems up to 40cm. Flowers scented, about 3cm long. For cool, well-drained soil, moist in summer. Photographed in W China by Chris Grey-Wilson.

Lilium bakerianum Collett & Hemsley var. **delavayanum** (Franch.) E.H. Wilson. Native of W Yunnan, on dry, rocky, often limestone slopes among boulders and scrub at 2500–3500m, flowering in July. Var. *bakerianum*, found at up to 1800m in Nepal, N Burma and W China, is taller, with up to 6 flowers, and petals white with reddish spots inside, recurved at their tips. Var. *delavayanum* is a dwarf, alpine variety with up to 3 flowers on stems to 20cm. For well-drained soil, moist in summer, dryish in winter. Photographed in W China by Chris Grey-Wilson.

Lilium lophophorum Franch., syn. *Fritillaria lophophora* (Bur. & Franch.) Balf. fil. Native of W China, in SE Xizang, NW Yunnan and W Sichuan, in alpine meadows and on the edges of forest on limestone at 3800–4500m, flowering in June to August. Stem to 15cm. Flowers rarely 2, sometimes spotted with red inside. Not difficult to grow in well-drained, peaty soil, but has proved shy-flowering. Photographed in W China by Chris Grey-Wilson.

Lilium nanum Klotzsch, syn. *Nomocharis nana* (Klotzsch) E.H. Wilson. Native of the Himalayas from Garhwal east to Bhutan and W Yunnan, on open grassy, rocky hillsides, among dwarf *Rhododendron* scrub, at 3300–4500m, flowering in June to August. Stems to 15cm; flowers spotted inside, purplish to pinkish. For peaty, well-drained soil, moist and cool in summer. This species grows well in cool climates such as Scotland, but dislikes warm summer weather. Photographed in Sikkim by Brian Mathew.

Nomocharis pardanthina Franchet (incl. *N. mairei* Leveille) *Liliaceae*. Native of the E Himalayas in Yunnan and Sichuan, often on rather dry limestone slopes, in clearings in pine forest or bamboo scrub, and in alpine meadows, at 3000–4000m, flowering from May to July. Stem to 1.1m, with up to 8 flowers, 5–9cm, rarely to 12cm across. Grows best on well-drained, N-facing slopes in a cool climate such as Scotland, in leafy or peaty, well-drained soil. This is the plant usually grown as *N. mairei* Lev., but it has lately been recognised that it was the heavily spotted form that Franchet called *N. pardanthina*.

Nomocharis pardanthina Franch. forma **punctulata** Sealy. This is the form formerly considered typical *N. pardanthina*, with white or pale pink flowers finely spotted only near the centre. A pure white form is also known.

Nomocharis saluenensis Balfour. Native of SW China in Yunnan, W Sichuan and SE Xizang in scrub and moist alpine meadows at 2800–4000m, flowering in July to September. Stem to 1m, with up to 5 flowers, rarely white, pale yellow or 'rose-scarlet'. Cultivation as for *N. pardanthina*.

Nomocharis pardanthina forma **punctulata** at Kildrummy Castle Garden, Aberdeenshire

Nomocharis pardanthina

Lilium nanum

Nomocharis saluenensis

Notholirion bulbiferum in the Savill Garden, Windsor

Lilium alexandrae

Lilium sargentiae

Notholirion bulbiferum (Lingels.) Stearn syn. *N. hyacinthinum* (Wilson) Stapf (*Liliaceae*). Native of Nepal, eastwards to W China in Shensi, and Gansu, growing in alpine meadows at 3000–3750m, flowering in June and July. Stem 60–100cm, to 150cm in gardens. Flowers 2–4cm long. For deep, rich soil, in semi-shade. *N. campanulatum* Cotton & Stearn, differs in its deep reddish-purple bells.

Lilium alexandrae (Wallace) Coutts (*Liliaceae*). Native of the Liukiu Islands, Ukishima and Kawanabe, growing in humus-filled pockets in coral rocks. This area has a warm, wet and frost-free climate. A rare species for a greenhouse or Florida-like climate.

Lilium sargentiae Wilson. Native of China, in W Sichuan, especially around Kangding, at 600–1500m, growing in scrub, usually on shale in leafy soil, with good drainage and heavy rainfall in summer. Stems to 1.5m, with scattered narrowly oblong leaves with bulbils in their axils. Flowers 2–5, or up to 18 in cultivation, scented, 12–15cm long. Requires a warm growing season with an alkaline or neutral soil, and reported to be very susceptible to botrytis.

Lilium henrici Franch., syn. *Nomocharis henrici* (Franch.) E.H. Wilson. The specimen shown here growing in Edinburgh Botanic Garden is more typical than that on p.210. True *Nomocharis* is now restricted to those species with greatly flattened anther filaments. *L. henrici* is confined to W Yunnan, on the mountains either side of the Salween valley, flowering in July and August.

Cardiocrinum cordatum (Thunb.) Mak., syn. *Lilium cordatum* (Thunb.) Koidz. (*Liliaceae*). Native of S Honshu, Shikoku and Kyushu, with var. *glehnii* (F. Schmidt) Hara in N Honshu, Hokkaido and Sakhalin growing in moist woods of conifers, oaks and bamboos, flowering in July and August. Stem to 1.5m. Leaves in a whorl on lower part of stem, as wide as long; flowers zygomorphic. Usually with 4–10 flowers, or up to 20 in var. *glehnii*. For moist leafy soil; hardy but the new shoots need protection from late frost.

Cardiocrinum giganteum (Wall.) Mak. var. **yunnanense** (Elwes) Stearn. Native of W and C China in Yunnan and Sichuan, in woods, scrub and grassy gullies in gorges at c.2500m, flowering in May and June. The commonly cultivated form has bronze-purple stems, leaves and young shoots, and probably originated from near Dali in NW Yunnan. The other form shown here, growing in Sichuan, was more slender, and often without purple leaves.

Cardiocrinum giganteum in Sichuan

Cardiocrinum giganteum var. **yunnanense**

Lilium henrici

Cardiocrinum cordatum in Edinburgh Botanic Garden

Lilium grayi in Edinburgh Botanic Garden

Lilium maritimum

Lilium occidentale near Brooking in north California

Lilium grayi S. Wats. (*Liliaceae*). Native of Virginia south to N Carolina and Tennessee, and reported from the Roan Mts of SE Utah, in moist lime-free soil among shrubs and in open woods, flowering in June and July. Stem to 1.5m. Flowers 4–4.5cm long, always red outside, sometimes yellowish inside. Photographed on the peat banks at Edinburgh Botanic Garden, growing among dwarf shrubs in peaty well-drained soil.

Lilium maritimum Kell. Native of NW California, from Marin Co. to Mendocino Co., in the drier parts of bogs and in the undergrowth of open woods, on moist, sandy soil near the coast, flowering in May to July. Stems to 120cm. Flowers 1-6, 3–4cm long. Photographed in the Krause Rhododendron Reserve in late May.

Lilium occidentale Purdy. Native of NW California in Humboldt Co. and S Oregon, in scrub, dry bogs and by streams, among ferns, sphagnum moss, azaleas etc, in sandy peaty soil, near the coast, flowering in June and July. Stem to 180cm, with narrowly oblanceolate, whorled leaves. Flowers up to 10, with petals 3.5–5.5cm long. A graceful species, not often cultivated, requiring moist but well-drained, peaty soil. Photographed by Derek Fox near Brooking, California, growing among *Spiraea douglasii*.

Lilium michiganense Farwell. Native of Michigan and Minnesota, south to Missouri and Kentucky west of the Allegheny Mts, in meadows and prairies, surviving though seldom flowering in woods. Stems to 1.5m, with up to 6 flowers. This lily is said to be lime-tolerant and requires full sun, unlike its close relatives *L. canadense* and *L. superbum*, which require moist acid soil, and tolerate some shade.

Lilium washingtonianum Kell. var. **purpurascens** Stearn. This variety of *L. washingtonianum* (p.209), is found in chaparral of *Arctostaphylos* and *Ceanothus*, and on open slopes at 800–1800m in NW California and

Lilium washingtonianum var. **purpurascens**

Lilium catesbaei

Lilium pardalinum in Quarry Wood, Berkshire

Lilium pardalinum

Lilium michiganense

Lilium vollmeri

Lilium canadense var. **rubrum**

Oregon northwards to Mt Hood, flowering in July. It differs from the normal variety in its broader inner petals and flowers which open white or pinkish, turning deep purple as they fade. Difficult to grow, requiring well-drained but deep soil, rather dry in summer. Photographed by Derek Fox.

Lilium catesbaei Walter (*Liliaceae*). Native of Florida, Louisiana, S Carolina, SE Virginia and S Illinois, in marshes or open places in pine woods. Stems to 60cm; leaves scattered. Flowers to 23cm across. For moist peaty and sandy soil.

Lilium pardalinum Kellogg. Native of S Oregon, W Utah and California S to Kern Co. in the Sierra foothills, and in the coast ranges to Santa Barbara Co., at up to 1800m, by streams, on mossy rocks and fallen trees, with ferns, *Caltha* and azaleas, just above the water level, flowering from May to July. Stems to 2.5m. Bulbs rhizomatous, branching to form clumps, with 1– jointed scales. Flowers yellow to red with maroon spots; petals 5–8cm long. Easily cultivated in moist soil, both peat and clay; tolerant of lime. Photographed by M.Woodgates at Quarry Wood.

Lilium vollmeri Eastw. Native of NW California, in Humboldt and Del Norte Counties and in S Oregon in Josephine Co., growing in wet flushes in Redwood forest, flowering in July and August. Stems to 1m; flowers yellow to reddish-orange, with petals 6–8cm long. Differs from *L. pardalinum* in having bulbs with unbranched rhizomes and 3-4 joints on each scale.

Lilium canadense L. Native of Québec and Nova Scotia south to Georgia east of the Allegheny Mts, in wet woods among ferns, in moist fields and along the edges of streams, flowering in June and July. Stem to 1.5m. Flowers up to 20, 5–7.5cm long, usually deep yellow, spotted inside, but sometimes red in var. *rubrum* Britton (shown here), rarely orange or unspotted. Not easy to cultivate in Europe, but said to grow best in well-drained, peaty, preferably acid soil, moist in summer and never allowed to dry out, in sun or partial shade.

Lilium henryi

Lilium hansonii

Lilium leichtlinii var. maximowiczii

Lilium ciliatum

Lilium concolor

Lilium henryi Baker. Native of C China, in W Hubei and Guizhou, among scrub on limestone cliffs, often in shade on humus-rich soil, at up to 1100m, flowering in July. Stems to 3m, with leaves scattered, shining green. Flowers up to 20, not scented, with petals 6–8cm long. Easily grown on both acid and limey soil, and one of the most virus-tolerant of all lilies.

Lilium leichtlinii Hook. fil. var. **maximowiczii** (Regel) Baker. Native of S Korea and Japan in Honshu, Shikoku and Kyushu, in moist, peaty but well-drained soil by streams among shrubs and grass, at 300–600m, flowering in July and August. This is probably one of the parents of the well-known Tiger Lily (*L. lancifolium*) see p.213. Stem to 2.5m, with scattered leaves and up to 10 flowers with petals 6.5–8.5cm long. Should be planted in almost pure leafmould and partial shade in a cool position. Photographed in Japan by Mikinori Ogisu.

Lilium hansonii Moore. Native of Korea and E Siberia near Vladivostock, in scrub and forest in well-drained humus-rich soil, at up to 1000m, flowering in June and July. Stems to 1.5m, with leaves in whorls and up to 12 scented flowers, 6.5–8.5cm across. Easily grown and very hardy, doing well in partial shade.

Lilium ciliatum P.H. Davis (*Liliaceae*). Native of NE Turkey in the mountains above the Black Sea coast from near Giresun east to Rize, at 1500–2400m, growing in beech and fir forest, in scrub and on alpine meadows, flowering in June–July. Stem to 150cm, with up to 15 flowers. Upper leaves ciliate, with long wavy hairs. Photographed at Quarry Wood by Martyn Simmons.

Lilium concolor (*Liliaceae*). Native of China, in N Yunnan, Hunan and Hubei, growing in scrub in pockets of humus on carboniferous limestone and in heavy limey soil, at 1500–2200m, flowering in June and July. Stem to 90cm, with up to 10 scented flowers. Leaves scattered. Flowers 6.5–8.5cm across. Var. *pulchellum* (Fischer) Regel, is found in NE China, Korea and E Siberia.

Lilium chalcedonicum L. incl. *L. heldreichii* Freyn. Native of Albania and Greece, on cliffs, stony hillsides and in *Abies* forests, often on limestone, at 1100–1800m, flowering in June. Stems to 1.2m with up to 12 flowers, but often only one or two; leaves numerous, the lower usually withering by flowering time, the upper appressed to the stem. Requires a very well-drained soil, preferably with lime and in full sun, or partial shade.

Lilium pumilum D.C. syn. *L. tenuifolium* Fisch. Native of the Altai Mts in Siberia and Mongolia, of NE China and N Korea, growing in grassland and low scrub in shallow humus-rich soil, at 400–900m, flowering in July. Stems to 45cm, with narrow scattered leaves and up to 30 flowers, but usually about 10 flowers. Petals 3–3.5cm long. Easily grown in light soil in full sun, but reported to be short-lived though easily raised from seed.

Lilium rubellum Baker. Native of Japan in N Honshu at 700–1800m, growing in grass and dwarf shrubs, and at higher altitudes among low conifers and dwarf *Rhododendron* scrub, in well-drained but heavy soil with a surface layer of leafmould. This beautiful lily survived for about 50 years in the wild garden at Wisley, in moist very acid sandy soil.

Lilium rubellum

Lilium chalcedonicum

Lilium pumilum

Lilium 'Bellingham Hybrids'

Lilium 'Pumpkin'

Lilium 'Bellingham Hybrids'. A race of hybrids involving *L. humboldtii*, *L. pardalinum* and *L. parryi* raised by the US Department of Agriculture at Bellingham before 1933. Robust and healthy plants with stems to 2.5m, flowering in July. Easily grown in moist soil, tolerant of clay and not requiring an acid soil.

Lilium 'Coachella'. Raised by Derek Fox.

Lilium 'Lake Tulare'. Raised by Derek Fox of Bullwood Nursery, Essex, before 1977. A cross between a Bullwood hybrid and *L. bolanderi* p.209. Stems around 2m; leaves whorled, flowering in July. For moist, acid soil. 'Bullwood hybrids' are complex crosses involving *L. pardalinum* var. *giganteum*, *L. pardalinum* and *L. bolanderi*. Photographed by D. Fox.

Lilium 'Iona'. Raised by Dr Chris North at the Invergowrie Research Station near Dundee, and named and introduced by Mr and Mrs Martyn Simmons in 1982. A hybrid of *lankongense* and Asiatic parentage. Stems to 1.6m. Easily grown in well-drained garden soil. Hardy.

Lilium 'Lake Tahoe'. Raised by Derek Fox before 1977. A cross betweeen 'Peachwood', a Bullwood hybrid selection and *L. bolanderi*. Stem around 2m; leaves whorled. Flowering in July. Photographed by D. Fox.

Lilium 'Pumpkin'. Raised by Derek Fox around 1972. A cross between a Bullwood hybrid and *L. parryi*. Stems to 2.3m. Photographed by D. Fox.

Lilium 'Ariadne'. A hybrid between *L. lankongense* and *L.* 'Maxwill', raised by Dr Chris North at the Invergowrie Research Station at Mynlefield near Dundee before 1976. Stems to 1.5m, with 20–30 flowers. Combines the elegant long pedicels of *L. lankongense*, with the robustness of *L.* 'Maxwill', a hybrid between *L. leichtlinii* var. *maximowiczii* and *L. willmottiae*. Photographed by Martyn Simmons.

Lilium 'Lake Tulare'

Lilium 'Iona'

Dr North's **Lilium lankongense** hybrids at Quarry Wood, Berkshire

Lilium 'Lake Tahoe'

Lilium 'Coachella'

Lilium 'Ariadne'

Lilium 'Pink Perfection' strain

Lilium 'Casa Blanca'

Lilium 'Golden Splendour' strain

Lilium 'Casa Blanca'. An auratum-type hybrid, raised by Gebr. Vletter & J.A. den Haan, in around 1975 and introduced in 1984. A selection from Jamboree grex × a seedling white oriental. Height to 1.5m; flowering in July.

Lilium 'Pink Perfection' strain. Raised by de Graaf in c.1950, from seedlings of *L. leucanthemum* var. *centifolium* and *L. sargentiae*. Flowers in various shades of pinkish-purple or violet. Easily grown, long-lasting and well-scented. It is reported that the seedlings sent out by Oregon Bulb Farms were the result of controlled crosses between two distinct clones which were repeated regularly, producing what were in effect F_1 hybrids.

Lilium 'Golden Splendour' strain. Raised by Oregon Bulb Farms in c.1957; selected from the 'Golden Clarion' strain, a complex cross of *L. sargentiae*, *L. leucanthemum* and *L. henryi*. Seed was produced annually by controlled crossing between selected parents.

Lilium 'Theodore Haber'. Raised by J. Petruske before 1975, by crossing *L. martagon* var. *dalmaticum* and *L. tsingtauense*. Stems up to 1.5m, flowering in July. This is one of the first of a new race of *martagon*-like hybrids which have larger, orange or red flowers owing to the influence of *L. tsingtauense*. Very hardy.

Lilium 'Stargazer'. A complex *auratum–speciosum* cross of unknown parentage, unusual in its upward facing flowers. Raised by Sun Valley Bulb Farms in California, and introduced in 1975.

Lilium 'Bright Star'. A selection from aurelian hybrids of complex *L. henryi*, *sargentiae* and *leucanthemum* ancestry, raised by Oregon Bulb Farms in 1959. Height to 1.5m. Easily grown.

Lilium 'Connecticut King'. A cross between 'Connecticut Lass' and 'Keystone' of complex *L. lancifolium*, *dauricum* and *davidii* ancestry, raised by Stone and Payne c.1967. Height to about 1m.

Lilium 'Theodore Haber'

Lilium 'Connecticut King'

Lilium 'Stargazer'

Lilium 'Bright Star'

Lilium columbianum

Lilium parvum

Lilium columbianum

Lilium kelloggii

Lilium bolanderi

Lilium washingtonianum

(a), (b) **Lilium martagon** L. (*Liliaceae*). Native of Europe from France and Portugal eastwards to Turkey, the Caucasus and Siberia, growing in subalpine meadows, woods and scrub, flowering from May to July. The dark wine-red forms (a) have been called *L. cattaniae* (Vis.) Vis. and var. *dalmaticum* Elwes. They come mainly from N Greece, Bulgaria and Yugoslavia, and are stronger growing, earlier flowering and usually have very hairy buds. White forms are frequent in cultivation and particularly beautiful, and other colour forms have been selected. The dull pinkish form shown here (b) is commonest in N Europe. Grows best in good leafy soil in sun or shade, tolerant of lime and probably better in a neutral or alkaline soil.

(c) **Lilium pomponium** L. Native of S France and NW Italy, growing on steep limestone screes and in scrub, flowering in May. Easily distinguished by its very narrow ciliate leaves and scarlet flowers. Best grown in a warm sunny spot in stony soil, protected from slugs. Source France, near Puget-Theniers, and shot near Vence by Brinsley Burbidge.

Lilium candidum L. Madonna Lily. Native of S Yugoslavia and Greece south to the Lebanon, growing in scrub and on cliffs and rocky slopes at up to 600m, flowering in May. Grows best in a well-drained chalky soil with good fertility, but is rather capricious as to where it will thrive. It often grows very well in cottage gardens, well manured and away from other lilies. The basal leaves usually appear in autumn and remain green through the winter. Photographed at Great Dixter, Sussex.

Lilium columbianum Hanson. Native of western N America from central British Columbia to northern California, in moist soil among rocks, on screes and in scrub and woodland at up to 1600m, flowering in June. Up to 2m high in the wild. Grow in moist well-drained soil, between shrubs. Photographed in California, del Norte Co., in June 1966 by Roger Macfarlane, and (single flower) on Mayne Is., BC, in June 1974 by Brinsley Burbidge.

Lilium kelloggii Purdy. Native of NW California, growing in grassy places, scrub and clearings in redwood forest. Grows in moist well-drained soil between shrubs in half-shade. Photographed in California by Roger Macfarlane.

Lilium parvum Kellogg. Native of California and S Oregon from 1600 to 3000m, growing in wet places and along mountain streams, flowering in June and July. Flowers yellow or orange, to red. Stem up to 2m. Grows best in deep moist sandy soil. Photographed in California by Roger Macfarlane.

Lilium bolanderi S. Watson. Native of the Siskiyou mountains of south Oregon and north California, growing on dry hillsides. Not easy to grow, requiring very well drained, gritty soil, and rather deep planting, about 15cm down. Photographed in California at French Hill in June 1966 by Roger Macfarlane.

Lilium washingtonianum Kellogg, var. **minor**. Native of Oregon and northern California, growing on dry slopes in scrub between 1000 and 2000m flowering in June and July. Flowers white, fading to pinkish-purple in var *purpurascens*. Bulb not creeping. Not easy to grow, requiring very well drained soil in a warm position, with ample moisture before flowering. Photographed in California on Mt Shasta in June 1966 by Roger Macfarlane.

1/5 life size Photographed 10 July

Lilium candidum

Lilium pomponium

¼ life size Photographed 12 July

Lilium nepalense

Notholirion macrophyllum

Cardiocrinum giganteum at Inverewe, Scotland

Lilium maculatum var. **dauricum**

(a), (d) **Lilium duchartrei** Franchet (*Liliaceae*). Native of western China from SW Kansu to N Yunnan, growing in moist places, at the edge of forest, in scrub and alpine meadows, flowering in July. The almost umbellate inflorescence is typical. Grow in moist peaty soil among shrubs such as dwarf rhododendrons. The form from Kansu, var. *farreri*, has pure white flowers, and is apparently tolerant of lime. *L. lankongense* Franchet is rather similar, with pink flowers and a stem which creeps underground before emerging with flowers held on horizontal pedicels.

(b) **Lilium tsingtauense** Gilg. Native of Korea and north-eastern China, growing on grassy banks and in open woods. It grows best in a cool peaty soil among dwarf rhododendrons.

(c) **Lilium henrici** Franchet. Native of western China, especially W Yunnan, at 3000–3600m, growing on steep grassy slopes, scrub and pine forest. The flowers are spotted in var. *maculatum* (Evans) Woodcock & Stearn. Stems to 135cm high with up to 9 flowers. This very rare species was derived from seed collected by Forrest's collectors after his death, and has been grown at Keillour Castle since 1954. It requires a moist well-drained soil and some protection from shrubs.

(e) **Lilium parryi** S. Watson. Native of southern California and Arizona, growing in rich soil by mountain streams at 2000–3000m, flowering in June. Plant in half-shade in very well drained sandy soil with a good quantity of peat or leafmould, in a moist situation. A seedling is shown here. The stem can be up to 2m with over fifteen flowers.

Lilium maculatum Thunb. var. **dauricum**. Native of Japan, mostly around the northern coasts of Honshu, with one locality in the mountains, growing in grassy places and on cliffs. Photographed in Japan, E. Hokkaido, near Shari, c.100m, in July 1978 by Peter Barnes.

Cardiocrinum giganteum (Wallich) Baker, syn. *Lilium giganteum* Wallich (*Liliaceae*). Native of the Himalayas, westwards to Nepal, growing in wet forests and scrub at 1600–3300m, flowering in June and July. Height 2–4m in cultivation. A variety from western China, var. *yunnanense* Leichtlin, has black slightly shorter stems and bronzy young leaves. Easily grown in rich moist soil with plenty of leafmould. Best in shade. Slugs are very fond of the young leaves, which should also be protected from late frosts. Photographed in Inverewe Gardens, Invernessshire.

Notholirion macrophyllum (D. Don) Boiss. (*Liliaceae*). Native of Nepal, Sikkim, Bhutan and Tibet, growing on grassy slopes at 2700–4400m, flowering in July. Not easy to grow, probably requiring very well drained soil in full light but not hot sun. Photographed in western Nepal by Oleg Polunin.

Lilium nepalense D. Don. Native of Nepal and Kumaon, east to Assam and NE India, growing on steep slopes, often among limestone rocks and bamboos, at 2300–3000m, flowering in June and July. Flower colour varies from all green to about half the flower marked with brown-crimson. The stem often creeps underground before emerging. Keep the bulbs dry in winter, but water well while in growth. Photographed in western Nepal by Oleg Polunin.

Lilium lancifolium Thunb.

Lilium 'Cover Girl'

Lilium 'Black Beauty'

Lilium auratum

Lilium bulbiferum

Lilium mackliniae

Nomocharis aperta

Lilium × testaceum

Lilium lancifolium Thunb., syn. *Lilium tigrinum* Ker-Gawler. This familiar garden lily is sterile triploid, long grown in Japan, and probably originally of hybrid origin, the likely parents being *L. leichtlinii* and *L. maculatum*. It is very tolerant of virus and grows particularly well in northern gardens, in well-drained but rich moist soil, flowering in August and September. It has numerous black stem bulbils. Photographed at Pitmedden, Aberdeenshire.

Lilium 'Cover Girl'. Raised by Oregon Bulb Farms in 1967. A hybrid between *L. speciosum* × *auratum* and *L. auratum* and still one of the finest pink *auratum*-type hybrids. Stems up to 2m, flowers c.25cm in diameter.

Lilium 'Black Beauty'. Raised by L. Woodruff in Oregon in 1957. A hybrid between *L. henryi* and *L. speciosum* which is very vigorous and long lived, with resistance to virus disease inherited from *L. henryi*. Very late flowering, usually August–September in southern England.

Lilium auratum Lindl. Native of Japan, especially Honshu, growing in scrub and grassy places in the mountains. Flowers with broader petals (var. *platyphyllum* Baker) and with red rather than yellow bands (var. *rubrovittatum* Duchartre) occur in the wild, the latter sporadically among the normal form, the former in the south-east of Honshu, growing in volcanic ash. Requires a very well drained acid soil and a warm place in half-shade or among shrubs. Grows better in warmer climates than in England.

Lilium bulbiferum L., syn. *L. croceum* Chaix (*Liliaceae*). Native of central Europe from Spain eastwards to Poland and Yugoslavia, growing in scrub, among bracken and on rocky slopes, flowering in June. Flowers orange to red, with or without bulbils (var. *croceum* (Chaix) Pers.) on the stem. Easily grown in any well-drained soil in sun or half-shade. Tolerant of lime. Photographed in S Switzerland in June 1964.

Lilium mackliniae Sealy. Native of Manipur on Sirhoi peak near Ukrhul, growing on grassy and rocky slopes from 2150 to 2600m, flowering in June. Discovered in 1948 by F. Kingdon Ward, and named after his wife. Plant in leafy well-drained soil in sun or half-shade. Photographed in cultivation by Brian Mathew.

Nomocharis aperta (Franchet) E. H. Wilson (*Liliaceae*). Native of western China, in SW Szechwan and NW Yunnan, and on the Burma–Tibet border, growing in alpine pastures at c.2700m. Flowers usually paler pink than shown here, with scattered spots. Grow in well-drained leaf soil with plenty of moisture at the roots. All *Nomocharis* are alpine plants and grow especially well in E Scotland.

Lilium × testaceum. A hybrid between *L. chalcedonicum* and *L. candidum*, requiring a good well-drained soil in full sun to grow well. It is one of the oldest lily hybrids in cultivation being recorded before 1841. Photographed at Great Dixter, Sussex.

Lilium monadelphum

⅓ life size Photographed 12 July

(a) **Lilium monadelphum** Bieb., syn. *L. szovitsianum* Fisch & Lall. (*Liliaceae*). Native of the Crimea, the northern side of the Caucasus from the Black to the Caspian sea, and the central Caucasus on the south side as far as N Turkey. It grows in woods, scrub and in subalpine meadows, on very steep slopes, at up to 2500m, flowering from June to August. The distinctions between *L. monadelphum* and *L. szovitsianum* do not seem to hold good in the wild. In the large population of several thousand plants shown here, plants were found with spotted and unspotted flowers, yellow or orange pollen, and the depth of the flower colour varied somewhat. No flowers with united filaments were seen. The plant shown in (a) is a fine specimen of the cultivated plant grown as *L. szovitsianum*. Photographed in the northern Caucasus, Dongus Orun, near Mt Elbrus, in June 1980, c.2000m. Grow in good garden soil. Long-lived but not easy to establish.

(b) **Lilium pardalinum** Kellogg (*Liliaceae*). Native of western N America from California to British Columbia, growing in marshes and in scrub in the coast ranges, flowering in June and July. Very variable in the wild, in colour from red to orange and yellow and in the amount of spotting. The bulbs creep horizontally, and can increase and make a dense mass if happy. They grow best in wet soil on a slope or in a well-drained soil in a place with a high water table. Stem up to 2.3m high.

Lilium carniolicum Bernh. ex Koch (*Liliaceae*). Native of the SE Alps in Italy and Austria, southwards to Greece, growing on limestone cliffs, in open pine forest, and in mountain meadows, flowering in May and June. The typical plant has red or orange flowers and leaves pubescent on the veins beneath. It comes from the north part of the species range. The more southerly forms have yellow flowers as shown here, and have been called *L. jankae* A. Kerner. Grows best in a very well drained peaty soil in full sun or half-shade. Photographed in Yugoslavia, Somuborsko Gorge, by Oleg Polunin.

Lilium pyrenaicum L. (*Liliaceae*). Native of the Pyrenees in France and Spain (and naturalised in Scotland), growing in alpine meadows and open woods, flowering in June and July. One of the easiest species to grow in northern England and Scotland, growing well in grass in well-drained peaty soil. There is also a reddish form, var. *rubrum* Stocker. Photographed in Andorra by Brinsley Burbidge.

Lilium monadelphum in the northwestern Caucasus above Itkol

Lilium pyrenaicum

Lilium carniolicum

Romulea thodei

Tulbaghia violacea

Wurmbea elatior

Romulea macowanii var. oreophila

Rhodohypoxis rubella

Rhodohypoxis deflexa

Tulbaghia violacea Harvey (*Liliaceae*). Native of Cape Province from Kynsha eastwards and north to Transvaal, flowering in December to March. Stems 20–35cm, to 60cm in cultivation. Flowers 12–25mm across, purple or white, in umbels of 12–30. One of the showiest and hardiest species, surviving −10°C. Photographed in Edinburgh Botanic Garden.

Wurmbea elatior B. Nordenst. (*Liliaceae*). Native of S Africa, in the NE Cape and Natal in the Drakensberg and nearby mountains, in wet, grassy places at 1800–2500m, flowering in January and February. Stems to 15cm. Flowers c.1.5cm across. An unusual genus of about 40 species, in Africa and Australia, related to *Colchicum*. Photographed in the NE Cape, near Rhodes.

Romulea macowanii Baker var. **oreophila** De Vos (*Iridaceae*). Native of S Africa, in the NE Cape, Lesotho and the central Drakensberg in Natal, in shallow soil and turf over rock, at 2400–2900m, flowering in January to March. Flowers 27–55mm long. Var. *macowanii* has larger flowers and is found further west in the E Karoo and the Cape. Photographed on Naude's Nek, the type locality. Flowers in cultivation in early autumn; hardy and easy to raise from seed.

Romulea thodei Schltr. (*Iridaceae*). Native of the central Drakensberg south to NE Cape Province, in short turf and shallow gravelly soil over rock, at 2100–3000m, flowering in January and February. Stems to 15cm. Flowers 15–28mm long. For well-drained soil, moist in summer, dry in winter.

Rhodohypoxis deflexa Hilliard & Burtt (*Hypoxidaceae*). Native of Lesotho and the NE corner of Cape Province, growing in alpine turf at 2600–3230m, flowering in late December to February. A minute plant, with relatively broad leaves to 5mm wide. Flowers 6–12mm across, usually reddish-pink, sometimes pale pink or white. Ovary not subterranean. Photographed in Lesotho, near Sani Pass, growing with *Lobelia galpinii*, flowering in January.

Rhodohypoxis rubella (Bak.) Nel (*Hypoxidaceae*). Native of Lesotho and S Africa from Mont-aux-Sources along the Drakensberg to Naude's Nek in NE Cape Province, growing in bare mud and shallow water, at 2700–3230m, flowering from November to February. Leaves narrow, 1–1.5mm wide. Flower tube 1–4.5cm long, with the stem and ovary remaining below ground. Flowers 10–18mm across, usually reddish-pink, rarely pale pink or white. Photographed on Naude's Nek, in bare wet ground over basalt in early February.

Pachycarpus grandiflorus (L. fil) E. Meyer (*Asclepiadaceae*). Native of Cape Province near Humansdorp, north to Natal and Transvaal, growing in grassland, often on steep slopes, flowering in January to February. Rootstock tuberous; stems to 50cm, variably hairy. Flowers c.4.5cm across, variably spotted. Photographed on Ngeli Mountain, Natal.

Pachycarpus concolor E. Mey. (*Asclepiadaceae*). Native of NE Cape Province, northwards to Natal, Transvaal, Swaziland and S Botswana, growing in grassland and on rocky slopes at up to 2000m, flowering in October to January. Stems to 45cm; root tuberous. Leaves broadly linear, obtuse. Flowers reddish-violet to purplish- or greenish-yellow. For well-drained soil in a warm position, dry in winter, moist in summer. Photographed in NE Cape Province, near Barkly Pass. The pollinating bluebottle has become trapped by its tongue

Androcymbium striatum Hochst. (*Liliaceae*). Native of the mountains of southern Africa, from Malawi where it is common, as far south as the E Cape, Lesotho and the Natal Drakensberg, at 2400–2700m, in wet gravelly places and on sheet rock in areas of seepage, flowering in December to February. An unusual genus, related to *Colchicum*, with large whitish bracts surrounding a head of small flowers. Most species are found in the Cape region, but three are found in the Canaries, in N Africa, and in SE Spain, and on the island of Elaphonisson near Crete. Photographed in Lesotho at 3000m.

Pachycarpus concolor near Bustervoepad, northwest Cape Province

Pachycarpus concolor

Androcymbium striatum

Pachycarpus grandiflorus on Ngeli mountain, Natal

¼ life size Photographed 4 August

Galtonia candicans Dcne. (*Liliaceae*). Native of S Africa in SE Transvaal and Natal as far south as the central Drakensberg, growing on grassy slopes and wet hillsides, at up to 2600m, flowering in December to February. Easy to grow, especially if raised from seed, and best in deep moist sandy soil in full sun. Very prone to damage by slugs.

Galtonia princeps Dcne. (*Liliaceae*). Native of S Africa, from Natal near Pietermaritzburg to the S Transkei, growing in wet meadows, flowering in November to January. Stems to 2m. Distinct in its flowers with a narrow tube and spreading segments. Seen here growing well in a sandy border at Wisley.

(a) **Galtonia regalis** Hilliard & Burtt (*Liliaceae*). Native of Natal on the N half of the Drakensberg escarpment on wet mountain cliffs at 1900–3000m, flowering in January and February. Differs from *G. viridiflora* in its larger size, and in having filaments with a ridge running down the inner face. For well-drained sandy but rich soil, dry in winter, moist in summer.

Galtonia viridiflora Verdoorn (*Liliaceae*). Native of S Africa, in the Orange Free State, W Lesotho and the NE Cape (Witteberg). Leaves glaucous. Stems shorter than *G. regalis*, up to 40cm. Grows best in sandy soil, and apparently hardy at least to −10°C.

(b) **Crocosmia × crocosmiflora** (Lemoine) N.E. Br. syn. *Tritonia × crocosmiflora* (Lemoine) Nicholson (*Iridaceae*). Montbretia. A hybrid between *Crocosmia pottsii* and *Crocosmia aurea* first raised in France in 1880. It is now common in western Europe in gardens and frequently naturalised along the Atlantic coast, especially in Ireland, by streams and on roadsides. Numerous other colour forms from yellow to red were developed in cultivation; see p.222.

(c) **Crinum × powellii** Baker (*Amaryllidaceae*). A garden hybrid between *Crinum moorei* and *C. bulbispermum*, both from S Africa. It is hardy in S England and W Scotland, growing in any rich moist soil, flowering in July and August. A position in full sun produces more flowers and less of the very lush foliage. Stems up to 1.5m, bulbs up to 20cm in diameter.

(d) **Habranthus brachyandrus** (Baker) Sealy (*Amaryllidaceae*). Native of S Brazil, Paraguay and NE Argentina, near the Parana River, flowering in January. The long pedicel and large pink flower, purple at the base, are characteristic. Easy to raise from seed and free-flowering in a warm sunny place. Will survive some frost if kept dry in winter.

(e) **Hippeastrum advenum** (Ker Gawl.) Herbert, syn. *Amaryllis advena* Ker Gawler (*Amaryllidaceae*). Native of S Argentina and Chile. This species is hardy to around −10°C, and easily grown in a pot or in a raised bed, kept dry in winter. Source Chile, B.C. & W. 4999.

Galtonia candicans on a marshy bank near Pietermaritzburg, Natal

Galtonia princeps

Galtonia viridiflora

Crocosmia pottsii in a stream on Ngeli mountain, Natal

Crocosmia pearsii near Mont-aux-Sources, Natal

Crocosmia masonorum

Crocosmia pottsii (Baker) N.E. Br. Native of Natal and Transkei, growing on stream banks and on rocks in streams, flowering in December to February. Flowers deep orange to orange-yellow, 2.8–3.5cm long. Easily grown in moist peaty soil. Photographed on Ngeli Mountain, C Natal.

Crocosmia pearsii Oberm. Native of the Drakensberg, in the Cathedral Peak and Mont-aux-Sources areas, growing in rock crevices, at 2200–3000m, flowering in January and February. Stems to 1m, not clump-forming. Flowers 7–9cm long, reddish-orange. For well-drained peaty soil. Photographed above Witzieshoek, near Mont-aux-Sources.

Crocosmia masonorum (L. Bol.) N.E. Br. Native of the S Drakensberg, in mountains in the Edgcobo district of Transkei near Santana Nek, flowering in December and January. Stems to 1.5m. Flowers scarlet-orange to orange-yellow, to 5cm long. Grows best in moist sandy soil, with some protection in winter. Hardy to −10°C.

Tritonia drakensbergensis de Vos. Native of the Drakensberg Mts in the Transkei and NE Cape Province, growing on grassy mountain ledges at c.2500m, flowering in January and February. Stem 25–50cm. Flowers c.4cm across. Probably hardy. Photographed on Naude's Nek, Cape Province.

Crocosmia aurea (Hooker) Planchon (*Iridaceae*). Native of S Africa in E Cape Province, north to Malawi, Zambia and

Tritonia drakensbergensis on Naude's Nek, South Africa

Tritonia drakensbergensis

Crocosmia aurea

Crocosmia aurea

Crocosmia paniculata

Tanzania, growing in woods, along streams and in shady gorges, at up to 2500m; especially common in conifer plantations, flowering in December to March. Stems to 1m. Flowers to 5.5cm across. Hardy to −10°C, and growing best in a warm, moist and shady position. Flowering in late summer in gardens.

Crocosmia paniculata (Klatt) Goldblatt syn. *Tritonia paniculata* Klatt, *Cyrtonus paniculatus* (Klatt) N.E. Br. Native of the Drakensberg of E Transvaal, Swaziland, the Orange Free State and E Zimbabwe, in moist, grassy places and on the margins of forest at up to c.1800m, flowering in December to March. Stem to 1.8m; flowers 5–7.5cm long. Easy to grow in rich, moist, sandy soil; it grows especially well in E Scotland where the photograph shown here was taken.

Tritonia disticha Baker subsp. **rubrolucens** (Foster) de Vos syn. *Tritonia rubrolucens* Foster, *T. rosea* Klatt (*Iridaceae*). Native of Natal in the Drakensberg, of Transvaal, the Orange Free State, Transkei and Swaziland, growing in grassland and rock crevices at up to 2000m, flowering in October to March, according to locality. Stems to 50cm, wiry, not upright. Flowers 2.5–3.5cm long, distinctly veined, rose-pink to pinkish-orange. For moist, well-drained, sandy soil. Hardy.

Tritonia disticha subsp. **rubrolucens**

⅓ life size photographed 17 August

Crocosmia 'Emily McKenzie'

Crocosmia 'Ember Glow'

Crocosmia hybrids. In addition to the common Montbretia (see p.218) which was raised in France by Lémoine of Nancy in 1882 and has become naturalised along the west coast of the British Isles, several large-flowered or differently coloured hybrids were raised both in France and later in England. Most of them are now very rare, but a few of those which have survived are shown below. Recently Alan Bloom of Bressingham has raised a new race of taller hybrids using different species. These are generally hardier with flowers in various shades of intense red.

(a) **Crocosmia masonorum**. (see p.221)

(g) **'Lucifer'**. (h) **'Spitfire'**. (b) **'Bressingham Blaze'**. These three are selections made by Alan Bloom from hybrids between *Crocosmia masonorum*, *C*. 'Jackanapes' and *C. paniculata*. All are tall, up to 1m, and hardy, surviving −10°C with a little dry peat or leaves for protection. They prefer a rich, moist and sandy soil, and flower in late summer. The leaves are generally pleated like those of *C.paniculata* (see p.221), but the flowers are larger.

'Ember Glow'. A hybrid between *C. masonorum* and *C. paniculata*, raised by Alan Bloom. Up to 1m high; Should be hardy.

(e) **'Citronella'**. A yellow variety with green leaves. According to Graham Thomas in *Perennial Garden Plants*, the original 'Citronella' had flowers with a dark eye.

Crocosmia 'Lucifer' at Wisley

'Emily McKenzie'. Raised by K. McKenzie in Northumberland before 1950 and said to be hardy there. A low-growing variety, to 60cm, but has the largest flowers of the common varieties, up to 6cm across, with red markings inside.

(c) **'Firebird'**. A good form of *C. masonorum*, see p.221, selected by Alan Bloom at Bressingham.

(f) **'Solfatare'**. A distinct variety with its greyish-brown leaves and yellow flowers. Stems to 60cm. Known since 1897, but not very hardy.

(d) **'George Davison'**. Another old yellow-flowered variety. George Davison was head gardener at Westwick Hall, near Norwich, and a successful hybridiser of *Crocosmia*.

Cytanthus falcatus

Cytanthus breviflorus

Amarygia parkeri

Americrinum corsii

Cyrtanthus breviflorus Harv. syn. *Anoiganthus breviflorus* (Harv.) Baker. (*Amaryllidaceae*). Native of S Africa in the E Transvaal, the Transvaal Highveldt, throughout the Natal Drakensberg and in NE Cape Province, in small streams and in wet grassland or on marshy slopes at up to 3000m, flowering in October to February. Stems to 30cm. Flowers c.3cm long, but sweetly scented. Very variable, and easily grown in moist soil.

Cyrtanthus falcatus R.A. Dyer. Native of C Natal, growing in crevices of S-facing cliffs, especially by waterfalls, at c.1800m, flowering in September: Stem 25–30cm, itself downcurved at apex. Leaves growing edge on, semi-horizontal, appearing at the same time as the flowers. Well-established in cultivation in Europe, thanks to the plants shown here, growing in an unheated greenhouse in Surrey. They survive freezing in winter if kept dry, and the seed produced germinates freely.

× **Amarcrinum corsii** Coutts, syn. × *Crinadonna corsii* hort. (*Amaryllidaceae*). A

Brunsvigia natalensis showing the fruiting head which acts as a tumbleweed

Brunsvigia undulata

Brunsvigia grandiflora

hybrid between *Amaryllis belladonna* and *Crinum moorei*. Shorter and stouter than *C. moorei* and *C.* × *powellii*, with stems up to 60cm, flowering in late summer, and early autumn. Hardy to −15°C if the bulbs are protected from freezing by deep planting against a warm wall.

× **Amarygia parkeri** hort. syn. × *Brunsdonna parkeri* hort. Hybrids between *Amaryllis belladonna* (seed) amd *Brunsvigia josephinae* (pollen). Flowers only slightly smaller than *Amaryllis*, deeper pink, but more numerous, facing all round the umbel. The cross in which *Brunsvigia* was the seed parent is called 'Tubergen's variety'. It is much closer to *Brunsvigia*, but has pinkish-purple flowers, larger than *Brunsvigia*, about 30 in an umbel; it is very rare, and possibly extinct in cultivation.

Brunsvigia grandiflora Lindl. (*Amaryllidaceae*). Native of Transkei and neighbouring Natal, to the NE Cape, in the Drakensberg and nearby mountains, growing in damp grassland at up to 2200m, flowering in January and February. Stems to 40cm; umbel to 40cm across. From its habitat this should be hardy to −10°C but will require warm summer weather to flower. Photographed in C Natal, on Ngeli Mtn.

Brunsvigia natalensis Baker. Native of Natal, in the foothills of the Drakensberg, but its exact range is uncertain, growing in grassland at up to 2200m, flowering in December and January. Umbel c.30cm across; flowers pink. Leaves very broad, flat on the ground. Photographed at Witzieshoek, showing the leaves and the fruiting inflorescence which acts as a tumbleweed, blowing along to disperse the seeds.

Brunsvigia undulata Leighton. Native of C Natal, growing in grassland at up to 1500m, flowering in January and February. Umbel to 45cm across, with up to 80 flowers. Leaves upright. Should be hardy to −10°C, with the bulb protected against hard frost. Photographed near Nottingham Road, C.D. & R. 225.

⅓ life size Photographed 24 September

(a), (b), (c) Nerine bowdenii W. Watson (*Amaryllidaceae*). Native of S Africa in E Cape Province north to Orange Free State and N Natal in the Drakensberg Mts up to 3000m on Mont-aux-Sources, where it grows in great quantity on cliffs and rocks, even in dry soil beneath overhangs, flowering in February to May. It is also recorded near Engcobo, growing in open woods in leafmould. Stems to 80cm. The variety commonly cultivated in Europe has leaves emerging in late winter, deciduous in late summer, and flowers in autumn; it originated on mountains behind King William's Town. The variety *wellsii*, also called 'Quinton Wells', is the one common in the N Drakensberg. It has larger bulbs, leaves which appear later and remain green all summer, and flowers in late summer, earlier than the variety from the Cape. It also has more, smaller flowers in the umbel, and the petals are more wrinkled. Both grow and flower best when planted under a warm wall. There is also a white variety which usually has a flush of pink, and a deeper pink clone 'Fenwick's var.'

(d) Nerine undulata (L.) Herbert. Native of Cape Province from Humansdorp eastwards and the Orange Free State, at low altitudes, flowering in April to June. Stems to 45cm. Leaves 6–13mm wide, appearing at the same time as the flowers. Petals 1.7–2cm. Less hardy than *N. bowdenii*, down to −5°C or so.

Nerine filifolia Baker. Native of the Orange Free State and Natal, growing in large numbers in wet grassy meadows or on rocks in streams, under a few inches of water at flowering time, though probably dry in winter, flowering in January and February. Stems 15–45cm, with short glandular hairs. Leaves thread-like. Petals 2.5–3cm long. Probably hardy if deeply planted, as it is dormant in winter.

(e) Amaryllis belladonna L., syn. *Brunsvigia rosea* (Lam.) Hannibal (*Amaryllidaceae*). Native of S Africa, in the Cape Province from Olifants River to Cape Town, and east to George, growing on rocky hillsides, in scrub and by rivers, flowering in February to April, especially after bush fires. Hardy in S England, surviving to −15°C, but requires a very warm position to flower well.

(f) Colchicum speciosum 'Album' (see p.241) Very easy and one of the finest of all autumn-flowering bulbs.

(g) Schizostylis coccinea Backh. & Harvey (*Iridaceae*). Native of S Africa, especially in the Drakensberg Mts, growing on the banks of streams among grasses at up to 1800m, flowering from January to March. Usually red in the wild, but pink forms are common in cultivation; there is also a white form, but its flowers are very small. In gardens it requires a moist soil, and is very valuable for its late flowering.

Crinum bulbispermum (Burm.) Milne-Redhead & Schweickerdt (*Amaryllidaceae*). Orange River Lily. Native of S Africa in the valleys of the Orange and Vaal Rivers, in the S Transvaal and in N Natal, near Ladysmith, growing in vleis (seasonal pools), marshes and on the banks of rivers, flowering in October to December. Stems to 50cm, about as high as the leaves. Flowers 17–20cm long, white with a red stripe, or entirely red. Anthers white or greyish. Easily grown in a moist place or an ordinary border; hardy to −10°C, but better protected by dry leaves or peat in winter. Photographed in Bermuda.

Nerine filifolia

Nerine filifolia

Nerine bowdenii var. **wellsii**

Crinum bulbispermum

Nerine bowdenii var. **wellsii**

Tigridia pavonia and **Galtonia candicans** at Trengwainton Cornwall

Tropaeolum tuberosum subsp. **silvestre**

Hippeastrum pratense

Tigridia pavonia

Tropaeolum ciliatum

Tigridia pavonia (L. fil.) DC. (*Iridaceae*). Native of Mexico and probably Guatemala, but cultivated by the Aztecs over 1000 years ago, so that its natural distribution is obscured. It is also naturalised elsewhere in C & S America south to Peru and Brazil. It is usually found wild in oak and pine forest, but is also frequent on roadsides and in semi-wild habitats, at 2000–3000m, flowering in July to October. Stem 30–150cm, usually near 50cm in cultivation in Europe. Flowers 10–15cm across, red, pink, orange, yellow or white, variously spotted and blotched, especially in the centre of the flower. Easily grown in a warm place and hardy if kept rather dry, and protected from extreme frost in winter. Or it may be brought indoors and kept dry, before being planted out in spring. Easily raised from seed.

Tropaeolum tuberosum

Tropaeolum speciosum

Tropaeolum azureum

Tropaeolum polyphyllum

Codonoposis convolvulacea

Hippeastrum pratense (Poeppig) Baker (*Amaryllidaceae*). Native of S Chile, recorded from meadows near Autuco (c.37°N), in the foothills of the Andes. Leaves 30–50cm × 6–13mm bright green. Flowers 2–8 in an umbel, bright red or purplish. This species is hardy in the milder parts of the British Isles and N America; it has grown well and is established in cultivation in Ireland, usually grown at the foot of a wall, flowering in May. It requires rich sandy soil and moisture in summer, and some protection in winter to keep it rather dry.

Tropaeolum ciliatum Ruiz & Pavon (*Tropaeolaceae*). Native of Chile, around Concepcion and Valparaiso, from 38°S north to 33°S, overlapping the area of *T. speciosum* which extends south to 42°S, in shady places and by streams, flowering in October to January. A delicate climber to 3m. Leaves 5-lobed, the middle lobe to 4cm long. Flowers up to 4cm across. Roots tuberous, rather thin, far spreading. Appears to be hardy in S England, and easily grown on a sunny wall or hedge.

Tropaeolum tuberosum Ruiz & Pavon subsp. **silvestre** Sparre. Native of the Andes, from Colombia south to Argentina, growing in scrub at 2400–3950m, flowering in February to July. A rampant climber to 4m, producing not tubers but fleshy overwintering rhizomes. Requires a cool position in summer as it soon dies or goes dormant if it becomes hot or dry. Hardy to −10°C, but safer if the roots are protected by a deep mulch in winter.

Tropaeolum speciosum Poepp. & Endl. Perthweed (*Tropaeolaceae*). Native of southern Chile, and the island of Chiloe, growing in wet forest and scrub, flowering in January and February. The tubers are thin, branched and very brittle. Hardy, and grows better in Scotland or the west of Britain than in SE England, but will grow in a cool shady situation in loose peaty soil. Stems up to 5m. Photographed in Scotland in September 1980.

Tropaeolum polyphyllum Cav. Native of the Andes in Chile, growing in screes. The tubers are elongated; the stems trailing not climbing, up to 40cm long. Hardy in well-drained soil, the tubers planted deeply. Photographed in cultivation by Valerie Finnis.

Tropaeolum tuberosum Ruiz & Pavon. Native of the Andes in Peru and Bolivia, growing on mountain slopes and valleys flowering in autumn. New tubers are formed annually, at ground level, and if the plant is left outside it should be protected or replanted more deeply. Two forms are cultivated, a short-day plant which begins to flower in October, and day-neutral form which can flower from late June to October (shown here). Height up to 3m. Photographed in cultivation by Valerie Finnis.

Tropaeolum azureum Miers ex Lindl. Native of central Chile, growing in scrub on dry rocky hillsides, flowering in October. The climate here is of Mediterranean type, hot and dry in summer. Tubers spindle-shaped. Tricky in cultivation and hardy only in the warmest gardens. Safer in a pot in the alpine house, kept frost-free. Seeds germinate easily.

Codonopsis convolvulacea Kurz (*Campanulaceae*). Native of Tibet and western China, especially Yunnan and Szechwan, growing in grassland, scrub and bamboo thickets from 1600 to 3500m, flowering in August and September. The climbing stems up to 1.5m long arise from an elongated tuber. Easily grown in sandy peaty soil, kept rather dry in winter, either in a pot or among low shrubs. Var. *forrestii* has larger leaves and a purple ring near the centre of the flower.

⅓ life size Photographed 1 September

(a) Aconitum volubile Pallas ex Koelle (*Ranunculaceae*). Native of E Siberia, Mongolia and W China, growing in thickets in the subalpine zone at up to 4000m, flowering from July to September. Easily grown in sun or shade, climbing through dwarf shrubs, and simple to raise from seed.

(b) Colchicum 'Princess Beatrix' (? = 'Princess Astrid'). One of the earliest of the large flowered hybrids, often flowering in early August. These hybrids were raised in Holland at the beginning of the century by crossing *C. speciosum* with *C. bivonae* (q.v.). All are robust and easily grown, showing great vigour in good soil. The leaves are large and resemble *C. speciosum*. Raised by Zocher & Co., Haarlem, c.1905.

(c) Eucomis comosa (Houttuyn) Wehrhan syn. *E. punctata* L'Herit. (*Liliaceae*) Native from Cape Province (Uitenhage) to Natal, flowering in December to February. Stems to 1m, often spotted. Flowers green or whitish, to pink and red, fading to deep purple and with purple leaves in some cultivars. The tuft of leaves at the stem apex is inconspicuous in this species and the long stems with flowers on the upper 30cm are often floppy in gardens. Hardy if planted deeply and needing a warm sunny position.

(d) Colchicum byzantinum Ker-Gawler (*Liliaceae*). An old garden plant of uncertain origin, possibly a hybrid between *C. autumnale* and *C. cilicicum*. Very free-flowering and robust, increasing well. The leaves are large, pleated, up to 30cm high. The flowers appear in late August. The long stigmas with bright crimson tips are characteristic, and distinguish it from large forms of *C. autumnale* or small forms of *C. cilicicum* in which the stigmas are shaded purplish towards the end. It was named by Clusius in 1601, who grew corms which had originally come from Constantinople in 1588.

(e) Gladiolus papilio Hooker fil. (*Iridaceae*). Native of southern Africa, especially the Transvaal and Natal, growing in damp grassy places, at up to 1600m, flowering in February. Easily grown in good soil in the open and apparently hardy. In poor soils it will increase well, but not flower freely. Often damaged by slugs which eat the young shoots underground.

Urginea maritima (L.) Baker (*Liliaceae*). Squill. Native of the Mediterranean region and Portugal, south to Israel and Jordan, growing on rocks, dry hills and sandy places, flowering in August and September. Stem 50–150cm. Leaves 30–100cm long, up to 10cm wide. Easy to grow in a warm sunny place, but not free-flowering in N Europe. Photographed in Greece, Itea near Delphi, by Oleg Polunin.

Pancratium maritimum L. (*Amaryllidaceae*). Native of the Mediterranean region, Portugal and the S Black Sea coast, growing in sand dunes by the sea, flowering from August to October. Leaves narrower than *P. illyricum*, up to 50cm long, evergreen. Easy to grow, but the leaves are damaged by hard frost, and the English summers are not usually warm enough to induce flowering. Photographed by Oleg Polunin.

Cypella herbertii Herbert (*Iridaceae*). Native of Argentine and Uruguay, growing in damp grassy places. The hardiest of the species *Cypella*, surviving outside in the south of England if planted in a warm spot, where it flowers in August. Photographed by Brian Mathew.

Urginea maritima in central Greece, near Delphi

Cypella herbertii

Pancratium maritimum

Pelargonium luridum

Pelargonium luridum

Pelargonium luridum

Eucomis autumnalis subsp. **autumnalis**

Eucomis autumnalis subsp. **clavata**

Pelargonium luridum (Andr.) Sweet (*Geraniaceae*). Native of S Africa in Natal northwards to Tanzania, growing in grassland and on roadsides, flowering in December to February. A member of subgenus *Polyactium* with a large underground tuber, and leaves which vary from lobed, to deeply divided and dissected later in the season. Flowers white to yellow or pink. Forms of this variable species from high altitudes may be frost-tolerant if kept dry in winter.

Eucomis autumnalis (Miller) Chitt. subsp. **autumnalis** syn. *E. undulata* Aiton (*Liliaceae*). Native of S Africa from the E Cape (Kynsha), north to Transvaal and to Malawi, growing in montane grassland, flowering in December and January. Stem to 30cm. Flowers all green. Easily cultivated, but requiring protection from frost in winter. Photographed on the Nyika plateau in Malawi, in January.

Eucomis autumnalis (Miller) Chitt. subsp. **clavata** (Bak.) Reyneke. Native of Natal, north to the Orange Free State, Transvaal, Botswana, Swaziland, in damp grassland and on moist rocky slopes and cliffs at up to 2700m, flowering in December to January. Stem club-shaped, 7–13cm long. Petals 1.2–1.7cm long, usually longer than subsp. *autumnalis*. Photographed near Mont-aux-Sources in February.

Eucomis bicolor Baker. Native of Natal, from the Mont-aux-Sources region southwards, growing on lush, moist, grassy slopes, often in seeping water and by streams, at up to 2750m, flowering in January and February. Stem usually spotted, to 60cm, with the flowers on the top 8–10cm. Petals usually with a dark purple edge. For good soil with ample moisture in the growing season. Forms originating from high altitude should be hardy. Photographed near Cathedral Peak, Natal.

Eucomis comosa (Houttuyn) Wehrhan syn. *E. punctata* L'Herit. (*Liliaceae*) Native from Cape province (Uitenhage) to Natal, flowering in December to February. Stems to 1m, often spotted. Flowers green or whitish, to pink and red, fading to deep purple and with purple leaves in some cultivars. The tuft of leaves at the stem apex is inconspicuous in this species and the long stems with flowers on the upper 30cm are often floppy in gardens. Hardy if planted deeply and needing a warm sunny position.

Eucomis schijffii Reyneke. Native of the Natal Drakensberg and nearby mountains, the Transkei and the NE Cape, growing on wet rock faces or below cliffs on steep slopes at 2300–3000m, flowering in January and February. A dwarf species with flowering spikes to 20cm, the whole plant purplish and glaucous. As it comes from such a high altitude, this species should be hardy, and it has, in England, survived c.3°C of frost without even the leaves being spoiled. Photographed on the Sani Pass, Natal, and, a larger form, near Mont-aux-Sources, in early February.

Eucomis bicolor near Mont-aux-Sources, Natal

Eucomis bicolor

Eucomis comosa

Eucomis schijffii near Mont-aux-Sources, Natal

Eucomis schijffii on the Sani Pass

life size Photographed 1 September

½ life size Photographed 19 November

⅔ life size Photographed 19 November

(a) **Leucojum roseum** F. Martin (*Amaryllidaceae*). Native of Corsica and Sardinia, growing in dry grassy and rocky places, flowering in autumn. Stem up to 12cm; petals 5–9mm. Grow in a sunny bulb frame or pot in the alpine house.

(b) **Crocus scharojanii** Ruprecht, syn. *C. lazicus* (Boiss. & Bal.), Boiss. (*Iridaceae*). Native of the Caucasus and NE Turkey, growing in alpine meadows at up to 3500m, flowering in August and September. Will grow well in peaty soil in a bulb frame, but should be happy in sandy peaty soil outside. Source SW Caucasus, Klukorsky pass, 1800m, Rix s.n.

(c) **Crocus ochroleucus** Boiss. Native of S Syria, Lebanon and Israel, growing on rocky hillsides up to 1000m, flowering in November. Leaves appearing with the flowers. Cultivation as (a).

(d) **Narcissus viridiflorus** Schousboe (*Amaryllidaceae*). Native of SW Spain and Morocco, on either side of the Straits of Gibralter, growing in damp fields, flowering in autumn. Flowers very sweet scented. Cultivation as (a).

(e) **Crocus biflorus** subsp. **melantherus** (Boiss. & Orph.) B. Mathew. Native of south Greece, the Cyclades and western Turkey, growing in rocky places and scrub, flowering from October to January (see p.21 (a)). Source Peloponnese, SE of Megalopolis, Rix 2108.

(f) Crocus longiflorus Rafin. Native of SW Italy, Sicily and Malta, growing in rocky and grassy places and the edges of woods, flowering in October and November. Cultivation as for (a) (see p.239 (p)). Shown here: a feathered form from Malta.

(g), (h) Crocus laevigatus Bory & Chaub. Native of S Greece, growing in scrub and on stony slopes, flowering from October to January. Corm tunic very hard. Cultivation as for (a) (see p.239 (q)). Shown here are two forms: (g) from Euboea, near Khalkis, Rix 556, and (h) a small pale form from Crete.

(i) Crocus nudiflorus Smith. Native of SW France and Spain, growing in meadows, flowering in September and October. The bulb is usually stoloniferous. Leaves three to four, appearing long after the flowers have faded. Cultivation as for (b). Will naturalise if happy, in thin grass.

(j) Crocus speciosus Bieb. Native of the Crimea, S Caucasus, Turkey and Iran, growing in woods, scrub, meadows and stony hillsides, flowering in October and November. Filaments glabrous. Easily grown in a sunny place or in thin grass on sandy soil (see p.245). Shown here, a small form from Crimea.

(k) Crocus serotinus Salisb. subsp. **salzmannii** (Gay) Mathew, syn. *C. asturicus* Herbert. Native of west, central and southern Spain, growing on stony slopes, in scrub and open pine woods, flowering from September to December. Cultivation as (b). Source Sierra de Guadderrama, c.2000m, Rix s.n.

(l) Colchicum corsicum Baker (*Liliaceae*). Native of Corsica, where it grows in sandy places in the mountains, flowering in September. The leaves which appear in winter are three or four in number, up to 8cm long and 9mm wide, linear lanceolate. The stigmatic hairs extend a little down from the tips of the styles. The very similar *C. alpinum* DC., from the Alps and mountains of Italy, Corsica, Sardinia and Sicily, has styles with stigmatic hairs only on the tip, and usually only two leaves. Cultivation as for (b).

(m) Habranthus andersonii Herbert (*Amaryllidaceae*). Native of temperate S America, probably introduced in Texas. Flowers may also be pinkish or white with yellowish apex. Easily grown in a bulb frame, kept dry in summer, flowering in cultivation from August to October, and seeding very freely.

(n) Colchicum boissieri Orph. (*Liliaceae*). Native of S Greece, especially the Taygetos mountains in the Peloponnese, where it grows in scrub and stony hillsides up to 1500m, flowering from September to December. Usually two leaves, up to 20cm long and 12cm wide, develop in winter. Easily distinguished from all other species except *C. psaridis* Heldr. ex Halacsy by its strange stoloniferous corm. Cultivation as for (a). Source Greece, Peloponnese, Brickell 2169.

(o) Colchicum cilicicum Dammer (*Liliaceae*). Native of southern Turkey in the foothills of the Tauros mountains at around 1000m, growing among rocks and on screes in pine woods and scrub, flowering from October to November. The leaves are large, up to 30cm high, broadly lanceolate. Easy to grow in dry sunny places in well-drained soil.

(p) Colchicum autumnale L. var. **album** (see p.239 (g)).

½ life size Photographed 17 September

½ life size Photographed 1 September

Colchicum pusillum

Crocus karduchorum

(a) **Allium callimischon** Link (*Liliaceae*). Native of Greece, Turkey and Crete, growing among rocks, flowering September to November. The leaves appear in early autumn; the flower stalk grows in spring, but remains throughout the summer covered in the dead remains of leaves, and the flowers appear from the top of the apparently dead stalk. Subsp. *callimischon* from the Peloponnese has unspotted flowers; subsp. *haemostictum* Stearn illustrated here, from Crete, has spotted petals.

(b) **Umbilicus erectus** DC., syn *Cotyledon lutea* Huds. (*Crassulaceae*). Native of S Italy to NW Africa and E Turkey, growing in rocky places and in woods, at 600–2300m, flowering from June to August. The fleshy kidney-shaped leaves appear in spring from the short tuber. Hardy. Source W Turkey, Izmir, 600m, Rix 1230.

(c) **Crocus kotschyanus** Herbert, subsp. **kotschyanus** (*Iridaceae*). Native of central Turkey, to Lebanon, growing in scrub and rocky places from 500 to 2600m, flowering in September and October. Easily grown in a bulb frame, or sunny place outside.

(d) **Biarum tenuifolium** (L.) Schott (*Araceae*). Native of the Mediterranean region, but absent from France, growing on rocky hillsides at up to 1000m, flowering in late summer or autumn. Here the spathe has been cut open to show the flowers, female below, male above, with sterile filament-like flowers between. Source NW Greece, near Joannina, Rix 1030.

(e) **Sternbergia lutea** (L.) Ker-Gawler (*Amaryllidaceae*). Native of the Mediterranean region, though probably naturalised in France, and west Asia east to Iran and the Pamir Alai, flowering in September and October. The form shown here is unusually tall. Easily grown outside in a sunny spot.

(f) **Merendera pyrenaica** (Pourret) P. Fourn. syn. *M. montana* Lange, *M. bulbocodium* Ramond. (*Liliaceae*). Native of the central Pyrenees, Spain and Portugal, flowering in autumn, on stony hillsides and in dry turf. Easily grown in well-drained soil. Source Sierra de Guadderrama, Rix s.n.

(g) **Sternbergia clusiana** Ker-Gawl ex Spreng. (*Amaryllidaceae*). Native of S Turkey, southwards to Israel and eastwards to Iran, growing on steep rocky slopes and deserts, flowering in October. Leaves about 30cm long, 1cm wide. Cultivation as (h).

Colchicum macrophyllum

Crocus kotschyanus subsp. **cappadocicus**

(h) **Colchicum variegatum** L. (*Liliaceae*). Native of Greece, especially the Aegean islands, Crete, Rhodes and S Turkey, where it grows on rocky hillsides up to 1500m, flowering from September to December. The leaves develop during winter and spring and are three or four in number, spreading, 10–15cm long, 10–20mm wide, with very wavy edges. In nature the flower would have a longer tube than that shown here. *C. agrippinum* hort. ex Baker (see p.241) is probably a hybrid between this and *C. autumnale* L. Easy to grow in dry sunny places in very well drained soil. Source Rhodes, Attaviros, Rix 1262.

(i) **Colchicum parlatoris** Orph. Native of the Peloponnese in southern Greece, growing on rocky hills, flowering from August to November. About four leaves appear in winter or early spring, and are c.1cm wide, and 5–10cm long. This is an unusually broad-leaved form, whereas p.247 (h) is typical. Source S Peloponnese, hills between Neapolis and Monemvasia, Rix 2127.

Crocus karduchorum Kotschy ex Maw (*Iridaceae*). Native of SE Turkey, south of Lake Van, growing on stony slopes in oak scrub c.2000m, flowering in September and October. A beautiful crocus recently rediscovered after over one hundred years, characterised by its finely divided white stigmata. Photographed near Hizan, by Brian Mathew, BM 9037.

Colchicum macrophyllum B. L. Burtt. Native of Crete, Rhodes and SW Turkey, growing in scrub and on rocky hillsides, flowering from September to November. Leaves three to four, very large, up to 35 × 14cm. Anthers purple, pollen green. Photographed in N Crete near Rethimnon in November 1980 by C. D. Brickell, B. & M. 10,116.

Colchicum pusillum Sieber. Native of Greece and Crete, growing in scrub and on rocky hillsides, flowering in October and November. Leaves three to six, appearing with the flowers, up to 14cm × 2mm. For a bulb frame, or pot in the alpine house. Photographed in NE Crete near Agios Nicolaios by C. D. Brickell in November 1980, B. & M. 10,142.

Crocus kotschyanus Koch, subsp. **cappadocicus** Mathew. Native of central Turkey especially between Kayseri and Malatya, growing on rocky limestone slopes and in alpine turf from 2000 to 2700m, flowering in September. See also p.245 (k). Throat glabrous. Cultivation as for (c). Photographed between Darende and Pinarbaşi by Brian Mathew.

½ life size Photographed 1 September

(a), (b) Cyclamen hederifolium Aiton, syn. *C. neapolitanum* Ten. (*Primulaceae*). Native from S France to Greece and Turkey, growing in woods and among rocks, flowering in autumn. The leaves are variously marked and marbled with silver. Easily grown in sun or shade in stony leafy soil.

(c) Leucojum autumnale L. (*Amaryllidaceae*). Native of Spain, Portugal, Sardinia, Sicily and N Africa, growing in open woods, scrub and grassy places, flowering from August to November. Easy in a sunny place outside.

(d) Cyclamen intaminatum (Meikle) Grey Wilson. Native of south and west Turkey, growing in pine woods and scrub at around 1000m. Leaves usually dark green, unmarked. A flower of *C. cilicium* (p.247) is shown for comparison.

(e) Cyclamen africanum Boiss. & Reut. Native of Algeria. Not hardy.

(f) Cyclamen purpurascens Miller, syn. *C. europaeum* L., *C. colchicum* Albov, *C. ponticum* (Albov) Pobed., *C. fratrense* Halda & Sojak. Native of France to Yugoslavia and Poland and in the S Caucasus, growing in alpine woods on limestone, flowering from June to October. Tuber rooting all over. Cultivation as (a).

(g) Colchicum autumnale L. (*Liliaceae*). Native of most of Europe from southern England and Portugal to Russia, growing in meadows and flowering in autumn. Easy to grow in grass. Source NE Italy, subalpine meadows above Udine, Rix s.n.

(h) Colchicum kotschyi Boiss. (*Liliaceae*).

(i) Crocus kotschyanus subsp. **hakkariensis** Mathew (*Iridaceae*). Native of SE Turkey, at 1000–3000m, flowering in September. Rix 161.

(j) Scilla autumnalis L. (*Liliaceae*). Native of Europe from England and Hungary southwards, growing in dry grassy places, flowering from August to October.

(k) Crocus robertianus C. D. Brickell. Native of the Pindus mountains of N Greece, growing in clearings in scrub at c.850m, flowering in October. Leaves three to four, 4–6mm wide. Marr 3580.

(l) Crocus tournefortii Gay. Native of most of the Aegean islands, Crete, Karpathos and Rhodes, growing in scrub and crevices in rocks, flowering from September to December. Cultivation as (i). Source Rhodes, Rix 1251.

(m) Crocus boryi Gay. Native of S and W Greece to Crete, on stony hillsides in scrub, flowering in autumn. Cultivation as (i). Source Peloponnese, near Githion, Rix 512.

(n) Crocus kotschyanus var. **leucopharynx** B. L. Burtt. Not known in the wild, but commonly grown. Cultivation as (c).

(o) Crocus caspius Fischer & Meyer. Native of Iran, on the south coast of the Caspian Sea up to 1300m, in sandy places, meadows and the edges of forests, flowering in October and November. Source Iran, Farah Abad, P. Furse 5083.

(p) Crocus longiflorus Rafin (see p.235).

(q) Crocus laevigatus Bory & Chaub. (see p.235 (g)). Source S Peloponnese, Rix 2128.

2/3 life size Photographed 14 October

⅓ life size Photographed 17 September

Crocus vallicola and **Colchicum speciosum** above Trabzon

Crocus vallicola

Crocus kotschyanus subsp. **suwarowianus**

(a) **Colchicum speciosum** Steven (*Liliaceae*). Native of the Caucasus, northern Turkey and Iran, growing in subalpine meadows and stony slopes, often in huge numbers, at up to 3000m. The flowers appear from August to October, the leaves in spring. They are up to 30cm high, 10cm wide, lanceolate, shining green, four in number. The petals are untessellated, and in the wild vary from deep purplish pink to white with pink tips. White throated forms, as shown here, are often wrongly called *C. bornmuelleri*, a distinct species from northern Turkey, with brownish anthers and a swollen apex to the style. Easily grown in grass or in normal garden soil, and increases freely when happy. Photographed in NE Turkey, Zigana pass, north of Trabzon, by Brian Mathew.

(b) **Colchicum agrippinum** hort. ex. Baker (*Liliaceae*). An old garden plant, a hybrid between *C. variegatum* and another species, possibly *C. autumnale*. It differs from *C. variegatum* in its larger flowers with more wavy petals, less strongly tessellated, which do not open as wide; the leaves are narrowly lanceolate, upright, with only slightly wavy edges. Easily grown in dry sunny places such as grassy banks or ledges in the rock garden, and increases well by proliferation of the corms.

(c) **Colchicum lusitanum** Brot., syn. *C. tenorii* hort. (*Liliaceae*). Native of Portugal, Spain and Italy, growing on dry, stony hillsides, flowering from September to November. The leaves which appear in spring are four to five in number, narrowly linear-lanceolate, up to 35cm long, 4cm wide, rather smaller than *C. autumnale*. The flowers are faintly tessellated. The plant shown here was grown under the name *C. tenorii*, but it appears to agree well with *C. lusitanum*. Easy to grow in sunny places in good well-drained soil.

(d) **Colchicum 'The Giant'.** This hybrid is one of the largest of all Colchicums, raised at the same time as many of the other hybrids. The tall white-centred flower is derived from the *speciosum* parent, the tessellation and brown anthers from *bivonae*. The leaves are large, similar to those of *C. speciosum*. Easy to grow in any good soil, but flowers better in a warm place in sun. Raised by Zocker & Co., Haarlem, c.1905.

(e), (f) **Colchicum bivonae** Guss., syn. *C. bowlesianum* Burtt, *C. visianii* Parl., *C. latifolium* Sibth. & Sm. (*Liliaceae*). Native of Sardinia, Italy and Yugoslavia to Greece and NW Turkey, growing in pine woods, and in scrub at c.500m, flowering from August to October. The leaves appear in spring, are five to nine in number spreading and tapering from the base, up to 25cm long and 4cm wide. A variable species; the two forms shown here differ in the number and shape of the flowers and size of the leaves. Easy to grow in a bulb frame, but less satisfactory in the open because it is much eaten by slugs. It requires a very sunny spot and well-drained soil. Source (e) Greece, foothills of Mt Olympus, Rix 631 (*C. bowlesianum*): this form increases very slowly; (f) NW Turkey, S of Çanakkale, Rix 1217: this form increases quickly.

(g) **Colchicum laetum** Steven (*Liliaceae*). Originally described from S Russia; a species under this name is grown in gardens, but the country of origin of the cultivated plants is not known. The characteristics of the garden plant shown here are the large bulb and the many narrow-petalled flowers. The leaves, which emerge in spring, are large, up to 40cm high and 10cm wide, similar to *C. autumnale*. Easily grown in sunny places in good well-drained soil.

(h) **Colchicum 'Conquest'** (*Liliaceae*). This is one of the richest-coloured of all the large-flowered hybrids, derived from *C. speciosum* and *C. bivonae*. It is not as large as the other hybrids, but equally easy to grow in any sunny place in good soil. Raised by Zocher & Co., Haarlem, c.1905.

Crocus vallicola Herbert (*Iridaceae*). Native of the Caucasus and NE Turkey, growing in mountain meadows at 1000-3000m, flowering in August and September. Shoot arising straight from the centre of the corm (see p.245). Easily grown outside in sandy peaty soil, but probably has to be increased by seed. Photographed in NE Turkey, Zigana pass, above Trabzon, by Brian Mathew.

Crocus kotschyanus subsp. suwarowianus (C. Koch) Mathew (*Iridaceae*). Native of western Transcaucasus and NE Turkey, growing in grassy and earthy places at 2000–3000m, flowering in September and October. Shoot arising obliquely from the corm. Petals purple-veined inside. Easy to grow in a bulb frame. Photographed in NE Turkey, Ikizdere to Ispir, 2600m, by Brian Mathew, 9022.

Colchicum 'General Grant'

Colchicum 'Waterlily'

Colchicum umbrosum Steven (*Liliaceae*). Native of the Black Sea region from Ulu Dağ in NW Turkey east to the Crimea, and in Romania, in beech woods and grassy meadows often on heavy clay soils, at up to 1400m, flowering in August to October. Flowers up to 3cm. Leaves 3–4, to 15 × 2cm. A very dwarf species suited to a heavy soil.

Colchicum 'General Grant'. A hybrid between *C. speciosum* and *C. bivonae*, raised by J.J. Kerbert, head of Messrs Zocher & Co of Haarlem, in c.1905.

Colchicum 'Waterlily'. A hybrid between a form of *C. autumnale* with double white flowers and *C. speciosum* 'Album', raised by Kerbert in c.1905.

Crocus asumaniae Mathew & T. Baytop (*Iridaceae*). Native of S Turkey, around Akseki, in evergreen and deciduous oak scrub on limestone, at 900–1250m, flowering in October to November. Flowers lilac to white, 8–11cm long; style divided at the level of the anthers. Leaves just showing at flowering time. A relative of the saffron crocus. Easily grown in a bulb frame.

Crocus cartwrightianus Herbert. Native of Greece, in Attica, Crete and the Cyclades, growing on rocky hillsides and in open woods, at up to 1000m, flowering in October to December. Flowers white or bluish, 4.5–8cm long. This is probably the wild form of the saffron crocus which is larger, and is a sterile triploid, unknown in the wild.

Crocus moabiticus Bornm. & Dins. Native of Jordan, in the hills of Moab and north towards Madaba, growing on rocky slopes at 600–750m, flowering in November and December. Leaves appearing with the flowers, which are variably veined, sometimes with a striking dark throat, 3.5–6.5cm long, with styles divided in the throat. Another relative of the saffron. Photographed in Jordan.

Narcissus serotinus L. (*Amaryllidaceae*). Native of the Mediterranean region, from Portugal to Israel and North Africa, at up to 300m in garrigue and among rocks on dry hills, flowering in September to December, either before or with the leaves. (Indeed, it is reported that leaves are usually not produced by flowering bulbs.) Flowers 1–2, rarely 3 in an umbel, 22–34mm across; stem to 25cm. Not easy to grow and probably better in a frost-free greenhouse than in a bulb frame.

Ungernia severtzovii (Regel) B. Fedtsch. (*Amaryllidaceae*). Native of C Asia, in the Tien Shan, especially around Tashkent, on rich earthy slopes at c.2000m, flowering in June to July. The leaves appear in spring, the flowers in summer after the leaves have died down. For the bulb frame, but only flowers in a very hot summer. Two similar species, *U. trisphaera* with brownish-red flowers and *U. flava* with yellowish flowers are found in the desert regions of Iran. Source: Chimgan valley near Tashkent.

Colchicum umbrosum

Crocus cartwrightianus

Crocus asumaniae

Crocus moabiticus in Jordan

Ungernia severtzovii

Narcissus serotinus in Corsica

½ life size Photographed 14 October

(a) **Crocus pulchellus** Herbert (*Iridaceae*). Native of the southern Balkans and W Turkey, growing in open woods or meadows, flowering in September and October. Will grow outside, but happier in a bulb frame.

(b)–(e) **Crocus speciosus** Bieb (see p.235). Source (b) wild form, MPR/79/27; (c) 'Oxonian'; (d) commercial form; (e) white form.

(f) **Crocus pallasii** Goldb. Native of E Europe from Crimea, and Romania to Turkey and Syria, growing on stony hillsides, flowering from October to December. Stigma usually red; leaves nine to fourteen, very narrow, greyish. Grow as (a). Source S Turkey, near Malatya, 2000m, Rix 1623.

(g) **Crocus vallicola** Herbert (see p.241).

(h) **Crocus goulimyi** Turrill. Native of the southern Peloponnese growing in rocky places and olive groves, flowering in October and November. Grow as (a).

(i) **Crocus hadriaticus** Herbert. Native of southern Greece, growing on open hillsides and scrub, flowering from October to December. Grow as (a). Source near Sparta, Brickell s.n.

(j) **Crocus cancellatus** Herbert. Native of Greece and Turkey, growing on stony hillsides and in scrub up to 1800m, flowering in October and November. Shown here are subsp. *cancellatus* from south Turkey (mauve), and subsp. *mazziaricus* (Herbert) Maw from Greece (white). Cultivation as for (a). Source Turkey, Maraş, Berit Dağ, Rix 700, and Greece, SE Peloponnese, Rix 2128.

(k) **Crocus kotschyanus** Koch subsp. **cappadocicus** Mathew (see p.237). Source Kayseri, Binboğa Da., on limestone, Rix 676.

(l) **Crocus banaticus** Gay. Native of Romania, Yugoslavia and western Russia, growing in meadows, woods and scrub, flowering in September and October. Leaves flat, up to 7mm wide. Grows well outside in leafy soil. Source W Romania, c.500m, Marr 3630.

(m) **Crocus niveus** Bowles. Native of the southern Peloponnese, growing among limestone rock and in olive groves, sometimes in great quantity. Flowers white to pale mauve. Grow as (a). Source S Greece, Rix 2135.

(n) **Crocus sativus** L. Saffron. Native range not known. The cultivated Saffron is a sterile triploid, increased vegetatively. Easily grown, but not free-flowering in northern Europe.

(o) **Galanthus nivalis** subsp. **reginae-olgae** (Orph.) Gottl.-Tann., syn. *G. corcyrensis* (G. Beck) F. C. Stern (*Amaryllidaceae*). Native of Sicily and Greece, growing among rocks and in oak scrub, flowering from October to December. Source Greece: shorter plant, Corfu, Rix 464; taller, near Igoumenitsa, Rix 2100.

(p) **Oxalis lobata** Sims (*Oxalidaceae*). Native of Chile, at up to 2000m. Has proved hardy for many years growing in a bulb frame at Wisley.

(q) **Argyropsis candida** (Lindl.) Roem., syn. *Zephyranthes candida* (Lindl.) Herbert (*Amaryllidaceae*). Native of Argentina, growing especially in marshy places along the Rio de la Plata. Hardy and grows best in rich moist soil.

(r) **Crocus medius** Balbis. Native of SE France and NW Italy, growing in grassy places and woods, flowering September to November.

½ life size Photographed 19 November

½ life size Photographed 14 October

(a) **Cyclamen graecum** Link, syn *C. maritimum* Hildebr., *C. pseudomaritimum* Hildebr. *C. pseudograecum* Hildebr. (*Primulaceae*). Native of Greece, Turkey and Cyprus, growing in rocky woods, scrub and clefts in rocks from sea level to c.500m, flowering from September to November. The leaves generally have fine fleshy teeth on the edge; the tuber is very rough with about six fleshy roots emerging from the base. *C. pseudograecum* was described from Crete, *C. maritimum* from wave-splashed limestone rocks in southern Turkey: they are merely minor variants. Easy to grow in a pot or bulb frame, but sometimes shy flowering. Should be very dry and baked in summer and kept rather dry in winter.

(b) **Cyclamen cyprium** Schott & Kotschy. Native of Cyprus, where it grows in woods and rocky places, especially in the Kyrenia range at from 300 to 1200m, flowering in autumn. Reputed to be tender, it is safer grown in a pot and protected from hard frost, but would probably survive in a bulb frame.

(c) **Cyclamen rohlfsianum** Aschers. Native of Libya from Benghazi to Derna, growing on limestone rocks at low altitudes. Not hardy and should be grown in a pot, kept dry in summer and not watered till growth begins. Detailed instructions for the management of this beautiful and rare species are given in the Alpine Garden Society guide, *Cyclamen*.

(d) **Cyclamen cilicium** Boiss. & Held. Native of southern Turkey from Antalya to Adana, growing in pine woods in pockets in limestone rocks at between 700 and 2000m, flowering from September to November. See also var. *intaminatum* Meikle (p.152). Hardy and easy to grow in rather dry places in sun or half-shade in stony soil. Source S Turkey near Akseki, Rix 1325.

(e) **Cyclamen mirabile** Hildebr. Native of SW Turkey around Muğla and Isparta, in pine forest and scrub at between 500 and 1000m, flowering from September to November. Very similar to *C. cilicium*, but the leaves are often clearly toothed and the upper edges of the petals are finely toothed. Grows in the same conditions as suit *C. cilicium* but possibly slightly less hardy.

(f) **Colchicum troodii** Kotschy, syn. *C. decaisnei* Boiss., (*Liliaceae*). Native of southern Turkey, Syria, Cyprus, Lebanon and Israel, growing on stony hillsides and among oak scrub, flowering from September to November. The leaves may be up to ten in number, and are narrow and linear, about 15cm long, 2.5cm wide. The flowers appear in succession. Has survived and flowered well for ten years in a bulb frame, but not increased, and is always on the point of being killed by botrytis which affects the dead flowers in winter. Source S Turkey, Adana to Gaziantep, Rix 1558.

(g) **Colchicum cupanii** Guss. Native of southern France to Crete, Tunisia and Algeria, growing on rocky hillsides, flowering from September to December. The usually two narrow leaves begin to emerge at the same time as the flowers, and are finally c.15cm long and c.1.5cm wide. Easy to grow in a bulb frame and increases well; not tried outdoors. Source S Italy, Matera to Taranto, Rix 454, and photographed in Crete near Agios Nicolaios by C. D. Brickell in November 1980, B. & M. 10149.

(h) **Colchicum parlatoris** Orph. Native of the Peloponnese in southern Greece, growing on rocky slopes flowering from August to November. Usually six to eight leaves appear in autumn after the flowers, and are very narrow (c.3mm wide) and glabrous. Easy to grow, but the dead flowers are susceptible to botrytis. Source S Peloponnese near Neapolis, Rix 2140a.

(i) **Sternbergia colchiciflora** Waldst. & Kit. (*Amaryllidaceae*) (see p.29 (e)). Source N Greece near Joannina, C. D. Brickell 2188.

(j) **Sternbergia lutea** (L.) Ker-Gawler (see p.177). Shown here a narrow-leaved form of subsp. *lutea*. Subspecies *sicula* (Tineo ex Guss.) D. A. Webb from S Italy, Sicily and Greece has even narrower leaves, 3–5mm wide. Source Greece, Peloponnese, Brickell and Mathew 8140, and subsp. *sicula* photographed in E Crete, Sitia province, in November 1980 by C. D. Brickell.

Biarum davisii Turrill (*Araceae*). Native of Crete and SW Turkey, growing in rocky places, flowering in October-November. The leaves are up to 4cm with a very short stalk and an ovate-oblong blade. Cultivation as for (b). Photographed in Sitia province in 1980 by C. C. Brickell, B. & M. 10,088.

Sternbergia lutea subsp. **sicula** in eastern Crete.

Colchicum cupanii

Biarum davisii

½ life size Photographed 12 January

Hyacinths are hardy and will grow successfully outside, but they are good for forcing indoors to flower from Christmas onwards. They are usually planted in 'bulb fibre', which consists of coarse peat, with shell and charcoal added to keep it 'sweet', in bowls without drainage holes. It is very important that the fibre be well moistened before the bulbs are planted, and that it should not be allowed to dry out; nor should it be sodden, but just moist enough for a drop or two to exude from it if it is squeezed. The bulbs should be planted with their tops on the surface, and when watered the shoot should never be wetted, or the buds will rot.

After planting the bulbs should be put in a dark, cool place (about 10°C) for at least two months while the roots develop. If they are expected to be in flower by Christmas, specially prepared bulbs must be bought, and they should be planted in early September, anyway before the 21st. If planted later the flower stem does not elongate properly as in (**d**) here, and the same happens if the bulbs are brought into heat too soon, or if they are allowed to become dry at any stage of growth. The bowls should be brought into a warmer temperature in as light a place as possible – but not in full sun – about four weeks before they are due to flower; and then after the shoot begins to elongate and the bud appear, they can be put in a warm room.

Varieties vary greatly in the ease with which they can be forced. Roman hyacinths (**g**) are the easiest, and of the other varieties shown here 'Rosalie' (**a**) was the earliest to flower. It is better to plant all bulbs of one variety in each bowl, since it is difficult to get different colours in flower together.

Narcissus are easier. 'Paper White' and 'Soleil d'Or' can be planted in gravel with water up to the base of the bulb. They grow very quickly and after a week or more in the cool can be brought into the house, where they will flower in about five weeks. As many bulbs as will fit should be crowded in for the best show, and it is especially important to get the largest possible bulbs for a good display of flowers. They are only satisfactory outside in the warmest gardens in England, but excellent in the Mediterranean.

Other daffodils, tulips, snowdrops and irises can be brought into flower in February and March if kept cool until late December, and forced according to the growers' instructions. *Iris histrioides* 'Major' and *I. danfordiae* are especially good. If the leaves grow up before the flowers appear, the plants should be moved into a cooler place.

(**a**) **'Rosalie'.** Raised by G. van Waveren-Kruyff 1948.

(**b**) **'L'Innocence'.** Raised by V. van der Vinne 1863.

(**c**) **'Pink Pearl'.** Raised by J. W. A. Lefeber 1922.

(**d**) **'Carnegie'.** Raised by A. Lefeber.

(**e**) **'Bismark'.** Raised by D. J. Ziegler 1875.

(**f**) **'Paper White'**, *Narcissus papyraceus* Ker-Gawler (*Amaryllidaceae*). Native of the Mediterranean region, growing in hills and grassy places, flowering from January to May.

(**g**) **'Roman Hyacinth'** *Hyacinthus orientalis* L. (*Liliaceae*). See p.47 for a wild form. There is also a pink form.

(**h**) **'Soleil d'Or'** *Narcissus tazetta* subsp. *aureus* (Loisl.) Baker (*Amaryllidaceae*). Native of S France, NW Italy and Sardinia; close to *N. tazetta*. Flowering January to March.

½ life size Photographed 12 January

General books on bulbs

The Smaller Bulbs, Brian Mathew (Batsford 1986)

The Larger Bulbs, Brian Mathew (Batsford 1978)

Collins Guide to Bulbs, Patrick M. Synge (Collins 1961)

Bulbs for the Gardener in the Southern Hemisphere, Sima Eliovson (Howard Timmins, Cape Town 1967)

The Royal Horticultural Society's Dictionary of Gardening, ed. P. M. Synge (OUP 2nd edn. 1965)

The Well-Tempered Garden, Christopher Lloyd (Collins 1970)

Seven Gardens . . ., E. B. Anderson (Michael Joseph 1973)

Growing Bulbs, Martyn Rix (Croom Helm 1983)

Hardy Bulbs, C. H. Grey, vols 1–3, (Williams and Norgate, London 1937–8)

The Bulb Book, John Weathers (John Murray 1911)

The European Garden Flora, Vol. 1, etc. (Cambridge University Press 1986–)

Floras

Flora Europaea, ed. T. G. Tutin *et al.* (Cambridge 1964–80)

Flora Iranica, ed. K. H. Rechinger (Graz 1963–)

Flora of Turkey, ed. P. H. Davis (Edinburgh 1965–84)

Flora of the USSR, ed. V. L. Komarov *et al.* (Moscow and Leningrad 1933–64) (translated into English by Israeli Program for Scientific Translations)

Additamenta et Corrigenda ad Floram URSS (tomi I–XXX), S. K. Czerepanov (Leningrad 1973)

Conspectus Florae Asiae Mediae (tomi II-VI) ed. A. I. Vvedensky (Tashkent 1971–76)

Flora of Japan (in English), J. Ohwi (Washington 1965)

A California Flora, P. A. Munz and D. D. Keck (Berkeley and Los Angeles 1959)

Vascular Plants of the Pacific Northwest, C. L. Hitchcock, A. Cronquist, *et al.* (Seattle 1955–69)

Gray's Manual of Botany, M. L. Fernald (New York 1950)

The Flora of South Africa, R. Marloth (Cape Town 1913–32)

Flowers of the Mediterranean, O. Polunin and A. Huxley (Chatto and Windus 1965)

Flowers of South-west Europe, a Field Guide, Oleg Polunin and B. E. Smithies (OUP 1973)

Flowers of Greece and the Balkans, a Field Guide, Oleg Polunin (OUP 1980)

An Enumeration of the Flowering Plants of Nepal (Vol I) H. Hara, W. T. Stearn and L. J. H. Williams (BM (NH) 1978)

Flowers of the Himalaya, Oleg Polunin and Adam Stainton (Oxford University Press 1984).

The Botany of the Southern Natal Drakensberg, O. M. Hilliard and B. L. Burtt. (National Botanic Gardens 1987).

Plants of the Cape Flora, a Descriptive Catalogue, Pauline Bond and Peter Goldblatt, (Journal of South African Botany, supplementary volume No. 13 1984)

Specialist books

Tulips and Irises of Iran, P. Wendelbo (Tehran 1977)

Lilies, P. M. Synge (Batsford 1980)

The Crocus, B. Mathew (Batsford 1983)

The Iris, B. Mathew (Batsford 1982)

Snowdrops and Snowflakes, F. C. Stern (Royal Horticultural Society 1956)

The Daffodil, M. J. Jefferson-Brown (Faber 1951)

Classified List and International Register of Tulip Names (Royal General Bulbgrowers' Association, Hillegom 1976)

Classified List and International Register of Daffodil Names (Royal Horticultural Society 1969 and later supplements)

The Bulbous Plants of Turkey, Brian Mathew and Turhan Baytop (Batsford and the Alpine Garden Society 1984)

The World of the Iridaceae, Clive Innes (Hollygate International 1985)

The Genus Cyclamen, Christopher Grey-Wilson, (Christopher Helm 1988)

Useful journals

The Botanical Magazine (London 1793–); almost every bulb species worth growing has been illustrated here

Hooker's Icones Plantarum (London 1836–); notably vol. XXXIX, parts I and II on Fritillaria, W. B. Turrill and J. R. Sealy 1980

Journal of the Royal Horticultural Society (London 1879–); since 1975 titled *The Garden*

The Plantsman (London 1979–)

Pacific Horticulture (San Francisco 1940–); formerly *Journal of the California Horticultural Society*

The Lily Yearbook (London 1932–); good articles on all genera of Liliaceae

The Daffodil and Tulip Yearbook (London 1933–); good articles on *Galanthus* and other Amaryllidaceae

The Iris Yearbook (London 1964–) and notes on Iris and Crocus distributed by the Iris Society Species Group

The Lily Yearbook of the North American Lily Society (New York 1948–); only articles on Lilies

The Bulletin of the Alpine Garden Society (London 1930–); many good articles on collecting bulbs

The Iranian Journal of Botany (Tehran 1976–)

Other articles

On the Genus Eremurus (Liliaceae) in South-west Asia, Per Wendelbo (Arb. Univ. Bergen no. 5, 1964)

Crocus tournefortii and its allies, Brian Mathew (Kew Bull. 31(4), 775–784, 1977)

Crocus vallicola and its allies, Brian Mathew, (Notes RBG Edinb. 38(3), 387-398, 1980)

Fritillaria in the Eastern Mediterranean region I-IV, E. M. Rix (Kew Bull. 33(4), 585-600, 1979)

Endangered Monocotyledons in Europe and South-west Asia, H. Synge, in C. D. Brickell, D. F. Cutler & M. Gregory (eds), *Petaloid Monocotyledons* (Academic Press 1980)

Neue Scilla-Arten aus dem östlichen Mittlemeerraum, F. Speta (Naturk. Jahrb. Stadt Linz 22, 65-72, 1976); eleven new species described!

Specialist horticultural societies in Great Britain

Royal Horticultural Society
Vincent Square, London SW1P 2PE

Alpine Garden Society
E. M. Upward, Lye End Link, St John's, Woking, Surrey

Scottish Rock Garden Club
Mrs I. Simpson, 48 St Alban's Road, Edinburgh EH9 2LU

British Gladiolus Society
Mrs M. Rowley, 10 Sandbach Road, Thurlwood, Rode Heath, Stoke-on-Trent ST7 3RN

British Iris Society
Species group, Prof. M. Bowley, Brook Orchard, Graffham, Petworth, Sussex

Daffodil Society
D. H. Pearce, 1 Dorset Cottages, Birch Road, Copford, Colchester, Essex

Lily Group of the RHS
c/o RHS, Vincent Square, London SW1P 2PE

Nerine Society
C. A. Norris, Brookend House, Welland, Worcs

Cyclamen Society
Miss G. Nightingale, Lavender House, 47 Lechmere Avenue, Chigwell, Essex

Specialist horticultural societies in America

The Species Iris group of North America,
c/o Elaine Hulbert, Rt 3, Box 57, Floyd, VA 24091

The Aril Society International,
(for oncocyclus and regelia irises),
111W. Magna Vista, Arcadia, CA 91006

The American Plant Life Society,
(for *Amaryllidaceae* and *Liliaceae*)
Box 985, National City, Ca 92050

The American Daffodil Society Inc.,
the Executive Director,
Rt. 3. 2302 Byhalia Road, Hernando, MS 38632

Bulb suppliers and nurseries in Britain and Europe

Avon Bulbs, Bathford, Bath BA1 8ED

Broadleigh Gardens, Barr House, Bishop's Hull, Taunton, Somerset

P. J. Christian, Pentre Cottages, Minera, Wrexham, Clwyd, N. Wales

Groom Bros Ltd, Spalding, Lincs

Jacques Amand, Beethoven Street, London W10 3LG

Cambridge Bulbs, Norman Stevens, 40 Whittlesford Road, Newton, Cambridge CB2 5BH

Walter Blom and Son Ltd, Leavesden, Watford, Herts WD2 7BH

Potterton and Martin, The Cottage Nursery, Moortown Road, Nettleton, Caistor, N. Lincs LN7 6HX

Rupert Bowlby, Gatton, Reigate, Surrey RH2 0TA

Michael Hoog, Huize Zwanenburg, Postbus 3217 NL-2001 DE Haarlem

Ole Sønderhousen, Brøvaenget 7, Denmark 3500, Vaerlose (for *Fritillaria*)

Albrecht Hoch, Ahornstrasse 2a, 1000 Berlin 37

Mrs Abel Smith, Orchard House, Letty Green, Hertford

Carncairn Daffodils Ltd, Carncairn Lodge, Broughshane, Ballymena, Co. Antrim BT43 7HS

John Lee, Durley Hall, Stourport-on-Severn, Worcs

Rathowen Daffodils, Knowehead, Dergmoney, Omagh, Co. Tyrone

Jack Drake, Inshriach, Aviemore, Inverness-shire (for *Nomocharis*)

E. Parker Jervis, Martens Hall Farm, Longworth, Abingdon, Berks (for *Colchicum*)

Washfield Nurseries, Hawkhurst, Kent (for Fritillaries).

Bulb suppliers and nurseries in the USA

B. &. D. Lilies, 330 P Street, Port Townsend, WA 98368, $2.00

Borbeleta Gardens, 15974 Canby Avenue, Route 5, Faribault, MN 55021, $3.00

Breck's, 6523 North Galena Road, Peoria, IL 61632, free

Daffodil Mart, Route 3, Box 794, Gloucester, VA 23061, $1.00

Doornbosch Bulb Co., 132 South Street, Hackensack, NJ 07601, free

French's Bulb Importer, Route 100, Pittsfield, VT 05762–0565, free

Dutch Gardens, Inc., P. O. Box 200, Adelphia, NJ 07710, free

Gladside Gardens, 61 Main Street, Northfield, MA 01360, $1.00

Russell Graham, 4030 Eagle Crest Road NW, Salem, OR 97304, $2.00

International Growers Exchange, Box 52248, Livonia, MI 48152, $5.00

John D. Lyon, 143 Alewife Brook Parkway, Cambridge MA 02140, free

McClure & Zimmerman, 1422 West Thorndale, Chicago, IL 60660, free

Messelaar Bulb Co., Inc., P. O. Box 269, Ipswich, MA 01938, free

Grant Mitsch Novelty Daffodils, P. O. Box 269, Ipswich, MA 01938, free

Charles H. Mueller, Star Route, Box 21, New Hope, PA 18938, free

Rex Bulb Farms, Box 774, Port Townsend, WA 98368, $1.00 (lilies)

Anthony J. Skittone, 2271 31st Avenue, San Francisco, CA 94116, $1.00

Spaulding Bulb Farm, 1811 Howey Road, Sebring, FL 33872, free (caladiums)

Ty Ty Plantation Bulb Co., Box 159, Ty Ty, GA 31798, free

Van Bourgondien Bros, P. O. Box 4, 245 Farmingdale Road, Route 109, Babylon, NY 11702, free

Van Engelen, Inc., 307 Maple Street, Litchfield, CT 06739, free

Mary Mattison Van Schaik, Route 1, Box 181, Cavendish VT 05142, $0.50

Vandenberg, Black Meadow Road, Chester, NY 10918, $2.00

Veldhoor Tulip Gardens, Inc., 12755 Quincy Street, Holland, MI 49423.

Mary Walker Bulb Co., P. O. Box 256, Omega, GA 31773, free

Wayside Gardens, Hodges, SC 29695–0001, $2.00

Bulb suppliers and nurseries in New Zealand

Palmers Garden World, (Auckland & Hamilton)

Sunhill Gardencentres (Auckland)

Botannix Garden Centres (Auckland & Hamilton)

Watkins Seeds, New Plymouth (Wholesale only)

Yates NZ Ltd, Henderson Place, Onehunga, Auckland

Daffodil Acre, PO Box 834, Tauranga

Gayborder Nurseries, PO Box 1496, Palmerston North

Glengary Gardens, Edmunds Road, Kaiapoi

Milburn Gardens, RD 2, Milton

Purdies Nurseries Ltd, PO Box 3051, Fitzroy, New Plymouth

Rangiora Nursery, Oxford Road, Rangiora

R.K.M. Plants Ltd, PO Box 9171, New Market, Auckland

Summergarden, PO Box 890, Whangarei

Van Eeden Tulip Farm, West Plains, RD4 Invercargill

Parra Plants Ltd, PO Box 549, Tauranga

Bulb suppliers and nurseries in Australia

The Blue Dandenongs Bulb Nursery, P O Box 8, Monbulk, Victoria 3793. Tel (03) 7566415

Schofields Garden and Floral Centre, 440 Moss Vale Road, Bowral, NSW 2576. Tel (048) 613058

Glossary

annulate splitting into rings at the base (of a Crocus corm).
anther the part of the stamen (q.v.) that contains the pollen.
axil angle between a leaf stalk and the stem.
bract a modified leaf below a flower.
bulb an underground storage organ consisting of modified leaves.
bulbil a small bulb which can be detached from the larger bulb on which it grows and form an independent plant.
canaliculate u-shaped in section (of leaf).
chaparral a low, dense scrub, characteristic of California.
ciliate fringed or surrounded with hairs.
clone vegetatively produced progeny of a single plant.
corm bulb-like subterraneous swollen stem of a plan, e.g. a crocus.
corona tubular structure on the inner side of the petals, e.g. the trumpet of a Daffodil.
cultivar a cultivated variety.
dehisce to burst open (of a stamen).
diploid containing twice the basic number of chromosomes (the usual complement).
emarginate with the apex indented.
fall the outer petals of an Iris.
filament that part of the stamen that supports the anther (q.v.).
garrigue scattered, low scrub common in limestone areas of the Mediterranean region.
glabrous smooth, i.e. hairless.
glaucous a greyish 'bloom' especially on leaves.
hybrid the offspring of two plants of different species or varieties.
inflorescence the part of the plant on which the flowers are borne.
loess a deposit of fine silt or dust (found in the arid interior of Asia, Eastern Europe and central USA).
maquis scrub consisting of small trees and shrubs and found in parts of the Mediterranean region.
nectary the part of the flower which secretes nectar, generally at the base of the petal.
ovary the lowest or innermost part of the flower, which ultimately becomes the seed vessel.
paniculate arranged in a panicle, i.e. a compound, pyramidal inflorescence.
papillose covered with small, fleshy projections.
pedicel the stalk of a flower.
perianth the outer ring of petals (q.v.).
petal generally the coloured part of the flower (often called tepals or perianth segments in the Lily family).
raceme a simple inflorescence (q.v.) in which the flowers are arranged on short nearly equal stalks on an elongated axis.
racemose arranged in racemes.
rhizome an underground modified stem, often swollen and fleshy.
scabrid rough, with small knobs.
scarious having a dry and papery appearance.
serpentine a dull green or dark reddish rock which, because of its mineral content, supports little but often interesting vegetation.
sessile without a stalk.
spadix form of inflorescence (q.v.) consisting of a thick, fleshy spike, closely set with minute flowers (in *Arum* family).
spathe large leafy bract wrapped round the inflorescence, particularly in the *Arum* family.
species group of individuals having common characteristics, distinct from other groups; the basic unit of botanical classification.
standard inner petals of an Iris flower, which are usually held erect.
stigma the part of the flower which receives the pollen, usually on the apex of the style which connects it to the ovary.
subspecies group within a species showing certain minor differences.
triploid with three times the basic number of chromosomes. (c.f. diploid q.v.). An unusual complement often producing a robust but sterile plant.
tuber swollen rhizome (see p.6).
tunic the outer skin of a bulb or corm, especially of Crocus.
umbel flat-topped inflorescence in which all the flower stalks arise from a single point.
whorl group of leaves or flowers arising at one level around the stem.

Index

Italic type indicates a synonym

CAMBRIDGESHIRE COLLEGE OF
AGRICULTURE & HORTICULTURE
LIBRARY
LANDBEACH ROAD, MILTON
CAMBRIDGE CB4 4DB